Cromwell and his Women

Cromwell and his Women

Julian Whitehead

First published in Great Britain in 2019 by
Pen and Sword History
An imprint of
Pen & Sword Books Ltd
Yorkshire - Philadelphia

Copyright © Julian Whitehead, 2019

ISBN 9781526719010

The right of Julian Whitehead to be identified as Author of this work has been asserted by him in accordance with the Copyright, Designs and Patents Act 1988.

A CIP catalogue record for this book is available from the British Library.

All rights reserved. No part of this book may be reproduced or transmitted in any form or by any means, electronic or mechanical including photocopying, recording or by any information storage and retrieval system, without permission from the Publisher in writing.

Typeset in India By IMPEC e Solutions

Printed and bound in Cornwall, United Kingdom By TJ International

Pen & Sword Books Ltd incorporates the Imprints of Pen & Sword Books Archaeology, Atlas, Aviation, Battleground, Discovery, Family History, History, Maritime, Military, Naval, Politics, Railways, Select, Transport, True Crime, Fiction, Frontline Books, Leo Cooper, Praetorian Press, Seaforth Publishing, Wharncliffe and White Owl.

For a complete list of Pen & Sword titles please contact

PEN & SWORD BOOKS LIMITED
47 Church Street, Barnsley, South Yorkshire, S70 2AS, England
E-mail: enquiries@pen-and-sword.co.uk
Website: www.pen-and-sword.co.uk

or

PEN AND SWORD BOOKS
1950 Lawrence Rd, Havertown, PA 19083, USA
E-mail: Uspen-and-sword@casematepublishers.com
Website: www.penandswordbooks.com

Dedication

To DM

Contents

List of Illustrations   ix
Acknowledgements   x
Introduction   xi

Part 1 A Fenland Family

Chapter 1	The First Elizabeth, 1599–1620	3
Chapter 2	A Second Elizabeth, 1620–1629	13
Chapter 3	Crisis and Redemption, 1629–1638	28
Chapter 4	An MP's Wife, 1638–1642	42

Part 2 A Soldier's Family

Chapter 5	A Good Army Wife, 1642–1643	59
Chapter 6	A General's Family, 1643–1644	75
Chapter 7	Two War Brides, 1645–1647	88
Chapter 8	Cruel Necessity, 1648–1650	100
Chapter 9	Finding a Settlement, 1651–1653	116

Part 3 The First Family

Chapter 10	Their Serene Highnesses, 1654–1655	133
Chapter 11	A Future Queen?, 1656–1657	150
Chapter 12	Uncertain and Giddy Times, 1657–1658	165
Chapter 13	A New Protector, 1658–1659	180
Chapter 14	Survival, 1660–1720	195

Epilogue   212
Appendix 1: Cromwell's Ancestors   214
Appendix 2: Cromwell's Siblings   215
Appendix 3: Cromwell's Children   216

viii Cromwell and his Women

Notes	217
Bibliography	226
Index	229

List of Illustrations

Hinchingbrooke House (picture courtesy of Hinchingbrooke School)
Cromwell's House in Ely (picture courtesy of Ely Tourist Board)
Elizabeth Cromwell née Steward, mother of Oliver, by Charles Turner (National Portrait Gallery)
Elizabeth Cromwell née Bouchier, wife of Oliver, by Robert Walker (Cromwell Museum)
Elizabeth ('Bettie') Claypole, daughter of Oliver, by John Michael Wright (National Portrait Gallery)
John Claypole, son-in-law, unknown artist (National Portrait Gallery)
Richard Cromwell, son of Oliver, unknown artist (National Portrait Gallery)
Dorothy Cromwell née Mayor, wife of Richard Cromwell, unknown artist (National Portrait Gallery)
Henry Cromwell, son of Oliver, unknown artist (Cromwell Museum)
Henry Ireton, first husband of Bridget Cromwell, by Robert Walker (National Portrait Gallery)
Bridget Fleetwood, daughter of Oliver, by Cornelius Johnson (Chequer's Trust)
Charles Fleetwood, second husband of Bridget Fleetwood, by Jocobus Houbraken after Robert White (National Portrait Gallery)
Cromwell's family interceding for the life of Charles the First, by James Scott (National Portrait Gallery)
Lady Frances Russell, daughter of Oliver, by William Bond (National Portrait Gallery)
Mary Countess of Fauconberg, daughter of Oliver, circle of Thomas Murray (Cromwell Museum)
Thomas Belasyse, Earl of Fauconberg, husband of Mary Cromwell, by Robert White (National Portrait Gallery)

Acknowledgements

I am indebted to all the authors of the books listed in the Bibliography, in particular for the various works of Antonia Fraser, Barry Coward, Peter Gaunt, John Morrill, Robert Ramsay, and Roy Sherwood. I would also like to thank the National Portrait Gallery, the Cromwell Museum, Chequer's Trust, Hinchingbrooke School and Ely Tourist Board for their assistance and agreement to me using their images for illustrations. Finally, I want to thank my wife for her help and support.

Introduction

Oliver Cromwell was born in the year 1599 when Shakespeare had just written *Henry V* and Elizabeth I had been on the throne for forty-one years. King Henry V was the epitome of a heroic monarch and although Elizabeth said she was 'a frail and feeble woman,' her subjects would have agreed with her that she had 'the heart and stomach of a king'. At once feared and revered, Elizabeth dominated the history of her time. That was not to be the case for a woman again until Anne became queen a 100 years later and ruled successfully, often with the advice of those formidable ladies, the Duchess of Marlborough and Lady Masham.

In the seventeenth century a woman could be credited with being beautiful, charming, and in mature years sometimes even wise, but would always be deemed inferior to a man. This was fully supported by the Bible based on Eve's unfortunate transgression in the Garden of Eden. The only real exceptions to this were queen consorts. They could enjoy power through having their own court and patronage and by sometimes exerting influence on their husbands. There was also a variation between classes. The wife of a tradesman might work as his unofficial junior partner in the shop or the wife of a husbandman would make an active contribution by feeding pigs, sheep shearing or helping with harvest. There was no question of a lady from the gentry or aristocratic classes being engaged in a profession.

A huge gulf existed between the lower orders and the wives of the gentry and aristocracy. A wealthy peer might have an income of £10,000 a year and a member of the gentry £500 to £1,000, but the common people, such as cottagers and servants, who comprised three-quarters of England's four million population, could expect 7s 15d per day. The ladies of the nobility and gentry may not have had to work in the same way as men, but they were not idle. They busied themselves with domestic management which, with a large household, required considerable attention. These households were almost self-supporting and their management required the supervision of everything from baking, brewing, butter and cheese making, to maintenance and the purchase of provisions. Then there was the matter of supervising and bringing up their many children. Ladies also had their own pastimes such as riding and needle work, as well as social activities with their neighbours. Although they wrote letters and very occasionally composed something longer, such as Lucy Hutchinson's memorial to her husband, they were never for publication. It was not until 1670 that Aphra Behn became the first English woman to be paid for her writing, and she was no lady.

A gentlewoman did not often assist in her husband's work. In fact, her husband would have had little work as we would recognise it today. He had his estates to manage, but this was often no more than the collection of rents, which might itself be delegated to a bailiff. A gentleman would spend his time hunting or hawking and taking up his duties as a local magistrate, officer in the militia or Member of Parliament. This affluent lifestyle could only be maintained by a family if there was a male heir to keep the estate intact and, if possible, enhance it by an advantageous marriage. A significant portion of the time of the gentry and aristocracy was spent in finding suitable wives and arranging agreeable marriage settlements. This is where women really came into the scheme of things, if only as chattels to be bargained over.

Oliver Cromwell described himself as being 'by birth a gentleman' and indeed he was a member of the gentry, albeit with fluctuating finances. Nearly all women from gentry families, such as Oliver's, could expect a similar pattern of life. As babies they would be wet nursed and then brought up by their mother and servants. They would be educated at home by their mother or possibly a tutor. This education would teach them to read and even write; the reading was especially important in a Puritan family, so they could study the bible. They also learnt needle work, and as they grew older, household management. Unlike their brothers, going to school was not for them. Still less attendance at one of the universities, usually followed by admission to an Inn of Court, which was the usual pattern for the sons of gentry. The next major step in a girl's life would be finding a suitor and arranging the marriage contract. Even if a suitable suiter were found, it could take months or even years to finalise the marriage contract and agreements concerning how much of her father's estate would be transferred to the husband as a dowry and how much her husband's parents would pay in dower to maintain her if he died.

The process of finding a husband could start quite early, as the age of consent was 12 for a girl and 14 for a boy. If parents were in haste to make an alliance, then the couple could be betrothed much earlier but would have to await the legal age before actual marriage. Despite the strong parental hand in arranging a marriage, it sometimes coincided with genuine love between the couple. Indeed, it was church teaching that no one could be married against their will, so both bride and groom were usually at least content to accept being united. If there was not love between them at first, it might grow with time and turn into deep affection, as was the case with Oliver and his wife Elizabeth. Once married, all the bride's property became that of her husbands by right. The wife became completely reliant on her husband and as her marriage vows said, she was obliged to: 'love, honour and obey'. How the husband treated his wife would be a matter of the way their relationship developed, but it was usually with respect and consideration, unless, of course, if she defied his wishes.

The foremost task of a new bride was to produce an heir and if the wife managed to survive the life-threatening experience of childbirth, then that was by no means the end of it. Most wives found themselves in an almost constant state of pregnancy and were faced with a high mortality rate, often followed by diseases in later years that remained incurable due to lack of modern medicine. Oliver and Elizabeth Cromwell lost at least one child at birth and disease took their eldest son at 15 and their second eldest at 21. A large progeny was insurance to ensure an heir would survive to inherit the estate. The other reason for pregnancy was lack of birth control. Birth control was seldom considered within marriage but reserved for extra marital relations where herbal potions such as oil of honeysuckle with marjoram were employed, usually resulting in unwanted consequences. The ravages of disease were naturally common to both sexes. Women of all classes faced the same horrors of child birth. This was ordained by God as was clearly stated in Genesis: 'unto the woman He [God] said I will greatly multiply thy sorrows and thy conception in sorrow shalt thy bring forth children'.

While sharing this ordeal with the rest of her sex, the life of a lady from the gentry was very different from that of women from the lower orders of society. Both could have happy and fulfilling lives enjoying the human pleasures of matrimonial and family love, friendships, amusements and pastimes. However, the lady had the added pleasures that can come with wealth; that is fine clothes and surroundings, servants to spare her physical work and time to pursue her interests whether it be riding, socialising, music or reading. One thing which women rich or poor had in common was that they were excluded from major decision making and were unable to have any direct impact on the world. These matters were exclusively the domain of men. It was usually members of the aristocracy and gentry who became the leaders who helped shape the country, but occasionally a man from a humble background could come to the fore as a soldier, priest or writer and make his mark. The fact that this option was never open to a woman of any class may have been a matter of resentment for some, but there was an outward compliance to this as the 'natural order'.

English history for the first half of the seventeenth century makes scant mention of women for the understandable reason that they did not have opportunities to shape events. They were unable to lead an army to victory, carry out a political coup, or leave their mark on legislation, literature, science or the arts. Nevertheless, they played their part in the important role of often encouraging, inspiring and influencing their husbands or sons to carry out great things. The lives of this neglected half of the population are worthy of examination and their contribution deserves more than an occasional historical footnote.

Women loomed large in Oliver Cromwell's life. At the age of 17 his father died, and he was the only male in a household consisting of his mother and six sisters. On marriage he and his wife Elizabeth had four daughters, as well as two surviving sons. He also had several aunts whose influences would be important in his career. Oliver was devoted to his wife and family. Their lives impacted on his and his amazing life certainly impacted on theirs. Oliver was to rise from being a middle-aged MP with no previous military experience to being one of Britain's greatest generals and then the powerful ruler of England, Scotland and Ireland, respected by the crowned heads of Europe. This book is about those forgotten women of Cromwell's family who rose from being minor gentry to semi-royal status and then plunged into lowly anonymity at the Restoration. It is now time for their remarkable story to be told.

PART 1

A Fenland Famiy

Chapter 1

The First Elizabeth
1599–1620

'I was by birth a gentleman, living neither in a considerable height, nor yet in obscurity.'

Oliver Cromwell, speech to Parliament, 1654

In the April of 1599 the news from London was dominated by the antics of Robert Devereux, the Earl of Essex. He was the popular, handsome 34-year-old soldier who had become Queen Elizabeth's principal favourite. She had made him Lord Lieutenant of Ireland with the task of putting down the rebellion of the Catholic Earl of Tyrone. Essex had just left London to command a 16,000 strong army. He had been seen off by cheering crowds and accompanied by members of the gentry and nobility who were hitching their wagon to this rising star. There were some who did not join in the general admiration of Essex and regarded him as a spoilt, petulant youth whose good looks had captured the heart of the 66-year-old queen. Essex's rise to royal favour threatened the position of those close to the queen, such as Sir Walter Raleigh and the Secretary of State, Robert Cecil. In the contest for Elizabeth's favour it was their hope that Essex would fail in Ireland as many had done before him. As it turned out, they were not to be disappointed.[1] The power struggle between the Essex and Cecil factions at court was to dominate news for the next two years until it ended with the earl's execution.

For many of the nobility and gentry there was great interest in the outcome of the Essex saga and which court faction would become dominant with the aging queen. For ordinary folk such gossip was of no interest as they were more concerned with matters directly affecting their everyday lives, such as the price of wheat. In a sleepy little town such as Huntingdon, which took two days to be reached by London news, nearly the only person who might have been interested in the Essex outcome was the owner of Hinchingbrooke House. This was the principal magnate of the area, the elderly Sir Henry Cromwell, who had once been an aspiring courtier.

4   Cromwell and his Women

In the early hours of the morning of 25 April 1599, when the good people of Huntingdon were fast asleep, candles would have been seen burning in the windows of a house in High Street. The room was the bedchamber of Elizabeth Cromwell and she was certainly not thinking about the fate of the Earl of Essex. She was in labour with her seventh child. Elizabeth was married to Robert Cromwell, the second son of Sir Henry. She was two years older than Robert and the match would have been arranged by their respective families. Elizabeth was the eldest daughter of Sir William Steward, a 'gentleman of comfortable fortune,'[2] who farmed the cathedral lands round Ely. Although brought up in comfort as the daughter of a prosperous member of the gentry, she was not an heiress. Primogeniture meant that when her father died her younger brother, Thomas, would inherit the estate. Elizabeth's future depended upon a favourable marriage facilitated by a reasonable dowry. After the usual parental haggling over the dowry, her marriage had been contracted with William Lynne, the heir of John Lynne of Bassingbourn. Elizabeth had settled in Bassingbourn with her husband and produced a little girl called Katherine. She might have reasonably expected a contented life of a country lady, but in the seventeenth century the spectre of incurable illness was never far away. First her baby girl died and then in 1589 John too died. Her brief time as a wife and mother now over, Elizabeth found herself a widow of 24. If she was to have any worthwhile life ahead of her it was important to attract a husband of some means or end her days as a poor relation.

Elizabeth had been fortunate in the quest for a second husband because, although she had no dowry to offer, she did have funds in the guise of her recently received 'jointure'. This was the sum agreed in the marriage contract which would be paid by the husband's family to the wife if she should become a widow. In Elizabeth's case this was the tithes of the rectory of Hartford providing an income of £60 a year. Not a huge sum, but enough to attract the interest of Sir Henry Cromwell as being of assistance to his younger son Robert. Sir Henry would, of course, pass the majority of this estate to his eldest son Oliver, but needed to find settlements for four other sons and dowries for three daughters. Even for a rich man this was quite a tall order. He had decided to settle an income of about £300 a year on Robert so an additional annual £60 would enable him to have just enough resources to live the life of a country gentleman. In 1591 the marriage was agreed, and Elizabeth's family gained the benefit of making an alliance with one of the most prominent families in the county.

Robert and Elizabeth settled down together in a house in Huntingdon High Street with an adjacent estate, given by Robert's father Sir Henry.

Both the house and the estate had been owned by the Austin cannons until Sir Henry's father got his hands on them as part of his spoils from the dissolution of the monasteries. The property had a large garden and a small stream running through which had been used for brewing. This modest house in Huntingdon was very different from the relative magnificence of Hinchingbrooke where Robert had been brought up. The Cromwell family wealth derived from the dissolution of the monasteries carried out by Henry VIII's chief minister, Thomas Cromwell, who became an earlier Earl of Essex.

Thomas Cromwell's sister Katherine had married a Morgan Williams and had a son, Richard, whose uncle Thomas appointed as one of his visitors for the monasteries. Richard not only carried out these duties with energetic efficiency but came into the king's favour through his skill at the tournament. He was allowed to buy the large nunnery of Hinchingbrooke with all its lands for the knock-down price of £18.9s.2d. Other undervalued parts of the monastic estate were also to come his way, such as Ramsey Abbey, nine miles north of Huntingdon. It was no wonder that Richard Williams decided to change his name to 'Cromwell' in honour of his illustrious uncle and benefactor. Thomas Cromwell fell from power and was executed in 1540, but Richard continued to flourish becoming a knight, High Sheriff and MP and marrying the daughter of a Lord Mayor of London. Despite his uncle's fall from grace Richard retained the name 'Cromwell,' as did his son Henry, to whom he was able to leave an estate worth the enormous sum of about £3,000.

Henry Cromwell had built Hinchingbrooke House next to the old nunnery and also built a manor house at Ramsey Abbey as a summer residence. Henry had been knighted by Queen Elizabeth, and he too married the daughter of a lord mayor and became a leading magnate in the area, being an MP and four times High Sheriff of Cambridgeshire and Huntingdonshire. He had entertained the queen at Hinchingbrooke and his opulent lifestyle resulted in him being referred to as 'the Golden Knight'. Such was the distinguished family Elizabeth had married into. She and her husband were of course frequent visitors to Hinchingbrooke and all the more welcome when she produced grandchildren for the 'Golden Knight' to add to his rapidly expanding family. Elizabeth had produced two girls, Joan in 1592 and Elizabeth two years later, and a year after that fulfilled her prime duty and gave birth to an heir for Robert in 1595. This boy was called Henry, but he sadly died in his first few months.

A grieving Elizabeth once more needed to produce an heir. Two years later she had another baby, but it was another daughter, who was named

Catherine, and it was possibly about this time her eldest daughter Joan seems to have died. Elizabeth had to wait another two years to again give birth and must have prayed through her contractions that this birth would at last provide a healthy son and heir. In the early hours of the morning of that 25 November 1599, Elizabeth's prayers were answered by the arrival of a baby boy. She and Robert must have been overjoyed to have a son, particularly after the tragedy of baby Henry's death. As they named Henry after his grandfather, it was only politic to name the new born boy 'Oliver' after the 'Golden Knight's' eldest son. This Oliver had already made a mark for himself and had been knighted the previous year. Sir Oliver lived in a property in nearby Godmanchester, was a Justice of the Peace and had followed his father by becoming an MP for Huntingdonshire and sheriff of Cambridgeshire and Huntingdonshire.

With the high rate of infant mortality, it was normal to have a child baptised as soon as possible after birth. Little Oliver was baptised at St John the Baptist Church, Huntingdon, four days after he was born with his uncle as godfather. For the next few years Elizabeth and Robert's lives then went on much as before punctuated by births, deaths and major events occurring at the big house. The fragility of life was once again made manifest to them when their nine-year-old daughter Joan died in 1601. Two years later the news arrived that death had even claimed the old queen, who seemed to have been on the throne as long as anyone could remember.

The death of the 'Virgin Queen' was seen by all as marking the end of an era. There would be a new dynasty with the son of Mary, Queen of Scots becoming king of England and Ireland. The throne passing to James VI of Scotland was greeted by most with a mixture of excitement and uncertainty. There was excitement about having a new monarch aged 37 compared with the revered, but $73\frac{1}{2}$-year-old Elizabeth, and uncertainty over what sort of rule could be expected from this Scottish king. There were many matters to be clarified, such as whether the new king would continue the long running war with Spain or not and the all-important question of his stance on religion. He had been brought up a strict Calvinist so was likely to favour the Puritan movement. On the other hand, his mother had been a Catholic, so he could be expected to ease the Penal Laws against Papists. There again, he was now head of the Anglican Church and would be likely to support it as an integral part of his royal authority.

James' views on these and the numerous other important matters would become clearer as the reign progressed, but perhaps the most pressing issue for ambitious members of society such as the Cromwells was how to win favour with the new king. The sovereign was not only the source of all honours and titles, posts in government and the royal household, but of virtually all positions of authority whether it was through the judiciary, army, navy, tax collection or the church. As such, a person in royal favour could expect considerable rewards both in status and financially. In the summer of 1603 the Cromwells had a heaven-sent opportunity to ingratiate themselves with the new king and lay claim to his bounty. It had been decided that James would stay at Hinchingbrooke on his slow progress from Scotland to London.

The excitement at this news must have been enormous not only for Sir Henry and his son, but also for the rest of the family. Elizabeth and her husband would be included among the first members of the English gentry to have direct contact with the new king. Fortunately, there was time for Hinchingbrooke to become ready for this great event. So many things to prepare, not least to build a large bow window in the dining-room. Scotland was a poor country and King James had to send to Robert Cecil, Secretary of State, in London for enough funds to cover his journey south in suitably regal style. James was the great-grandson of Henry VII through his daughter Margaret. She had married the ill-starred James IV of Scotland who had been killed at the battle of Flodden. Although closest in line to the English throne Queen Elizabeth had never acknowledged him as her heir. The news of her death and final confirmation that he was to take the throne of England was the realisation of a lifetime's ambition. He was over the moon to be leaving poor, damp Scotland, where he was lectured by his Presbyterian clergy and treated with over familiarity by his nobles. At last he would be moving to wealthy England where he could reign in majesty. In fact, as he crossed the border into England, James declared to those about him that he had indeed arrived at the Promised Land.

King James continued his high spirits as he journeyed southwards and was joined at York by Robert Cecil, who he made a baron. To express his satisfaction with the English gentry, James was to confer over 200 knighthoods on those who greeted him on his southward progress.[3] It was in this exuberant and generous mood that he arrived with his entourage at Hinchingbrooke House. As old Sir Henry Cromwell did not have the stamina to be an effective royal host, he delegated that position to his son, Sir Oliver. From the moment when the king arrived it was clear to all that Sir Oliver would prove an outstanding host. He provided King James with the flattery and luxury he had lacked in Scotland and laid it on with a trowel. Elizabeth and Robert would have taken part in the lavish feasting and entertainment for the royal visitor which easily surpassed everything that he had so far received in England. Like all those present they would have been amazed by the gifts that Sir Oliver lavished on the king. These included: 'a standing cup of gold,' 'goodly horses,' 'fleet and good mouthed hounds,' and 'divers hawks of excellent wing'.[4]

King James was a rather ungainly figure with a large body and small legs, but was an excellent horseman and stag hunting was his passion. Naturally, Sir Oliver took the king to his new red deer park and James was delighted to find that the Huntingdon area, with its plentiful deer and ideal terrain, provided some of the best sport he had ever enjoyed. The whole royal visit turned out to be a resounding success as King James found Hinchingbrooke House extremely comfortable, its estate and deer park excellent, and Sir Oliver a congenial and generous host. All too soon the two-day stay had to end as it was necessary for the king and his entourage to press on to London in preparation for his coronation. So magnificent had been the occasion of the king's visit that no one could have been left in doubt that the Cromwells were the leading family in the county.

Robert and Elizabeth Cromwell could bask in some of the reflected glory of being part of so prominent a family. The status and respect must have helped Robert in his capacity as a local landowner in advancing his interests, such as the draining of the Fens. Robert had been briefly the MP for the borough in 1597 and although by no means as prominent as his elder brother, was a person of some local consequence. A year after the king's visit Sir Henry Cromwell died. His heir, Sir Oliver, moved from his house in Godmanchester to Hinchingbrooke House and took over the family estate, the wealth of which was beginning to show signs of strain. Sir Oliver had no sooner moved in than King James returned to Hinchingbrooke. He had decided that Hinchingbrooke was a convenient place to stay to meet his son Charles.

Prince Charles was the frail 4-year-old younger son of the king who had been left in Edinburgh when James, the queen and their eldest son, Prince Henry Frederick, had gone to London. Charles was brought on the long journey to be reunited with the rest of the family and his father wanted to meet him on the last leg. Sir Oliver naturally organised lavish entertainment for the king and his party, but also wanted to arrange something for Charles. It is related that Sir Oliver thought the best way to look after the little boy prince was by having his brother Robert's son Oliver over to play. Charles had been slow to develop and was not yet able to walk or talk, so interaction in play would have been a bit limited. If the two boys did play together they would have been far too young to remember it, but it would have been a matter of some pride for Elizabeth and Robert to think that their son had played with a prince. As before, King James enjoyed his visit to Hinchingbrooke and this and subsequent visits reinforced the prominence of the Cromwells in the county and further depleted the coffers of Sir Oliver.

Elizabeth must have had the pleasant existence of a country gentlewoman and mother of a growing family. Another daughter, Jane, was born two years after the king's first visit and then a son, Robert, four years after that, but he died shortly after his birth. The next year, in 1610, Elizabeth had her last child, a baby girl who was christened Robina. The surviving children of Elizabeth and Robert now consisted of Elizabeth, Catherine, Margaret, Anna, Jane and Robina, with just one remaining son, young Oliver, who was Robert's heir.

Elizabeth's children would have received their basic education at home possibly with the assistance of a tutor. Her girls' education would not have extended outside their house, but for boys the next step was to go to school and learn Latin. Oliver was enrolled at Huntingdon Grammar School.[5] This was just down the road from Oliver's own house in Huntingdon High Street and consisted of the usual arrangement of a single classroom for all age groups with a headmaster and an assistant. The school was a good one with the redoubtable Dr Thomas Beard as headmaster and Warden of St John's Hospital (alms house) of which the school formed a part.[5]

Dr Beard was a clergyman fortunate in possessing several livings including being vicar of both All Saints and St John's churches in Huntingdon and two other churches in Suffolk and Essex. As a clergyman he used curates while he spent his time as a teacher and intellectual theologian. His writings, such as his best seller *The Theatre of God's Judgement* published in 1597, made a significant contribution to the development of Puritan thought. The Puritan movement had begun in Queen Elizabeth's reign. Puritans believed that the Reformation had not gone far enough and that the church needed to be 'purified' from the remaining offensive Roman Catholic practices. The practices Puritans wanted removed included the rule of bishops, the wearing of vestments by clergy and what remained of churches' statues and decorations. As a Puritan Dr Beard also regarded the pope as the Anti-Christ and believed that, as well as receiving judgement in after life, God intervened on earth to reward the righteous and punish the wicked. Whether much of this new thought rubbed off on young Oliver is difficult to say, but it was certainly true that Dr Beard was a close family friend of Robert and Elizabeth Cromwell. It is unlikely that the friendship would have existed if Robert and Elizabeth had not at least partially held the same beliefs.

When Oliver was 17 it was decided that he should continue his education in the customary manner for the son of a country gentleman of means and be sent to university. There was no question of which university to attend because Cambridge was much closer to Huntingdon than Oxford. The only question was, which Cambridge college? It was agreed that Oliver should attend Sidney Sussex college as a fellow commoner. The college was only three years older than Oliver and had been founded by the legacy of Frances Sidney, Countess of Sussex, as 'a good and godlie monument for the mainteynance of Francis Sidney good learning'. The 'godlie' bit of the mission statement implied its Protestant purpose and that was almost immediately translated into a strong Puritan ethos. The fact that Oliver was sent to Sidney Sussex makes it probable that it was at the suggestion of Dr Beard, and that the college's religious leaning was in accordance with that of Robert and Elizabeth.

How much the teenage Oliver subscribed to Puritan beliefs at this stage is hard to say. From what little evidence that exists he was more interested in enjoying his new freedom away from home among a lot of young, and no doubt boisterous, gentlemen of his age group. Oliver must have put some effort into his Latin study because he was in later life able to converse with the Dutch ambassador in that tongue. There were, however, other university pursuits, such as hunting, hawking and playing football, all of which were more to his taste.

Oliver had been enjoying life up at Cambridge for a year when tragedy again struck Elizabeth Cromwell's life. In June 1617 her eldest daughter, the 16-year-old Margaret, had been married by Dr Beard to Valentine Walton. It was a good match as the Waltons were an old knightly family whose estate was just eight miles south-west of Huntingdon in Great Staughton. The happy atmosphere for this wedding was to be completely dispelled just a few days later. Robert, who had been unwell, suddenly died. He was only 54 and Elizabeth was left a widow for the second time. Then just two weeks later Elizabeth received the news of the death of her father, Sir William Steward.[6] Having lost both husband and father, she obviously needed support and recalled Oliver from Cambridge, where he was never to return to complete his degree. Elizabeth had been left to shoulder the responsibilities of looking after her large family and running the estate single handedly. Dr Beard had been a witness to Robert's will and Elizabeth had been made sole executrix. Oliver was still three years under age, but the 18-year-old Oliver was Robert's heir and now assumed the position of head of the family.

Oliver, the youthful new patriarch, would have to work in a partnership with his mother and draw upon her maturity and experience. Taking over the running of the family would be no easy task. There was the estate to manage and as it was fairly small, Elizabeth and Oliver could ill afford to waste money by not running it effectively. The estate is thought to have included a brew house and Elizabeth appears to have taken personal charge of its management. Money would have been tight for Elizabeth, especially with her having six of her children still living at home. This was not just a matter of mouths to feed, but also of keeping up appearances as being members of the Cromwell family. Marrying so many daughters off to men of suitable means was an urgent challenge and brought with it the financial headache of finding six dowries. Elizabeth must have been very relieved to have Oliver back from Cambridge to share the responsibilities and, in some respects, take the position of her lost husband. Before Robert Cromwell's death, Oliver probably had the normal love and filial respect for his mother and the death of Robert seems to have created an even stronger bond between mother and son which would remain for the next thirty-eight years until it was Elizabeth's turn to be claimed by death.

However close Elizabeth was to Oliver it did not mean that their relationship was always entirely easy, any more than it is between many parents and their teenage children. Oliver had returned to Huntingdon having just experienced the freedom of being an undergraduate at Cambridge. He was also now officially head of his branch of the family and, although by no means rich, he had a certain amount of money and local status. It would not have been surprising if he had grasped his newly found independence and been tempted to show off his position to his former class mates in Huntingdon. Teenage exuberance sometimes leads to bad behaviour and Oliver appears to have gained a reputation in Huntingdon for gaming, wenching and generally carousing to excess.

It may be that Elizabeth felt that it would do him good to remove him from the Falcon Inn[7] and the other alehouses of Huntingdon and send him off to mature, by taking the next step in his education and attending one of the Inns of Court. It was the norm for young gentlemen to be sent to one of the Inns, not so much to train them for a career in the law, but rather to obtain some working knowledge of the law to assist in estate management and prepare them as potential magistrates and future MPs. A year after his father's death Oliver made this rite of passage and probably went to Lincoln's Inn which had been attended by his father, grandfather and two of his uncles.[8] Oliver was to remain studying the law in London for three years while Elizabeth was left to manage her family and estate by herself. No doubt he visited his mother and regularly wrote to her to provide what moral support he could. Although Elizabeth would have been able to discuss important family or business matters with Oliver, the fact remained that she was left to resolve the numerous everyday issues by herself. Of course, Elizabeth had her daughters and could turn to Sir Oliver or Dr Beard for advice, but that was not the same as having her son at her side. She must be given credit for her unselfishness and common sense in sending Oliver to study and mature in London so soon after becoming widowed.

The three years at the Inns of Court had brought Oliver in contact with the sons of the gentry from all over the kingdom. It also familiarised him with life in the capital and helped him to learn something of the ways of the City of London and the Royal Court. What Oliver made of all this is not known, but at the very least it would have broadened his experience and, hopefully, made him a more mature person upon his return to family responsibilities in Huntingdon. The completion of his three years coincided with his coming of age and another Elizabeth coming into his life.

Chapter 2

A Second Elizabeth
1620–1629

'I will govern according to the common weal, but not according to the common will.'

King James I

On 24 August 1620, four months after his coming of age, Oliver married Elizabeth Bourchier at St Giles' Cripplegate, in Fore Street, London. Elizabeth was roughly the same age as Oliver and came from a similar background. She was the eldest child of Sir James Bourchier and his wife Frances, who had a total of twelve children. As nine of them were sons, Elizabeth would certainly not be an heiress, but had been raised as a member of the gentry. Sir James was a wealthy London fur and leather merchant who owned extensive lands in Essex, as well as property around Tower Hill. Like others who had made their fortune in London he had joined the gentry by acquiring a country estate. Sir James had bought Little Stanbrook Hall near Felsted, and it was there that Elizabeth had been brought up.

It is not clear how Elizabeth and Oliver came together, but it is very likely to have been through a family connection. Elizabeth's maternal aunt, Eluzai Crane, had married Oliver's uncle, Henry Cromwell, who owned the Upwood estate seven miles north of Huntingdon.[1] Another possible connection was that Oliver's paternal aunt, Joan, had married Sir Francis Barrington of Barrington Hall near Hatfield Broad Oak which might have brought Oliver in contact with Essex society.[2] Although Eluzai had died in 1620, it is more probable that it was through her that the idea of marrying Oliver to Sir James Bourchier's daughter came about. With Oliver still a minor and his mother Elizabeth sole executrix of her husband's will, it would have been her decision to give the proposed marriage her blessing and begin the necessary marital negotiations. It was Elizabeth who arranged the jointure for Oliver's wife and used the jointure she had herself received on the death of her first husband. That was: 'all that parsonage house of Hartford with all the glebe-lands and tythes in the county of Huntingdon'.

Indeed, it is probable that Elizabeth was the driving force behind finding Oliver a suitable wife in the first place. Oliver was only just 21 and so still quite young for marriage. Elizabeth may well have decided that, young as he was, a wife was just what he needed to curb any of his remaining wanton ways and make him mature and responsible enough to be the head of the family. Eluzai's niece Elizabeth Bouchier must have come close to fitting the criteria for Oliver's wife. At 22-years-old it would have been high time for her to be married off and, being a year older than Oliver, might make her a steadying influence. What was more, she came from a respectable family and one that shared Elizabeth's Puritan beliefs. The actual extent to which the marriage between Oliver and Elizabeth was arranged and what dowry she brought is not known. Nor is it known whether they felt any love for one another prior to the wedding. Elizabeth was certainly not known for her beauty, but was a homely, pleasant looking girl. It should be remembered also that among those of a Puritan persuasion a woman was to be loved not for her beauty but for her virtue, and Elizabeth was certainly virtuous.

It is unlikely that Elizabeth found Oliver handsome, but rather a plainly dressed young man of acceptable looks. He had a reddish countenance, long brown hair parted in the middle and a light moustache. His nose was rather bulbous and for most of his life he suffered from boils, but he had a sturdy build of 5ft 10in and held himself well. They made a reasonably well-matched couple. What is known from the future letters between them is that they were to become completely devoted to each other. It is unlikely that Oliver would have achieved what he did in life without the firm foundation of love and support provided by Elizabeth. Oliver's mother deserves credit for her part in bringing about this successful union.

Following the marriage, Oliver returned to Huntingdon with his bride. Elizabeth had been used to living at Stanbrook Hall so the Cromwell's house in Huntingdon High Street must have seemed a come down in comparison. It was a former church property which was reasonably impressive by Huntingdon standards, but might have been more suitable for a successful merchant rather than a member of the gentry. Fortunately, Elizabeth was used to having numerous brothers and sisters around, so it would not have been a shock to find herself sharing the house with Oliver's five, as yet unmarried, sisters. Then there was the matter of Elizabeth, now married to the official head of the household, but with Elizabeth his mother still in residence. In fact, not just still in residence, but the person who had been largely managing the estate since her husband's death and certainly running the house and the lives of her children.

In the seventeenth century the running of a fairly substantial house was no small matter. So much of the necessities of life were produced at home, from brewing the small beer which accompanied all meals, to making malt, churning butter, processing cheese, baking bread, dressing meat, and preserving fruit and vegetables. There were also the mundane matters of laying fires, drawing and heating water, cooking, laundry and cleaning and making tallow candles. Naturally there would be some servants to carry out these activities, but they had to be taught and supervised. Also, the financial aspects of housekeeping would have fallen to the mistress of the house. This involved the payment of the servants and hired hands used for maintenance, as well as the purchase of provisions and minor luxuries from food to wax candles to cloth and clothes. Oliver's mother had been running the house for twenty years and would hardly immediately relinquish her position to Oliver's young bride.

In a richer family there might have been a dower house to where Oliver's mother would have moved on her son's marriage. Elizabeth was by now a 55-year-old widow, so would have been a suitable age for moving out, but clearly the Cromwells did not have the wealth to support a dower house. Had Elizabeth been much older and less active she might probably have been happy to spend her time quietly sitting in the inglenook fireplace doing some sewing. However, Elizabeth was in good health and active, so she would have had no intention of settling for the inglenook option. The situation that found Oliver's mother and wife both under the same roof had the makings for domestic tension. Both might have vied with each other for Oliver's attention and the position of mistress of the house. If any natural tension arose from the situation, it seems to have been resolved as both Elizabeths were to live together for many years to come. From all reports Oliver's mother Elizabeth was a sensible and practical woman and so we may assume that she made her daughter-in-law welcome and gradually handed over the reins of household management to her at a pace that was acceptable to them both.

Having moved to Huntingdon, Elizabeth was away from her family for perhaps the first time. There was the success and excitement of having become married, but there must have also been some apprehension about being united for life with a man she cannot have known well before hand. It must have been potentially pleasant to have her sisters-in-law living in the same house to provide her with young female company. Elizabeth probably became like an elder sister to Jane who was 15 and Robina who was only 10. The other two of Oliver's sisters living at home were Elizabeth, who was five years older than Oliver's wife, and Anna who was three years younger. It is probable that with these two that Elizabeth Bouchier found some companionship. There was also Oliver's married sister Margaret, who was now Mrs Valentine Walton, and who lived a short ride away. Although Margaret was only 19, she had been married for three years, so might have been a natural friend for Elizabeth and one with whom she could confide in about marital matters.

With time Elizabeth would have been introduced to others in their circle, including Oliver's former school master and family friend Dr Beard, who still ran the alms house and school. The good doctor had become an important figure in Huntingdon as he continued to prosper from his various livings, but he had also gone up in the world by being appointed a Royal Chaplain and be given a prebendary stall in Lincoln Cathedral. Much further up the social scale would have been the generous Sir Oliver Cromwell. He would have invited Oliver and Elizabeth to Hinchingbrooke soon after they arrived, and she would have begun to come into contact with the wide family network of Cromwells living in and around Hinchingbrooke. As Sir Oliver had ten children it is probable that some of them would have been of Elizabeth's age. The Cromwells of Hinchingbrooke were high-echelon gentry, but so were many of those that they had married into. There was Oliver's Aunt Mary, Lady Dunch, living at her late husband's estate at Little Wittenham, near Wantage. Then there was Aunt Elizabeth, married to Sir Richard Ingoldsby of Lenborough in Buckinghamshire. Also, another Aunt Elizabeth, married to the wealthy William Hampden of Hampden House, Great Hampden in Berkshire and Aunt Joan, as we have already mentioned, married to Sir Francis Barrington. Not to forget Aunt Frances who had married Richard Walley, a well-to-do local landowner.

It must have been gratifying for Elizabeth to have married into a well-connected family, as indeed was her own, but there was no getting away from the fact that she and Oliver were poor relations. They were minor gentry. Oliver's estate produced an income of £300 a year, but that was dependent upon the harvest and grain prices. Huntingdon was a wheat growing area and although recent harvests had been reasonable, wheat prices had fallen to their lowest point in twenty years. Oliver was principally an arable farmer, but he would also have had a few horses and sheep grazing on some of his own fields or on common land. This would have been supplemented with chickens, pigs and the odd cow for household use. On the face of it the Cromwells appeared reasonably prosperous.

This was a time when a parish priest would have a stipend of between £8 to £10 a year and a labourer might expect a wage of between 7d to 15d a day (without food) when they were fortunate enough to be in employment.[3]

Oliver's annual income of £300 would have been much envied by the cottagers and common folk of Huntingdon, but was at least £200 a year less than the income from that of the average estate of a member of the gentry. The situation was even worse than that. Oliver's father's will had stipulated that for the twenty-one years after his death, two-thirds of his estate would be held by his widow Elizabeth to provide for the maintenance of their daughters. So, in the longer term, Oliver and his wife ended up with an income of £100 a year, once the dowries had been paid for the five remaining sisters. However, those were all potential problems for the future and for the present they had enough on which to get by.

Oliver's mother was probably more aware than he was of how potentially precarious the family's finances were. Oliver had returned from London with his wife and was probably generally at ease with the world. His wife, Elizabeth, probably found her young husband a contented man. It is likely that he was less concerned with his wheat fields than he was with indulging his passion for horses and hunting. In the evenings he would have enjoyed a pipe and a leather tankard of ale by the fire, accompanied by the seven females consisting of his sisters, mother and wife. Oliver loved music so there would definitely have been some singing, which may have been accompanied by any musical instrument members of the family could play. As Oliver had a sense of humour and enjoyed boisterous fun, the periods of relaxation with Elizabeth and the other ladies of the household were likely to have been quite merry times.

A year after their marriage Elizabeth fulfilled her expected duty and gave birth to a baby boy. Oliver must have been delighted to have an heir, even if the expected inheritance was in decline. They called the boy Henry who was probably named after either Sir Henry 'the Golden Knight' or, more likely, after Oliver's uncle, Henry Cromwell of Upwood, whose wife Eluai may have been instrumental in bringing about Elizabeth and Oliver's marriage. The next year Elizabeth again fulfilled expectations by producing another son, this time rather unoriginally named Oliver. The birth was a welcome cause for joy in the year 1622, which saw a below average harvest and increasing inflation.[4]

The following year brought an equally poor harvest with wheat prices remaining some ten shillings a quarter less than normal, yet domestic life for Elizabeth and Oliver presumably continued in an agreeable fashion. They had the convenience of living in the small town of Huntingdon coupled with the pleasant circumstances that rural life offered to many landowners. It was a life marked by few excitements other than major functions at Hinchingbrooke, as when Sir Oliver entertained the king or other leading figures. It would have been an ordinary life marked by the seasons, births and deaths, sowing and reaping and events in the church calendar. In 1624, an eighth female, albeit in swaddling clothes, joined the ever-increasing Cromwell household. Her name was Bridget.

The year after Bridget's birth King James died. The death of the sovereign was always a major milestone for the country, but in truth, it did little to change the lives of the citizens of Huntingdon. King James' reign had been a break from the past. Rightly or wrongly, many looked back with nostalgia to the time of 'Queen Elizabeth of blessed memory,' and continued to name their daughters after her. James had wanted to create peace and religious settlement between the Puritans and Anglicans. He ended the war with Spain and to cement good relations even executed Sir Walter Raleigh at the request of the Spanish ambassador for attacking a Spanish outpost, Guiana. Yet, despite the fact that he presided over religious conferences, James failed to draw the diverging faiths together and decided to come down in favour of his established church. One of his religious initiatives resulted in the publication of the Authorised Version of the Bible. Previous to this were versions based on Tyndale's first English translation, but the wider publication of the improved Authorised Version made the bible more accessible. This enabled people to interpret the Scriptures themselves with the unintended result that meant their conclusions were not always in accord with the doctrine of the established church. Increasingly, they were uncomfortable with church ceremony interfering between the Christian individual and his or her maker. Feelings of this sort were essentially Puritan and during the course of King James' reign Puritanism spread and found favour among members of the gentry and, thus, in the House of Commons where many of them held seats.

During this time, the Commons also began to explore its perceived rights based on common law and started to assert them against those of both the king and the House of Lords. King James, on the other hand, was also conscious of his rights as sovereign, a position he was convinced he held by divine right. This is best explained in his own words from his book *Basilikon Doron*: 'Kings are the breathing images of God upon earth. They are not only God's lieutenants upon earth and set upon God's throne, but even by God himself are called gods.' As the king was answerable only to God, it was up to the monarch alone to decide how much he should respect the law or the wishes of either Houses of Parliament. Again, in his own words: 'A good king will frame his actions according to the law; yet is not bound thereto but of his good will and for the good example of his subjects.'

King James' beliefs might not have mattered so much if he had not been dependant on parliament for his finances. When Queen Elizabeth died the Crown had debts of £400,000 and she had only managed to keep her financial head above water through the sale of Crown lands. James had brought peace, but his extravagance increased government expenses and he had to rely on parliament to legally raise sufficient taxation. Parliament, the Commons in particular, became aware that their control of the purse strings gave them the leverage to assert their rights at the expense of the Crown.

Whether this conflict of interests between parliament and king might be amicably resolved was a matter for the future. It is probable that neither Elizabeth Cromwell nor her husband Oliver were even aware of this as a potential problem. However, there are two things that had stemmed from James' reign of which they might have been aware. These were the interrelated matters of the increased fear of popery and the growth of Puritanism. Although both of them were children at the time of the 1605 Gunpowder Plot, such was the horror over this attempted bloody coup by some Roman Catholics that it was neither forgiven nor forgotten. In 1606 Parliament had passed a law that every year, 5 November should be held as a day of thanksgiving and bonfires lit in all towns.[5] Whenever Elizabeth and Oliver attended the annual Huntingdon bonfire, their natural Protestant fear of popery was probably reinforced.

As the citizens of Huntingdon were against Catholicism and all the trappings of popery, it is likely that they became increasingly concerned that King James' Anglican Church had not gone far enough to purify itself from papist practices. One aspect of this was that Anglican clergy seldom gave sermons and when they did, they merely read from a book. Those of a Puritan persuasion regarded an inspired sermon as more important than formal liturgy in a church service. As in other towns with growing Puritan movements, they decided to remedy it themselves and appoint their own town preacher. The job of preaching was called a 'lectureship' and the Huntingdon Corporation did not need to look far for a member of the clergy who was up to the task. The Cromwell's old friend Dr Beard was appointed to the town lectureship in 1614 and given an annual payment for delivering sermons at All Saint's Church every Wednesday and Sunday morning.

All Saints was one of several benefices held by Beard, so to contemporary eyes it was surprising that he was actually paid to deliver sermons in a church for which he was the vicar. However, what this shows is that sermons were not normally given and that the Huntingdon Corporation was prepared to spend good money to have them. Beard for his part was, of course, happy to receive the revenue. Beard was puritanical in his beliefs, detesting Catholicism, and in the year King James died published his work *Anti-Christ the Pope of Rome*. The fact that he was so popular in Huntingdon shows how the town embraced the Puritan ethos. King James had been on the throne since Elizabeth and Oliver's early childhood, but apart from his visits to Hinchingbrooke, there was only one way in which their lives would have been affected by this reign. This was being part of a community that increasingly looked towards the Puritan faith.

It was a different story for Oliver's uncle, Sir Oliver. For him the reign of King James had been one of promise and expectation, having started so well with the royal visit in 1603. Those who lavished gifts and hospitality on a monarch to the extent that Sir Oliver did expected some recognition for their display of duty. Sir Oliver, although already a knight, had been appointed a Knight of the Bath at James' coronation. Although a good start, and despite the king's visits to Hinchingbrooke, it is where it seems to have ended. For King James' funeral Sir Oliver was given the honour of holding one of the royal standards. It may have been something that impressed other leading families in the county, but it did not translate into hard cash in the way a government appointment or the grant of a monopoly might have done.

Hard cash was something for which Sir Oliver was finding increasingly in need. He was beginning to negotiate loans from London money lenders to keep up his lifestyle when a means of raising funds occurred to him. As the king was so fond of Hinchingbrooke and was using it as his annual autumn residence, he might be prepared to buy the property for a good sum. It is probable that when King James visited Hinchingbrooke in 1620 this suggestion was first proposed. The king appeared to like the idea but did not rush into any decision. He already possessed hunting lodges such as his Manor of Woodstock and being a canny Scot was in no rush to buy Hinchingbrooke when he could stay there for free.

Despite delays, negotiations over the sale of Hinchingbrooke eventually began, but then continued in a rather desultory manner. King James' own family affairs had become a higher priority after his daughter Elizabeth had married Frederick the Elector Palatine. The Protestants of Bohemia revolted against their nominal ruler the Catholic Holy Roman Emperor and invited the Protestant Frederick to be their king. He accepted but was king for only a year before the Catholic League of Imperial states invaded first Bohemia and then the Palatinate, forcing Frederick and Elizabeth to flee as exiles to the Dutch Republic.

These events in Bohemia had sparked the Thirty Years War which was to dominate power politics for that period, devastate central Europe and result in 8,000,000 casualties. King James had naturally wanted to have his son-in-law restored to the Palatinate. He attempted to try to create an alliance with the king of Spain in order to get him to use his influence with his cousin the Emperor for Frederick's restoration. The king's eldest son, Prince Henry Frederick, had died of typhoid fever some years earlier so James decided to try to create an alliance with Spain by marrying his second son Charles to the Spanish Infanta. This scheme went horribly wrong, ending with Charles' ignominious rejection by the Infanta and James being persuaded to go to war with Spain to repay the slight. As France was the traditional enemy of Spain, James pursued an alliance with France to be cemented through the marriage of Charles to a French princess.

These affairs of state that so closely touched on his own children must have distracted James from thoughts of Hinchingbrooke. Added to this was a deterioration in the king's health, first with arthritis, soon to be accompanied by gout and kidney stones. Sir Oliver must have lived in the hope that the king would recover sufficiently enough to bring the sale to a satisfactory conclusion. But that was not to be; a stroke followed by severe dysentery brought the king's life to its end in 1625. The death of James had also brought an end to the Hinchingbrooke negotiations and the end of Sir Oliver's hopes. It was back to new negotiations, this time with the London money lenders.

Sir Oliver probably kept his financial troubles to himself and Elizabeth and Oliver continued their life unchanged by the king's death. As Prince Henry Frederick had died in 1612, his younger brother Charles had thirteen years in which to be educated in kingship. Charles was, of course, the former frail little boy who may have played with Oliver at Hinchingbrooke back in 1604. He was now a 25-year-old man with a refined and dignified manner, but his stammer and small stature hinted at that previous frailty. He had not only inherited the three kingdoms of England, Scotland and Ireland, but also his father's chief minister, the handsome and disastrous George Villiers, Duke of Buckingham. It was largely Buckingham's doing that caused James' peaceful reign to end with war against Spain and the agreement to provide 600 soldiers to fight with the Dutch. Both were costly ventures that could only be paid for with the support of parliament; a parliament that was none too pleased with a French alliance that was cemented by the marriage of Charles to a Catholic French princess. Oliver and Elizabeth would have been aware of these events but are unlikely to have paid much attention to them as they were far removed from their daily lives, which continued as normal with the birth of a third son called Richard the next year. A concern in their normal lives which still loomed at this time involved finding both husbands and dowries for Oliver's unmarried sisters. It was a matter of which Oliver's mother Elizabeth worked towards as a likely matter of urgency as her eldest daughter Elizabeth was now 31 years old and others were not far behind.

This was a time when daughters were often married off before they were twenty.

In 1627 there was a major blow to the whole Cromwell family. Sir Oliver, being unable to pay the interest on accumulated debts, was forced to sell Hinchingbrooke, which he sold to Sir Sidney Montagu, and move to his much lesser grand residence of Ramsay Manor. It was one thing to sell Hinchingbrooke to King James for a good price and probably continue to administrate it, and quite another to sell it to another member of the gentry. The Montagus were a Northamptonshire family who had raised themselves to prominence through law and parliament. Sir Sidney was the son of a judge and the grandson of a judge. He had himself gone into law and became a Member of Parliament. His brother Edward was MP for Nottinghamshire and had been made Baron Montagu. Another brother, Henry, was also a lawyer and politician who had become Lord High Treasurer and was created Earl of Manchester. In short, the Montagus were the epitome of how a talented family of the lower gentry were able to rise to prominence during the later-Tudor, early-Stuart period.

It was a great period for social mobility, but in the case of the Cromwells, the mobility was downwards. Sir Oliver, the son of the 'Golden Knight' and he himself the leading figure in the county, was renowned for his hospitality to the great and the good, including the king. He was still a respected knight, but his days of major local influence were over, having passed to Sir Sidney Montagu. Elizabeth and Oliver may have sometimes resented being poor relations to Sir Oliver, but at least he was a man of prominence. Now they were just poor relations of a fairly average landowner now living at Ramsay some twenty-five miles from Huntingdon. At a time when there were major gulfs between classes and social status meant so much, Elizabeth and Oliver must have felt that their own status, such as it was, had seriously declined in Huntingdon.

Just as Oliver must have thought that he and his family were sinking into obscurity, there was a surprising turn of events that helped shape his life for the better. It was decided that he should be one of the two MPs for Huntingdon in the next parliament which was to sit in March 1628. Oliver had displayed no previous interest in politics or civic affairs, nor was he a member of the senior gentry who might have been expected to become an MP. True, his father had been an MP briefly in 1593, but he was the younger son of the 'Golden Knight'. Oliver was merely the son of a younger son, and one whose finances looked decidedly precarious. No doubt Oliver's mother Elizabeth would have encouraged him to follow his father and become an MP. However, it would need more than enthusiasm or even aptitude for him to become an MP; a powerful patron was needed.

It is not known who gave Oliver the necessary vital support to ensure he was elected. It is just possible that it may have been Sir Sidney Montagu. Although he had not yet moved into Hinchingbrooke, he may have already decided to combine his desire to control a Huntingdon MP with an act of reconciliation towards the Cromwell family. Certainly, the other borough MP was a Montagu appointment as it was James Montagu, the second son of Sir Sidney's brother, the Earl of Manchester. Perhaps the more likely sponsor was Sir Oliver. Having moved from Huntingdon and having ceased being one of the county MPs himself, he may have wanted to retain influence in Huntingdon through his nephew. However it came about, no doubt Oliver's mother, wife and sisters would have had a feeling of pride that he was to represent the town. This feeling might have been modified by the fact that it would take him away. Oliver is not known to have left the Huntingdon area since his return with his bride eight years previously, having along the way produced a family of his own which that year had increased to five children when Elizabeth gave birth to another son, christened Henry.

Prior to attending parliament Oliver is likely to have brought himself up-to-date on the issues of the day, most of which probably concerned the disastrous management of King Charles' principal minister, the Duke of Buckingham who had instigated the unnecessary war with Spain. Among his many honours Buckingham had been made Lord High Admiral and, as such, he decided to launch the war by leading an expedition to attack Cadiz. This expedition, led by an admiral who had never previously put to sea, was a complete disaster.[6] When the poorly trained and undisciplined English troops landed they got so drunk on Spanish wine they were unable to fight effectively, and the expedition ended up limping home having run out of provisions. A little later, the country drifted into war with its ally, France, largely through Buckingham's stupidity which included trying to have an affair with the French queen. Buckingham also led another expedition, one in support of the Protestant French Huguenots at La Rochelle who had been holding out against the Catholic forces of King Louis. Buckingham's expedition of ninety ships and 10,000 men failed to capture its first objective, the town of St Martin on the Isle de Rhé, and he once again limped back to England having lost 4,000 men. It was the high cost of the simultaneous wars with France and Spain that had forced the king to call a new parliament, so it could vote for the necessary taxes to pay for them.

As Oliver knew London from his time at the Inns of Court, he may have stayed somewhere he had lodged before, like the town house owned by Elizabeth's father, Sir James Bourchier, near the Tower of London. Sir James may have introduced his son-in-law to some of the leading London merchants and gentry of his acquaintance who were interested in politics, such as Oliver St John, an up and coming lawyer with connections to John Pym. Pym was an experienced Parliamentarian who had first become an MP fourteen years previously and who had been one of the main leading MPs who had wanted to impeach Buckingham at the last parliament. We do not know whether Oliver met such people at this stage, but he is certainly likely to have been in contact with his cousin Edmund Dunch, the son of his father's sister, Mary. Edmund had been MP for Berkshire in 1624 and returned again in 1626, but for the 1628 parliament he had been elected MP for Wallingford. Oliver may have probably also contacted another cousin, John Hampden, the son of Elizabeth, another of his father's sisters. John was MP for Wendover who had also previously served in parliament and as such, he and Edmund may have advised Oliver on the procedures of the Commons and how to conduct himself.

Whether or not Oliver was acquainted with other MPs before attending parliament is not known. Either way, his first days in the House must have been slightly daunting. The Commons sat in the Chapel of St Stephen which was a high narrow building at right angles to Westminster Hall. It had been built by Edward III as a royal chapel but had been given to the Commons in 1547 as part of the general dissolution of unwanted religious sites.[7] At the east end of the building was the Speaker's oak chair with five tiers of benches behind it and steep rows of benches on either side. In the centre was a table with the mace and clerks and there was a small visitors gallery at the west end. Oliver was to come to know this building very well over the years, but as a newcomer it would have been difficult to feel at ease. This would be particularly so given his financial situation which would have been made worse by the added expenses of living in London.

Oliver was just one among the 400 MPs in the Commons, a large number of whom had previously sat in parliament and knew each other. For them, a parliamentary sitting must have been something of a social reunion whereas Oliver, like other new MPs, needed to get to know other members. A great many of his fellow MPs were knights, some were the sons of peers and nearly all of them had greater incomes than his own. Their dress and lifestyle must have been a constant reminder to him that he was something of an outsider and could have undermined both his confidence and morale. Nevertheless, Oliver would have felt some excitement and exaltation about being a member of the Commons, although this may have been tempered by him missing Elizabeth and his family in Huntingdon.

Life for Oliver's family must have been difficult with him away. His wife Elizabeth had been used to him being by her side for the whole eight years of their married life. Sisters and mother would also be missing the person that they looked up to as the head of the family, as would his five young children. Then there was the more practical matter of running the estate. Oliver's mother Elizabeth had managed this on her own when he had been in London before at the Inns of Court, so had no doubt taken up the reins, while her daughter-in-law, who was once again pregnant, continued to busy herself with her young family. Oliver may have been able to keep up with family and estate matters by post, but as it would take the best part of a week to exchange letters, this was not entirely satisfactory.

Oliver's mother would have continued her mission to find suitable husbands for her daughters, a probable matter of urgency as her eldest daughter, Elizabeth, was 34 and there were still four other unmarried daughters living at home who needed husbands. Even Robina, the youngest, was 18 and a suitable age for marriage. Elizabeth may have been regarded a lost cause when it came to match making, so her mother was likely to have been putting her efforts into husbands for Catherine, who at 31 was almost on the shelf, and Anna, a more promising 25-year-old. It may have been about this time that Catherine became betrothed to Roger Whetstone who appears to have been a reasonably prosperous member of the gentry of Puritan persuasion. Roger had done some service with the Dutch as part of the Thirty Years War which had become a bloody struggle not only between Protestantism and Catholicism, but between France and Spain. This would have been a good match for Catherine, but quite when it occurred is not recorded.

Oliver's family in Huntingdon must have tried as best they could to follow the events unfolding in parliament, relying on news from carriers after it had trundled its two-day journey up the Great North Road to the town. Such news as they received was important as Oliver had become an MP at a critical time. The king had called parliament because of the urgent need to agree the tonnage and poundage excise taxation to conduct the war against France and Spain. The House of Commons, for its part, was in no mood to vote for supplies for an unnecessary war until it had aired its grievances and obtained some concessions from the Crown.

The grievances were not just about the conduct of Buckingham, but the overstepping of his powers by billeting soldiers on wealthy families without payment, raising forced loans and imprisoning without trial those who refused to cough up money that was demanded. The Commons drew up a Petition of Rights cataloguing these arbitrary actions, requesting the king to put an end to them. On 7 June the king very reluctantly accepted the Petition in order to receive an agreement for the funding of war; it seemed that monarch and parliament could work in harmony. To Charles' surprise the Commons still did not grant the tonnage and poundage and demanded that the king remove Buckingham from his council. The king acted to save his minister and on 26 June prorogued parliament until October.

Oliver had been a mere spectator to this clash between the king and the Commons and had not spoken, but sensibly watched and listened to the proceedings. The surprising prorogation of parliament meant that he was able to return home after a merely three-month absence. When he first left it was for an indefinite time and his quick return must have been a relief to Elizabeth and the family. It was also good for them to know that he would remain home until parliament reassembled in October. As it happened, it was not until January the next year that it was necessary for Oliver to return to London, because a major event caused delay in reconvening parliament. The Commons objections to Buckingham had gained widespread support, especially in London where a mob attacked and killed the duke's physician, a Dr Lamb. A satirical notice had been nailed up in the city saying: 'Who rules the kingdom? –The king. Who rules the king? –The duke. Who rules the duke? –The devil. Let the duke look to it or he will be served as his doctor was served.'[8]

These were prophetic words. Buckingham was in Portsmouth preparing for another expedition to relieve La Rochelle when on 28 August he was assassinated by a dissatisfied officer called John Feltham. The assassin was arrested and eventually executed, but so great was the dislike of Buckingham that Feltham was cheered by many as a public hero. The assassination did not prevent the expedition sailing to relieve La Rochelle, but before it arrived, the Huguenots had surrendered and the war with France drew to a close. The end of the French war would save money for the Exchequer, but the bills from it still had to be paid and there remained the cost of the ongoing war with Spain.

When parliament met again on 20 January 1629 their mood should have improved now that Buckingham was no longer relevant. The king again requested a vote to raise the tonnage and poundage taxation. The Commons ignored the request and continued with their grievances, not least of which was that the king had been collecting taxes without parliamentary consent, contrary to the Petition of Rights. As the majority of MPs were, like Oliver, Puritan in their outlook, they turned their attention to what they considered the corruption of the Anglican Church by way of the introduction of papist practices. They established a Committee of Religion to look into the introduction of Arminianism[9] by people in high places in the church. What was meant by Arminianism is best described by what would later be called 'High Church,' that is emphasis on ritual and formality in services rather than on plain worship inspired by sermons. What was meant by 'high places' were bishops such as William Laud, Bishop of Bath and Wells, and Richard Neile, Bishop of Winchester, both of whom encouraged traditional ritual in services and decoration in churches. What Laud was later to describe as 'the beauty of holiness,' the Puritan gentlemen of the Commons regarded as idolatrous popery.

Those leading this attack on the 'Arminians' in the church were Sir John Eliot and John Pym. In February Oliver became a member of the Committee of Religion and made his maiden speech in the House of Commons. The speech was a short one recounting what he had heard from his old family friend Dr Beard about how Bishop Neile had reprimanded Beard when he had denounced a royal chaplain, the revered William Alabaster, for being an Arminian. The Speaker took sufficient enough notice of the speech to direct that Dr Beard should come to the House to give evidence against Neil. The king also took note of the Commons discussions of religion which he regarded as an insolent trespass on a subject that was his royal prerogative and for which he alone was answerable for to God.

When the MPs reassembled they were informed that they had been adjourned once again. Furious at this, two members held down the Speaker in his chair and refused to be dismissed. Instead they locked the Chamber and passed motions against popish practices in the church, taxation without parliamentary consent and made it treasonous for any merchant to pay such taxes. The king ordered Black Rod to restore the Commons to obedience and the Sergeant at Arms to seize the mace. After threats to break down the chamber door, and amid much noise and scuffling, the Commons was finally adjourned. Eight days later Charles formally dissolved parliament. Some MPs were then arrested for their opposition, amongst whom was Sir John Eliot, who was to remain in the Tower until his death three-and-a-half years later.

With parliament dissolved Oliver was no longer an MP. Indeed, although no one knew it at the time, there would be no more parliament for another eleven years. He had made just one short speech which had resulted in nothing as there had been no time for Dr Beard to attend the Commons before parliament had ended. It seemed that his short, undistinguished political career was over. Oliver returned to Huntingdon, no doubt to the delight of his family. That delight must have turned to concern when they realised that Oliver was changed. While in London he had consulted one of the great doctors of the day, Sir Theodore Mayerne. Sir Theodore had prescribed him a cocktail of drugs because he had noted Oliver suffered from '*valde melancholicus*', severe clinical depression.[10]

Chapter 3

Crisis and Redemption
1629–1638

'Poor intricated soul! Riddling, perplexed, labyrinthine soul!'

John Donne, *Sermon XLVIII*

We do not know what form Oliver's depression took. We may assume he exhibited at least a degree of listlessness, lack of interest, anxiety and loss of confidence. One symptom was later recounted by Dr Simcott, his doctor in Huntingdon, to Sir Philip Warwick and later recorded by him in his *Memoires of the Reign of Charles I*. This was that Oliver 'had been called upon him many times upon a strange fancy, which made him believe he was dying'.[1] The change in Oliver's personality must have been difficult for the whole of his family, but in particular for Elizabeth. Not only would she, as his wife, have been closest to him, but she may have personally suffered through nightly disturbance if, as is likely, Oliver suffered from insomnia. Also, we can only guess what side effects Oliver experienced on top of his illness as a result of the combination of seventeenth-century drugs that would have been prescribed for him. The family evenings together round the fireside may well have lost their previous merriment.

It might have been hoped that some positive circumstances could have helped lift Oliver out of his illness. After all, he was now home with a family who loved him and a recently born pretty baby girl. This baby had been christened Elizabeth, but was already being called 'Bettie,' to avoid confusion with Oliver's mother, wife and sister. On the subject of sisters, there must have been some celebration when his sister Anna got married at about this time. Once again, Oliver's mother seems to have arranged a good match. Anna's husband was John Sewster who was the nephew of Elizabeth's first husband, William Lynne. Sewster was a small landowner of knightly family who had no interest in public office, but who would have been able to provide Anna with a reasonably comfortable lifestyle. Although there would have been joy at this union, there also would have been cause for anxiety because of the dowry. The fairly recent marriage of Catherine to

Roger Whetstone, followed by that of Anna, must have been a double blow to Oliver's income. Financial worries can only have contributed to Oliver's depression.

Local affairs often seem trivial and boring to outsiders, especially when they occur in a small backwater town like Huntingdon. To those citizens who consider they might be adversely affected by change, such matters can assume a disproportionate importance, leading to dispute and bitter divisions. Such was the case in Huntingdon at about the time Oliver returned, which began with the good news of a major bequest to the town. The bequest was made by Richard Fishbourne who had been born in Huntingdon, who then went to London to join the Mercer's Guild and on to make his fortune. Fishbourne had authorised the Mercers to administer his estate and it was they who informed the Huntingdon Corporation that he had left £2,000 to his home town. This was a very large sum and it took some time to decide how it should be invested. Eventually land was bought which produced an annual income of £100 per year. This was all fairly uncontentious, but it was deciding how the income should be spent that was much more difficult.

The borough Common Council consisted of two bailiffs and twenty-four burgesses. It is probable that Oliver was one of the burgesses having been an MP and a prominent citizen. After considerable discussion the Common Council considered two options for using the income. One was to spend it all on the poor of the borough through a work creation programme. The other was to spend £60 on the poor and £40 on a preaching lectureship. Oliver appears to have supported all the charity income going to the poor. However, the majority of the Common Council felt that £40 should be spent on a continued lectureship for Dr Beard at All Souls. This would not only save them the cost of the fee that Beard was currently paid, but also meant that he would receive £40 instead of the lower fee he had received from the Council. Beard had ceased to run the school by this time but had added to his many benefices by being appointed Rector of Wistow, as well as becoming a JP for the county and a member of Huntingdon Common Council. Although a very prosperous cleric, Beard would have naturally wanted to increase his fee for the All Saints lectureship. Sir Sidney Montagu of Hinchingbrooke added his support to the majority of the Council who wanted the Beard preaching lectureship. To top it all, as Beard had been a royal chaplain to his father, King Charles let it be known that he too supported Beard.

Oliver put himself out on a limb by opposing that part of the bequest income be given to the All Saints lectureship. He also put himself in direct opposition to his old family friend, no doubt much to the concern of his mother Elizabeth. The dispute over this matter soon became very acrimonious and the case was taken to the Court of Mercers. After a visit to Huntingdon by a Mercer committee and more endless wrangling, the Mercers made their ruling. They directed that money should go to a preaching lectureship, but that it should not be at All Saints but instead at St Mary's Huntingdon where the benefactor Fishbourne had been baptised. What was more, they decided that this should be a second lectureship and the job of preacher should go to a Robert Proctor, with Beard continuing his All Saints lectureship at the Common Council's expense. After further haggling the Mercers ruled that Beard should receive a single payment of £40. The majority of the Common Council would have been furious that the Mercers had thwarted their designs, but at least Beard was reasonably happy with the outcome. He had retained the All Saints lectureship with its existing fee and had received the useful payment of £40. Also, he must have been gratified to have received so much support from the leading figures of the town despite any objections by Oliver.

The rift with an old family friend must have been difficult but worse was yet to come. The long dispute over the Fishbourne legacy had convinced the majority of the Common Council that they should have a more effective way of running the borough. In spring 1630 they petitioned the king for a new charter and this was subsequently granted. The charter stated that there should be a permanent body of aldermen to serve for life and a mayor, who was appointed by seniority among the aldermen, to serve for a year. In the new borough management Oliver was not made an alderman and was merely offered one of the town's five JP posts. A county JP, such as Dr Beard, had real authority, but to be just one of the borough JPs was one step above being a village constable. Oliver declined the appointment. He would have realised how far his position in the town rested on his uncle's standing. There were new occupants of Hinchingbrooke and he was no longer an MP, but a minor landowner with mounting financial difficulties; not a situation easy to bear for someone with bouts of depression.

Oliver had supported the new charter but was dismayed with the result. The new charter enabled a grab for power by a leading clique in Huntingdon of which he was not a part. Worse yet, he saw the new mayor and aldermen using their positions to further their own interests in the running of the borough. They began changing old established practises, such as the grazing of cattle on the commons, to their financial advantage. Oliver and his one ally, the town postmaster William Kilbourne, were angry enough not to take the aldermanic coup lying down. Supported by Kilbourne, Oliver made a public denunciation of Mayor Waldon and Robert Barnard, the recorder, for their misuse of the charter. The speech was both passionate and vitriolic.

In fact, it was sufficiently vitriolic for Robert Barnard to regard it as so 'disgraceful and unseemly' that he reported Oliver and Kilbourne to the Privy Council for attacking a charter granted by the king.[2]

Oliver's wife, mother and the rest of his family must have been extremely anxious and rather embarrassed at this turn of events. Oliver's mental state may have been partially responsible for his 'disgraceful and unseemly' action in challenging the leading figures of Huntingdon. His outburst then being reported to the Privy Council, would have been the talk of the town. It was a town in which the Cromwell family were well known; his actions must have been difficult for them as it put them at odds with their friends. No doubt some friends rallied round, but it is likely that the overall experience for the family was that of being marginalised, if not actually shunned.

Oliver and Kilbourne were summoned to the Privy Council and appeared before them on 26 November 1630 when they were remanded in custody for six days. For Oliver to find himself in gaol, even for this short time, must have been a further reminder how far he had fallen. On 1 December the case was handed to the Lord Privy Seal, Henry Montagu, Earl of Manchester. This would not have been a welcome development. The Earl of Manchester was the brother of Sir Sidney Montagu who had supported the corporation and Dr Beard so Oliver who opposed them might have well faced bias. Manchester asked Oliver and Kilbourne to explain their case against the mayor and aldermen. They described how the mayor and aldermen alone, without consultation of the burgesses, disposed of the inheritance of their town lands, altered the rate of cattle on the commons and fined even the poor £29 for disobedience. Manchester listened to their plea and also read submissions from the corporation. One of these was the following affidavit from Dr Beard: 'Oliver Cromwell, esquire, and William Kilbourne, gent, with a free assent and consent did agree to the renewing of our late charter and that it should be altered from Bailiffs to mayor as they did hope it would be for the good and quiet of the town.'[3]

Beard's evidence was damning and implied that Oliver only opposed the implementation of the charter because he had not himself been appointed an alderman. In the circumstances, the judgement given by Manchester on 6 December was reasonably even handed. He directed the aldermen agree to uphold the existing rights of the commons, and limit fines to twenty marks (£13 6s 8d). This addressed Oliver's objections, but was followed by a sting in the tail. Manchester exonerated the mayor and recorder, praised the new charter and required Oliver to make a cringing apology to Barnard.

Oliver and Kilbourne returned to Huntingdon in December as losers. Some of the townsfolk may well have been grateful to them for their success in preserving their common rights. However, the majority of those who mattered in Huntingdon would have been gleeful that they had been ignominiously put in their place. Barnard was sufficiently delighted as to have his new born son baptised 'Manchester Barnard' in All Saints Church.

Oliver's family would have found him returned home rejected and dejected. For a man who suffered bouts of depression, to be excluded from a position of authority in his own town only then to be publically humiliated by being placed in custody and forced to make an abject apology, this must have been a trying time. There can be little doubt that his mood made life equally difficult for his wife Elizabeth and the rest of the family. It was a situation compounded by the additional stress of financial worries and reduction in the family's status; hardly the ingredients for a happy family Christmas period.

Elizabeth and the family would have watched helplessly as the whole trivial matters of the Fishbourne legacy and the town charter had escalated out of hand and leading to the major crisis in Oliver's life and one that would affect all their lives. For Oliver's mother, the rift with her old friend Thomas Beard must have been particularly upsetting, especially as it was to be permanent. In 1631 a third edition was printed of Beard's popular *Theatre of God's Judgements* and in the preface, he thanks the burgesses for standing by him 'in the late business of the lecture' in the face of 'the opposition of some malign spirits'. It is very likely that Oliver was included amongst the malign spirits. With his honour and position in ruins, and finances in tatters, Oliver decided to sell up and leave.

Having made the decision to leave, Oliver focused on the major task of managing his affairs in order to make the big change. After what must have been a stressful period, in May 1631 Elizabeth and Oliver moved to St Ives, a small town on the River Great Ouse between Huntingdon and Ely. Oliver had sold all but four acres of his land in Huntingdon for £1,800. As this small sum probably provided an annual income of only £100, his financial circumstances brought him to well below that of gentry level and he became a tenant farmer. His being a yeoman working farmer reduced the status of his family to what was described as 'the middling sort'. This must have been difficult to bear for Elizabeth, the daughter of a knight. Oliver's mother Elizabeth was also the daughter of a knight and being of the older generation might well have felt the change even more keenly. In fact, for whatever reason, she decided not to move and stayed on in Huntingdon.

The land that Oliver tenanted was part of the Slepe Hall estate to the south-east of the town belonging to a distant relative, Henry Lawrence, and the house he rented as probably Wood Farm.[4] Oliver's Huntingdon lands had been largely used for wheat growing. The water meadows around St Ives were not suitable for arable farming and so he became a sheep grazier. Ironically it was just at a time when the price of wheat began to rise steeply after experiencing a depression in previous years. The Cromwell household was still large, consisting of Oliver and Elizabeth and their six children: Robert, Oliver, Bridgette, Richard, Henry and Elizabeth. There were also Oliver's unmarried aunts: Elizabeth, Jane and Robina. The major upheaval of the move and change of status must have made this a difficult time for the whole family. Although they had only moved five miles from Huntingdon and could continue to visit those friends who were still prepared to receive them, they needed to put down new roots and make new friends in St Ives. Oliver was fortunate in already having a friend in St Ives. This was the newly arrived rector, Henry Downhall, with whom he had been a close companion at Cambridge and one who Oliver had made godfather to his eldest son Robert. Having Downhall as a neighbour in St Ives must have given Oliver someone to confide in and may have helped to alleviate some bouts of depression.

We cannot be certain, but it is thought to be about this time of crisis in his life that Oliver had his spiritual conversion. Oliver was, of course, a practising Christian, as was virtually the whole of the population of the three kingdoms. He was a Protestant and a member of the Anglican Church but had been brought up in the Puritan tradition as his parents were friendly with his Puritan schoolmaster, Thomas Beard, and he had attended the Puritan leaning Sidney Sussex College. But what was a Puritan? All Protestants were anti-Catholic and against popery. Puritans took this a step further and wanted to purify the established church of remaining Catholic ceremonial and practices.

Puritans differed on exactly how much of the church still needed purification. Should it be the removal of church decoration, such as stained glass and carvings because they could be seen to be idolatrous? If so, how far should this go; should it entail whitewashing church wall paintings, the smashing of windows and the breaking up of statues? Should it merely entail dispensing with candles and incense? There was also the question of Christian practice in church; most would agree not to use the sign of the cross, but there were differing views on whether it was wrong to have the alter at the east end of a church and whether it was necessary to turn towards it. More fundamentally, Puritans questioned the sacraments and whether some or all should be abolished along with the Book of Common Prayer. There were many other important issues for those of a Puritan outlook, such as whether or not to abolish bishops or to continue to have bishops but make them accountable to lay leaders or merely to reduce some of the bishops' powers.

It is probable that when Oliver went to St Ives he was a fairly normal God-fearing Protestant who fell halfway along the Puritan spectrum of Anglicanism. This middle of the road Puritan faith suddenly changed to a climax of religious zeal that was to shape the rest of his life. This change was not so much concerned with any remaining papist trappings, such as the use of candles and keeping the alter at the east end of the church. Formal and external religion were of little matter to him compared with a sudden inner certainty that he had been specifically called by God. His friend, Henry Downhall, was no doubt someone he spoke to about his spiritual feelings, but this friendship is unlikely to have been a catalyst for the change. Downhall was a more formal Anglican and went on to serve as a chaplain in the Royalist army. In fact, he was later dispossessed of his parish in Cambridgeshire for hiring a curate who was 'one who observed ceremonies;' clearly not much of a Puritan.[5] If anyone did influence Oliver's ardent spiritual awakening it could have been Job Tookey or Walter Wells, both Calvinist leaning preachers at St Ives and Godmanchester respectively. We do not know what brought about this fundamental change. We can only speculate how it happened, but some idea of what form this awakening took is described by Oliver in a letter. The following is an extract from this letter to his cousin Elizabeth, the daughter of one of his uncles, Sir Henry Cromwell, written several years later in October 1638:

> 'My soul is in the congregation of the firstborn, my body rests in hope, and if here I may honour God either by doing or by suffering, I shall be most glad…the Lord accepts me in the light … Blessed be His Name for shining upon so dark a heart as mine! You know what my manner of life hath been. Oh, I have lived in and loved darkness, and hated the light. I was the chief of sinners. This is true; I hated Godliness, yet God had mercy on me. O the riches of His mercy. Praise Him for me, that He hath begun a good work should perfect it in the name of Christ.'[6]

Reading this it might be assumed that Oliver had led a dissolute and unchristian life before his spiritual conversion. Although he may have sown some wild oats as a young man, after his marriage Oliver became a sober and devout husband and father. What he was probably indicating in his letter is that he had previously lived an empty life unaware of that, despite his shortcomings, God had made him one of His elects, graced with the certainty of salvation. Once he had grasped the full assurance of God's promise to him he could only pour out his heart in praise and thanksgiving for this unmerited gift. Henceforth he would be constantly aware of his unrepayable debt to Almighty God to whom he would place his complete trust in all things.

Oliver had never been a keen reader, and, in fact, it was later said 'he preferred to read men rather than books', but the one book he seems to have had always enjoyed reading was Raleigh's virtuous Protestant work, *The History of the World*. He still occasionally dipped into Raleigh's book, but after his conversion he was firmly focussed on the bible. Like the normally religious man he had been in the past, he was naturally very familiar with the bible yet after his conversion it is likely he buried himself in his bible, pouring over close examination of the text, hour after hour. Over time he was to build a very deep knowledge of both the Old and New Testaments and able to quote large sections of them. It might be said that it was good that Oliver had found this compelling scholarly interest, but it had the effect that he began punctuating much of what he said with biblical references. Although such references were apt and informative, the habit could have been slightly wearing for those close to him. The impact of this spiritual awakening was such that no future event in his life would be untouched by God's presence and guiding will.

Oliver would have been overflowing with awe and excitement at the realisation that he was chosen for salvation and this seismic change in him must have had a major effect on the family. What Elizabeth thought of all this is not recorded, but his sudden burning religious zeal at so high a temperature must have been rather trying for her and the rest of the family. Elizabeth came from a Puritan leaning, God fearing family and was very probably a dutiful Christian who shared the same type of faith as Oliver before his conversion. Yet, Oliver's absolute conviction about God's salvation was a different order of faith and there can be little doubt that he talked to Elizabeth and the rest of the family at great length about his revelation. Having found God's grace for himself, it would have been imperative for him to ensure that those he loved were able to share in the divine knowledge they had been selected for redemption.

After a while, however, it must have become clear that Oliver had indeed been seized by the Holy Spirit and this would be no passing phase. At first Elizabeth and the adult members of the family may well have humoured Oliver by accepting his views and later perhaps changed their own views to conform to his. He was head of the family and it was after all their duty to comply with what he asked of them. They would never have his religious zeal and energy, but subsequent extant letters from them show that, at the very least, they joined him by placing their whole trust in God. Like Oliver, their trust in God would be absolute and accepting even of the mysterious ways in which the Lord moved to bring setbacks and tragedy into their lives. It must have been a little trying to be married to someone who had begun bringing God into nearly every utterance and at first Elizabeth may have wondered whether Oliver's new zeal was somehow linked with his bouts of depression and would pass with time.

Oliver's phases of depression seem to have passed and whether this occurred before or after his conversion is not known but must have been a huge relief to Elizabeth. In St Ives he and Elizabeth could start new lives, admittedly in reduced circumstances, but away from the backbiting and bad feeling that had arisen in Huntingdon. Oliver's joy in his new relationship with God might well have led him to accept his humbler financial and social position as a St Ives' tenant farmer. It would be enough to understand that it was God's will. Oliver may also have pondered the thought that if his elder brother Henry had not died in infancy he would have remained a younger son and ended up a tenant farmer in any case. Elizabeth and Oliver were to spend five years in St Ives and it is likely that having accepted this as God's will, the family began to enjoy happier times. His depression over, Oliver busied himself with his small holding consisting largely of sheep, but also chickens and with selling eggs and wool to support himself. For relaxation he was still able to enjoy his two loves of hunting and hawking. The year after the move to St Ives Elizabeth gave birth to her seventh baby who was called James. This baby died soon after birth, but sad as it was, Elizabeth no doubt sought consolation in the acceptance of God's will.

The Cromwell's family life appears to have continued uneventfully in St Ives during this period with Oliver becoming more interested in the town's religious affairs and attending the church vestry meetings. At the same time as maintaining his livelihood in St Ives, Oliver had to visit Huntingdon to look after his remaining few acres there and to see his mother. To begin with it must have been rather painful for Oliver to return to the town he had fled after so much animosity, but this probably eased with time. For Elizabeth and her sisters-in-law, visits to Huntingdon would have been much less difficult, except for the fact that they returned as the family of a mere farmer rather than that of the town's MP and relation of the great Cromwell family of Hinchingbrooke. The death of Dr Beard in 1632 eased the situation. It removed someone who might still have held a grudge over the Fishbourne lectureship feud and Oliver who would have been embarrassed to bump into on the streets of Huntingdon. There were, of course, others who remained, like Robert Barnard who was unlikely to forgive and forget Oliver's outspoken denunciation. Nevertheless, it seems that as time went on Cromwell re-established good relations with at least some of the towns folk for they were to support him in later years.

Oliver's mother Elizabeth must have looked forward to visits by Oliver and other members of the family as she had been used to living in a house shared with her three daughters, Oliver and his wife and their six children. Since Oliver had moved to St Ives, she lived alone, possibly with a live-in servant or two, but ultimately, she had also been left behind to face the social downfall of her son. The smug triumphalism that many of the aldermen would have displayed at that downfall would have been particularly hard to bear, but Elizabeth appears to have been made of sterner stuff and clearly weathered this situation with grace. Although the senior Cromwell family had moved far from Huntingdon, she probably had the support of some old friends in the town who stood by her. Whatever the case, Elizabeth's lonely stay in Huntingdon came to an end in early 1636 as Elizabeth's younger brother Sir Thomas Steward died childless and left his estate to Oliver.

It is probable that Sir Thomas' potential legacy had been known about for some long time and may have even been taken into consideration as part of Elizabeth's marriage settlement. However, neither Oliver nor anyone else would have taken the expectation of a legacy into account. After all, Elizabeth was Sir Thomas' elder sister and she would live for another eighteen years. Sir Thomas' estate was by no means huge but was sufficient enough to transform the lives of both Elizabeth and Oliver. What Sir Thomas left was not freehold land, but a reversion of long leases of tithe and glebe land from the Dean and Chapter of Ely Cathedral. Associated with this was lessee of the Manor of Stuntney, to the south of Ely, and lay rectorship (that is administrator) of the church lands and tithes of the parishes of Ely and their outlying chapelries. These lands would provide Oliver with an income of about £200 a year and came with a reasonably substantial house in the town; a black and white half-timbered house at 29 St Mary's Street, in the shadow of Ely Cathedral.[8]

Having received the good news of the inheritance, Oliver wasted little time in moving with his family to Ely and taking up his new responsibilities. His mother Elizabeth joined in the move and came back to live with the whole family in the house by the cathedral. The Cromwells were no longer rural yeomanry but town dwellers and returned to being minor gentry. Oliver ceased to be a full-time working farmer and became more of an estate manager farming some land himself and subletting the rest. After a while he expanded his lands by becoming the tenant of Cambridge University lands belonging to Clare College and Trinity Hall. With this additional revenue stream his annual income would have probably come to £250.

For Oliver's wife, Elizabeth, the unexpected inheritance must have been profoundly welcome. The family returned to their social position and there was, at last, sufficient money for the household to maintain a reasonable standard of living. However, there was a downside to the move. She had spent five years establishing roots in St Ives and keeping in touch with friends in nearby Huntingdon. The move meant starting again and with Ely some seventeen miles from St Ives and even further from Huntingdon, she certainly would be seeing less of those she had come to know. In St Ives she ran her own household, but now in Ely, she had to revert to sharing her new home with her mother-in-law. What is more, the home belonged to her mother-in-law's family and was one in which she had been born. It would have been only natural for Oliver's mother Elizabeth to have proprietorial feelings towards 29 St Mary's Street. As she is believed to have been a lady of strong personality, her daughter-in-law may have faced apprehensions about them both living under the same roof once more. Yet it seems that both Elizabeths worked hard to ensure a harmonious management of these 'new' living arrangements and the running of the household as Oliver's mother lived with them until her death.

Just as Oliver's household increased to welcome back his mother, so it decreased with bids of farewell to his sister. While in Huntingdon, Oliver's mother Elizabeth continued her search for suitable husbands for her daughters and had alighted John Desborough as a suitable match for Jane. Jane was, by then, 30 and John was 28 so there was only a slight age difference. The potential bridegroom was the second son of James Desborough, a prosperous landowner from Eltisley, about eight miles south of Huntingdon. John had been to the Inns of Court but being a younger son had decided to actually practice the law. He also had some prospects because it was known that when his father died, which he did two years later, he would inherit a small estate. John, a tall and burly fellow, who despite being born a gentleman had a gruff and rather aggressive manner. For all that, however, he was an honest man of the Puritan persuasion who was able to provide Jane with a reasonable lifestyle and Elizabeth had done well in finding John as a husband for Jane at a time when the family status was in decline.

The timing of the marriage was also beneficial because the financial shock of the dowry payment was offset against the improvement in Oliver's finances. Elizabeth had just two more daughters to marry off, Robina, 26, and Elizabeth, by then aged 42, who looked as though she would remain a spinster. Although there are no records of the event, it is possible that Robina was also married during this time to an academic called Dr Perter French who was a cannon of Christ Church, Oxford. This too was a reasonably good match, but how it came about is not known, although Elizabeth's hand must have featured at some point.

In February after the move to Ely there was another addition to the Cromwell household. Oliver's wife gave birth to a girl, five years after the death of her baby James. Although living in Ely, the family travelled to Huntingdon for the baptisms and the new baby was christened Mary at All Saints, the church attended by the leading figures of the town and whose lectureship had caused so much controversy. Most probably, Oliver and the family decided the journey to Huntingdon was worth the inconvenience as it allowed them to show the town that they had returned to their former status.

No doubt Oliver busied himself with establishing his position in Ely, but religion, of course, remained his consuming passion and he had mounting concerns that the work of completing the Reformation was actually going in reverse. In 1633 George Abbot, the puritan-leaning Archbishop of Canterbury, was replaced by William Laud. Archbishop Laud believed that the road to salvation was to be found in the restoration of the ancient sacraments and ceremonials of the church. He rejected the Puritan concept of predestination and felt that salvation would be granted as a result of good works and a godly life rather than individuals being specifically selected by God. Laud decided to appoint High Churchmen like himself to implement his views and tried to enforce his beliefs as a uniform standard across the Anglican Church. Naturally, he did not change the church overnight and the results were patchy, but to the horror of Puritans, altars began to be moved to the east end of churches, candles lit up and alter rails erected.

For Oliver these changes made by Laud were Arminian, if not downright Papist, and were in defiance of the will of God and having become one of God's 'chosen,' he felt moved by increased Puritan fervour to help complete the Reformation by changing church liturgy, abolishing bishops and popish practices such as saints' days. A minor member of the gentry working in close cooperation with the Dean and Chapter of Ely, there was little he could do except build up relations with others who shared his views. As he worked directly for the Anglican Church he presumably kept his more extreme views to himself, although no doubt Elizabeth heard about them both regularly and at some length. She and the family probably found that Oliver went out more to associate with likeminded Puritans with little explanation of who they were or where they were meeting.

In 1637 arrangements were made for another wedding, but this time in the senior branch of the Cromwell family. Oliver's uncle Sir Henry Cromwell of Upton married off his daughter Elizabeth to an attorney called

Oliver St John. He was the eldest son of Oliver St John of Clayshoe and had been educated at Cambridge and Lincoln's Inn before being called to the bar.[9] By age 39 he had started to make a name for himself as an attorney and was retained as a lawyer by some of the leading Puritans of the time including the Earl of Bedford and Viscount Saye and Sele. As St John's first wife had died, he was free to remarry and although an apparently rather cold and arrogant lawyer, he appeared an up and coming man suitable for Sir Henry's daughter Elizabeth.

The problem was, as so often the case, the dowry. Like his elder brother, Henry's fortune was depleted, and he had to mortgage half his Upton estate to one of his nephews to raise the agreed £2,000. The marriage did not take place until the next year, but it is likely that St John and Oliver became more closely acquainted during the period of the prolonged negotiations after having been at least aware of each other earlier. Although at different colleges, they were contemporaries at Cambridge and had a family connection of sorts. St John's first wife's mother was the sister of Oliver's Aunt Joanna, the dowager Lady Barrington. As Lady Barrington was very much involved with her brother and Sir Henry's marriage negotiations with St John over her niece Elizabeth, Oliver may have also been drawn to them as an acquaintance of St John.

By this time Oliver and Elizabeth had seven surviving children and the two eldest boys were Robert, aged 16 and Oliver, 14. It was time they were sent to school to learn Latin in preparation for university and although there must have been good schools in Ely, it was decided to send the boys to Felsted School in Essex. Oliver had only to walk down the street to get to Dr Beard's school in Huntingdon. To reach Felsted from Huntingdon would mean travelling fifty-six miles on the appalling roads. The reason Felsted was chosen was because it was close to Little Stanbrook Hall, the home of Elizabeth's father Sir James Bourchier. The idea that the boys could stay near their grandfather and strengthen the Cromwell Bouchier relationship was important. Further, the school also commended itself with its well-known Puritan ethos and sponsorship by the Earl of Warwick, one of the leading Puritan peers of the time. Warwick took a great interest in the school and personally appointed the headmaster. This was a Martin Holbeach who was a friend of Oliver St John and it may be that St John helped Oliver and Elizabeth with having children accepted to the school.

The marriage of Oliver's cousin Elizabeth to St John and the move of the boys to Essex was to bring Oliver into contact with the prominent Puritan gentry of the county. He already had one connection of his own with Essex through his aunt Joan, the dowager Lady Barrington living at

Hatfield Broad Oak. With the boys going to stay with his wife Elizabeth's father, more connections were created in Essex and the City of London as Sir James was both landed gentry of Essex and a wealthy London merchant. He knew the Earl of Warwick and was indeed the tenant of one of his manors. Warwick was very much involved with the London merchant community and put substantial investment in colonial ventures in New England and the Caribbean. He was, for example, a leading member of the Providence Island Company, as were two other leading Puritan peers, Viscounts Saye and Sele and Baron Brooke, together with the veteran MP and staunch Puritan, John Pym. This web of influential Puritan contacts was one in which Oliver found himself on the outer perimeters. This would have been a matter of little significance had not fate, or in Oliver's terms, 'Divine intervention', made these connections an important part in his future career.

In just a couple of years two changes had occurred in Oliver's life which potentially transformed his future. Through his mother he had received the funds necessary to return to gentry status, providing him the wherewithal to once again mix with the ruling classes and even be considered for public office. It was through other women in his family, notably his wife Elizabeth, cousin Elizabeth and aunt Joan, that he had also gained some entrée to the main leaders of the Puritan movement. These two changes provided the basis which, coupled with Oliver's passionate belief that he was an instrument of God, enabled him to build his subsequent career.

Chapter 4

An MP's Wife
1638–1642

'It is an atheism and blasphemy to dispute what God can do; it is presumption and high contempt to dispute what a king can do; or say that a king cannot do this or that.'

True Law of Free Monarchies – **James I**

'I must avow that I owe the account of my actions to God alone.'

Charles I, December 1641

In these early years in Ely, Oliver had established tenuous links through his mother to leaders of the Puritan movement. He shared their Calvinistic spiritual values and detestation of Arminianism but does not at this stage seem to have shared their opposition to the Crown. The earls of Warwick and Bedford and Viscount Say and Sele, together with their followers, such as John Pym and Oliver St John, were deeply disturbed about the way the king was exercising his power; Charles I had been ruling without parliament since 1629. It must be said that England had prospered during the period. The war with Spain had ended, the country was at peace, and trade picked up. Although the country was doing rather well economically, this was not the case for royal revenue. Despite making economies, Charles did not have enough money coming in to cover the costs of both maintaining his court and running the country.

With no parliament to vote for funds, the king had to resort to raising taxation through royal prerogative. He collected the tonnage and poundage excise revenue despite it not having been approved by parliament and then raised money through a series of creative financial devices based on quasi-legal interpretations of royal prerogative. These included forced loans and reinstating the thirteenth-century tradition of distrain of knighthood. For the forced loans, JPs were directed to induce citizens to 'lovingly, freely, and voluntarily' make a loan to the Crown with no prospect of repayment. Distrain of knighthood required anyone owning property worth over £40 at a time of a coronation to either accept a knighthood, and thus fall into the knightly tax bracket, or pay a fine. Those who refused to pay could be sent to prison without trial. The Puritan aristocrats who were already deeply concerned about the High Church practices being introduced by Archbishop Laud became equally concerned that the king was ruling as an absolute monarch contrary to the accepted laws of the land.

Oliver was a man of strong feelings and not one to keep those feelings to himself. Elizabeth and his family must have been used to him talking at length about the Church of England embracing popish practices. They were probably slightly relieved that Oliver had not also railed against the king, or at least his advisers, raising taxes without parliamentary consent and imprisoning people without trial. Few people welcomed taxation and no doubt Oliver grumbled about Crown fund raising, but he accepted the situation, albeit grudgingly. He paid what he was required to for the forced loan and, although tardy with the payment, had coughed up for the knighthood fine. In 1637 he also paid what he was assessed for Ship Money. This was a tax that was traditionally raised by the Crown from sea ports to build warships in times of national emergency. Charles began raising Ship Money from ports in 1634, despite the fact that the country was at peace. It was the king alone who had the prerogative to decide what was a national emergency, and the fact that Dunkirk pirates continued to attack shipping in the Channel and Barbary corsairs carried out raids on the coast of Ireland and Cornwall provided fairly legitimate reasons. It became less legitimate later in the year, however, when the tax was extended to the City of London and completely without precedent in August 1635 when it was extended to the whole kingdom.

Oliver's cousin, John Hampden, had previously refused to pay the commissioners collecting forced loans and had been briefly gaoled for his pains. He now took a stand against Ship Money. He paid the tax for about a dozen of his parishes, but as a matter of principle withheld just 20s owed by his parish of Stoke Mandeville. Other leading Puritans such as Lord Saye and Sele had also refused to pay, but Charles decided to pick on the less important figure of Hampden as a test case. In 1637 Hampden appeared before twelve judges and he selected Oliver St John to be his attorney. With great eloquence St John made the point that if the king could levy taxes whenever he wanted, all property was at 'the goodness and mercy of the king' and thus threatened the foundation of ownership itself.

Despite St John's strong case, the judgement went against Hampden, but by a narrow margin as five of the twelve judges found in Hampden's favour. The king had won, but it was a moral victory for Hampden who was given a spell in gaol, which transformed him from an unknown squire to a national hero. After the court case Ship Money continued, but the commissioners for its collection found more and more people refusing to pay.[1] Indeed a couple of years later one of Oliver's other cousins, Edmund Dunch (son of his Aunt Mary) refused to pay Ship Money and was arrested by Royal warrant. He was represented at his trial by John Hampden and escaped punishment. By the end of 1639 two thirds of Ship Money failed to be collected.

Presumably the Cromwell household would have followed this national case with some interest especially as the two leading protagonists were connected to the family. However, it does not seem to have inspired Oliver to actively move into opposition against the king. For John Hampden, the king's changes in religion and the constitution were much the same issue. Oliver had not at this stage made that link. The only non-religious issue which occupied him was the local matter of draining the Fens. He supported the draining of the Fens but was unhappy about how it was being carried out. The areas to be drained were divided into levels and royal licences were given to investors for organising the work. The investors were then able to enclose about half of the land that they had drained. This meant that the locals were deprived of their historic right of grazing the livestock on half the previously common land. It also meant that they could no longer collect fuel or go fishing and fowling; all particularly important in winter. The poor of the Fens were so incensed to this threat to their way of life there were angry demonstrations, and which looked as though they could lead to an uprising. Oliver was a strong conservative in many ways and took up the cause of those demanding the return of their ancient rights. He managed to win a local court case which resulted in the commoners being able to continue their rights for the next five years.

It is probable that Elizabeth and the other ladies of Oliver's household were affected by Oliver's support of the Fens commoners. There would have had to have been many meetings on the subject probably at their own house and Oliver's successful legal challenge would have brought him the gratitude and respect of those who felt wronged. The Fens commoners were humble cottagers, but it must have been pleasant for Elizabeth to feel that her husband had won local respect after the unfortunate events in Huntingdon. Nevertheless, there may have been a slight cloud on the horizon for Elizabeth and her mother-in-law. Oliver was interested in the cause of the commoners, but his main passion was religion and there was mounting anger over Archbishop Laud's programme for introducing High Church practices.

Oliver may have confined his anger within the intimacy of his immediate family, but in Scotland anger was all too public. Laud wanted to bring High Church religious uniformity across the three kingdoms and so had enforced the English Book of Common Prayer on the Church of Scotland. Rioting followed, and leading Presbyterian peers drafted a National Covenant to formalise their opposition. The National Covenant document professed loyalty to the king but opposed all:

> "Superstitious and papist rights" in worship and uphold their existing reformed church. In February 1638 the document was printed in Edinburgh for people to sign to swear their support of its principles. Soon copies were distributed around the country and the signatures grew and grew.'

The Covenant had the support of powerful clan chiefs, men such as James Graham, Earl of Montrose, and Archibald Campbell, Earl of Argyll. Later the leading Scottish soldier, General Alexander Leslie, returned from abroad to join them. The king sensed rebellion was in the air so played for time by ordering a meeting of the General Assembly (Governing body) of the Church of Scotland to discuss the matter. The General Assembly met in Glasgow in November 1638 and was dominated by Presbyterians. It quickly demonstrated its resolve to resist Anglican uniformity by abolishing the English Prayer Book and deposing bishops. The king realised that he could only bring these Scottish Covenanters to heal by force, so began to plan to raise an army.

The events in faraway Scotland would have been of little interest to the Cromwell family in Ely. They would have no way of knowing that the resistance to the king in Scotland would start a chain of events which would engulf the three kingdoms in a bloody civil war and change their lives out of all recognition. For the two Elizabeths, Oliver's mother and wife, there were more important events at home. In February 1638 Francis White, the Bishop of Ely, had died. White was a supporter of Archbishop Laud but had made few High Church changes to the diocese. Besides as a 74-year-old he did not have the energy to embark on change. It should be remembered that Oliver was, in many respects, working for the Bishop and Dean of Ely, so his relationship with them was of some importance. It would seem that Oliver and White had a perfectly good working relationship despite their differing religious outlooks, but the question remained if that relationship would continue with White's successor.

Matthew Wren, the Bishop of Norwich, was chosen as the new Bishop of Ely. Like any episcopal appointment it had been made with the agreement of Archbishop Laud and so it was no surprise that Wren was a High Churchman. This does not seem to have been a serious problem for Oliver at first and the two men appear to have continued the previous satisfactory working relationship. Oliver had been made a JP and Wren found him a useful go between with the fensmen who were still protesting in the Ely area about the drainages. In fact, towards the end of the year, Bishop Wren was asked by the Privy Council to prepare a report on the subject and Oliver was able to supply useful input.

Despite the apparently reasonable relationship between the Bishop and his leaseholder of cathedral land and dues, all was not well. When he was Bishop of Norwich, Wren had insisted on the clergy wearing surplices, that communion tables were moved to the east end of churches and that congregations received communion on their knees. Having moved to Ely, Wren began to demand similar High Church practices. For someone with Oliver's white-hot Calvinistic conversion, the introduction of such practices in his local church of St Mary's in Ely must have been hard to bear. He may have kept his council when dealing with the Bishop, but we may be assured that an emotional man like Oliver would have let off steam in the privacy of his family.

It is never a happy situation to fall out with your employer and the two Elizabeths must have been concerned that Oliver and Wren might be on a collision course and there could be no doubt which party would come off best if such a collision occurred. A related matter might also have given them grounds for further anxiety. There is some evidence that Oliver may have been attending secret Nonconformist conventicles in the Isle of Ely area.[2] What is more, there were reports that he was actually preaching at some conventicles. If his family suspected that this was happening it would have been a real worry to them. For a start, conventicles were illegal. Secondly, no one was allowed to preach anywhere without a licence from their bishop. If Oliver was indeed participating in conventicles it was a dangerous game for both him and his family. He was breaking the law and, if caught, could expect little mercy from a court of law and even less from his bishop.

Oliver's wife Elizabeth had other additional matters on her mind. She was pregnant again, at the age of 40. Although she probably had a couple of miscarriages, as was highly common, she had already successfully given birth to eight children counting baby James who had died fairly soon after birth. Given the state of hygiene and medical knowledge in the seventeenth century, child birth was a very dangerous business and Elizabeth would have known that the chances of mishap increased with age. This was a time when forceps had not yet been invented and midwives used a crotchet hook (stick with a hook) often before the waters had broken. There was of course no way to alleviate pain, but a Puritan woman in labour would at least know that the pain was being divinely inflicted as God's punishment of Eve. They might have been regarded as the weaker sex, but women who went through childbirth were made of stern stuff indeed and Elizabeth was no exception. At the end of the year she was brought to bed with a healthy baby girl. It was decided to call this new addition to the family 'Frances' and she was baptised on 6 December at St Mary's Ely.

As a person of Elizabeth's social background, she would probably have used a wet-nurse, but a decline in Cromwell's finances at their time in St Ives makes it more likely that she would have become used to feeding her babies herself. Elizabeth would have also been wise enough to know that breast feeding provided a form of birth control and we may assume that having gone through childbirth at least nine times, she was in no hurry to repeat the experience. As it turned out, baby Frances would be the last of Elizabeth and Oliver's children. This must have been an exhausting time for Elizabeth with a new baby and a large household still to run with, no doubt, plenty of gratuitous advice from her 73-year-old mother-in-law, never mind her concerns about her husband's activities.

Whatever the exact number of family members under the same roof in Ely, there were certainly quite a lot of them. During this time, Robert and Oliver junior were still at Felsted School in Essex and how often they visited home is not known. Most likely visits were few and their mother Elizabeth must have missed them terribly. It is also unknown if Richard had joined his brothers at Felsted by this time, but Henry certainly would have still been at home, as would his sisters Bridget, Bettie, Mary and the new baby Frances. Elizabeth's unmarried sister-in-law, the 34-year-old Elizabeth, also still remained in the house. Managing the household to ensure they were all fed and generally looked after must have been a taxing, but also rewarding activity, especially since they had the means to maintain a good lifestyle. After all, at a time of so many untreatable illnesses, it was indeed a blessing to have such a large and healthy family. But the Lord giveth and the Lord taketh away. The year 1639 turned out to be one of the most devastating of Elizabeth and Oliver's lives. In May news arrived from Felsted that their eldest son Robert had died. Of what we do not know, but it is presumed to have been from a sudden fever. Oliver was later to describe the news of his death as 'it went as a dagger to heart'. It was ironic that soon after God had blessed them by the birth of a healthy baby girl they should lose their first born out of the blue.

Elizabeth and Oliver loved all their children, but Robert must have been particularly special to them as the heir. To be robbed of him when, at the age of 17, he was just developing into manhood and about to make his way in the world, was cruel indeed. Robert was buried at Felsted Parish church where the register records that he was 'a boy of exceptional promise, fearing God in all things'.[3] The sudden death of this promising young man, the object of their hopes and expectations, must have severely tested Oliver and Elizabeth's faith, but Oliver's faith was strong enough to carry them both through as twenty years later he would recall that they found solace in a passage of the Bible from St Paul: 'I have learned in whatever state I am, therewith to be content, I know both how to be debased, and how to abound ... I can do all things through Christ that strengthen me.' That they still had three sons, with Oliver junior now moving to the position of heir, also surely offered them further consolation.

The Cromwell family would have been too wrapped up in the tragedy of Robert's death to have taken much notice of the king's continued problems with the Covenanter Scots that summer. Charles had scraped together enough money to raise a rag-tag army of 20,000 and dispatch it to Berwick-upon-Tweed. This force remained on the English side of the border and a Scots army of 12,000 under General Leslie remained on the other side. Various skirmishes took place with few casualties as neither side wanted to do battle. In June this military posturing known as 'The First Bishops' War' was brought to an end by an agreement called the Pacification of Berwick in which it was agreed that disputed issues should be resolved by either another General Assembly or the Scottish Parliament. This merely served to postpone a resolution of the religious differences. The General Assembly eventually gathered, this time in Edinburgh, and took precisely the same stance as that in Glasgow. This was followed by a session of the Scottish Parliament which passed a bill abolishing the episcopacy.

The Scots had defied their king and Charles was faced with either accepting the situation and giving in gracefully to the Covenanters or bringing them to obedience by force. It was not Charles' way to give in to those who questioned his divine authority as ruler, so a second and more determined Bishops' War was the obvious result. However, the king had no money and the only way of raising sufficient to cover the cost of war was to call parliament to vote on the necessary taxation. In January 1640 Charles summoned his first parliament since he had dissolved the last one eleven years previously. In some ways, rather surprisingly, Oliver decided to stand for election for this new parliament. He had of course been an MP for Huntingdon back in 1628, but that had been for only one year and he had not particularly distinguished himself. He had since burned his boats in Huntingdon and there was no question of trying to be elected there. It is probable, that despite all this, Oliver was so full of religious zeal that he wanted to seize the possibility of becoming an MP in order to help further the Puritan cause. As an MP he could unite with likeminded individuals to help reverse Archbishop Laud's High Church measures and complete the reformation of the church based on the Puritan model. This might have been a reasonable enough objective, and a welcome distraction from Robert's death, but Oliver needed a seat which he had a chance of winning.

It is hard to know what Elizabeth thought when Oliver told her that he intended to stand in the forthcoming election. She probably felt that the likelihood of him being accepted as a candidate slim and tried to forget the matter altogether. But, in a surprising turn of events, Oliver became a candidate for one of the two parliamentary burgesses of Cambridge. It was surprising for a number of reasons. Oliver did not live in Cambridge; indeed, it was seventeen miles from Ely. Nevertheless, this difficulty was overcome through him becoming a freeman of the town paying the sum of one penny to the poor and putting a few of his possessions in the yard of the White Bull Inn in Bridge Street. The other surprise was that he was considered for the position of MP for a city that, for at least 150 years, had only returned to parliament either long serving members of the city's corporation or the nominees of the city's High Steward.[4] Oliver was neither.

The nominee for one of the burgesses was Thomas Meautys, Clerk of the Privy Council, who had been nominated by the High Steward, Lord Keeper Finch—one of the judges who had found against John Hampden. A possible explanation as to why an outsider like Oliver was selected is that the situation in Cambridge seems to have been one of 'town versus gown,' with the university and its chancellor Holland being overbearing to the townsfolk. Holland's elder brother was the Earl of Warwick who might be able to use his influence on Holland to the city's benefit. As Oliver was a known local Puritan activist who had connections with Warwick, he may have been selected to gain Warwick's support to curb Holland. Conversely, there is also the possibility that Warwick might have identified Oliver as someone who could further the Puritan cause and used his and his brother's influence to have him elected. What might have also been a factor was that the Mayor of Cambridge was Thomas French who could well have been a relation of Oliver's sister Robina's husband, Dr Peter French.

However it came about, Oliver found himself elected by the mayor and burgesses as one of the two MPs for Cambridge. It was miraculous or in Oliver's terms, down to God's guiding hand. Elizabeth would have been pleased and also a little proud that her husband was once again an MP, but there may well have been some apprehension. The last time Oliver had served as an MP he had begun his bout of depression. She may have worried that with him out of her sight and the pressures of politics, these problems might return. She may also have wondered how Oliver's business interests would be carried out in his absence in London and there was no way of telling how long this parliament would last. Elizabeth already had a lot on her plate with managing so large a household and a new baby, which was hardly conducive to her being able to take over the family business on his behalf. It would have been quite a problem. As it happened, the new parliament was to be appropriately named the 'Short Parliament', so Oliver's protracted absence turned out to be of little issue.

We know that Oliver decided to sell up his cathedral leases sometime in 1640 and it may have been the thought of long absences in parliament that made him decide to do so. Nevertheless, another perhaps more important issue behind the sale was that Oliver was finding it increasingly difficult to work in cooperation with Bishop Wren and his High Church cathedral dean and cannons. No doubt they had found it equally difficult to deal with a man who provided one of the main sources of the cathedral income, but who was increasingly known as not only a Puritan, but one rumoured to be taking part in illegal Nonconformist conventicles. The leases were transferred to the archdeacon and were probably purchased by the cathedral chapter. The sale would have been a welcome relief to both the cathedral and Oliver. Unburdened from the management of the cathedral lands and tithes, the sale would have allowed Cromwell a new sense of freedom to take action, granting him spare time to pursue politics with a clear conscience, having distanced himself from a bishopric and deanery he had come to despise.

Oliver would probably have retained the small amount of his uncle's own land in the Ely area, but this would have been no great difficulty for Elizabeth to oversee in his absence. When Oliver left Ely in April, Elizabeth and the family are likely to have seen him in high spirits over what appeared to be a new chapter in his life. He was about to become a member of the House of Commons and so join with cousins such as Hampden and associates such as John Pym in trying to undo the spread of Arminianism and help complete the Calvinist reformation of the church. It was God's work and exciting to be able to play a part in it. Oliver took up lodgings in Long Acre near Covent Garden which was close to the Inns of Court and, importantly, in the area chosen by Pym and most of the other leading Puritans.

Parliament was opened by the king on 13 April with a patriotic call for funding for a military expedition to deal with the Scots. This fell on the deaf ears of members of a parliament who had a large accumulation of grievances that had been unable to be voiced over the last eleven years. Pym provided them the opportunity to raise their collective voice with a two-hour long speech detailing those grievances both political and religious, which ended in demands for the establishment of annual parliaments. Pym's oration received general support and during the next few days the king understood he was to expect no cooperation from his parliament and so dissolved it on 4 May. Such a quick dissolution meant that there had been no time for Oliver to even begin taking part in parliamentary proceedings. The great promise of at last participating in a parliament that could right the many religious and other secular wrongs of the Crown had come to nothing. Cromwell must have returned home to Elizabeth a very disappointed man indeed. It had appeared that God had called him to take part in the great work of promoting the true Protestant religion. Within the space of a mere twenty days parliament had come and gone with nothing to show for it. It had been eleven years since the previous parliament and who knew when, or indeed if, there would be another one and if there were, whether Oliver would even manage to become a member again.

He would have been pleased to be reunited with his family after his time in London, but a man renowned for his emotions, he would not have hidden his despair over parliament's dissolution. He was no longer an MP and, assuming the sale of his cathedral interests had gone through, he no longer held a position of authority in Ely. By this time, he was aged 43-years-old with no obvious future, let alone one in which he could act as an instrument of God's will. We should spare a thought for his family having to deal with an emotional man in distress. Based on past experience, Elizabeth must have been more than a little concerned that her returned husband would again sink into clinical depression.

No letters have survived. Oliver may have been in correspondence with John Hampden and other parliamentary colleagues about their future plans and hopes, which, if true, may have given him some encouragement. In the past he had not shown any interest in the Scottish situation, but following his brief time among like-minded men in London he realised that the pressure the Covenanters exerted upon the king could be to parliament's benefit. Pym was almost definitely in touch with the Covenanter leaders with the intention of finding ways to cooperate that were mutually advantageous. If the Scots army threatened England, the king would be forced to turn to parliament to fund a royal army and so enable Pym and the opposition to extract concessions in return.

The king, for his part, was taking action to bring his Scottish subjects to heal. He recalled Viscount Wentworth as Lord Deputy of Ireland to make him his principal adviser and gave him the title Earl of Stafford. Wentworth was a highly efficient and loyal Crown servant, but his authoritarian policies and manner had made him many enemies. As Wentworth, now Stafford, had become the king's principal minister, he became the focus of blame for his master's actions. Stafford returned to Ireland briefly in March and, with Catholic support, persuaded the Irish Parliament to vote to provide both money and troops for a campaign against the Scots. Encouraged by this Charles set out for York, but before he arrived, the Covenanter army under Leslie crossed the Tweed, scattered the northern royal forces at Newburn, then occupied Newcastle and took control of the counties of Northumberland and Durham. With no army from Ireland likely to arrive in the immediate future and completely out of funds, the king was obliged to sign a humiliating treaty at Ripon on 26 October. The treaty stipulated that until a final settlement was reached the Scots would continue their occupation and should be paid £850 a day to maintain their army on English soil. As the king had no other way of finding this sum of money he was forced to once again call Parliament and hope it would provide the funds needed to solve the Scottish crisis.

When writs were issued for a new parliament, Oliver's spirits must have revived. Although the matter of being elected to parliament loomed, in this there would be no difficulty; the mayor and corporation of Cambridge were firmly behind Oliver's election as their MP. Reflecting the mood of much of the country they even refused to select Thomas Meautys, the government nominee, and elected instead John Lawry, a Puritan and long serving member of their common council. Within a few days of the election Oliver said another farewell to his family and returned to London to play his part in what would be the longest parliament in English history.

The king opened Parliament on 3 November with another call for funding. Pym and the opposition realised that they had Charles over a barrel and sought to exploit the situation for all it was worth. As well as enumerating the same objections that had been previously raised in the last parliament, Pym also called for the impeachment of the king's 'evil advisor', the Earl of Stafford, for 'high misdemeanours' in Ireland. The new year of 1641 was to see major events in Parliament. Stafford appeared before the Lords to answer the accusations and was released on insufficient evidence. Undeterred, Pym pushed a bill attainder through the Commons, meaning that Stafford could be merely pronounced guilty by Parliament. Oliver St John put the case for attainder to the Lords, who passed it as most members had deep dislike of Stafford. Charles signed the warrant on 10 May and two days later Thomas Wentworth, Earl of Stafford, had his head struck off on Tower Hill—a triumph for Pym and the opposition, if not for English justice.

The other most 'evil advisor' of the king was Archbishop Laud. Denzil Holles, a leading aristocratic member of the opposition, moved that Laud should be impeached by the Lords. In March Laud was placed in the Tower where he was to remain as a pawn in negotiations with the king until he was executed nearly four years later. Oliver must have rejoiced to see the removal of the man responsible for the introduction of so many popish practices and shed no tears for his final demise.

Towards the end of 1641 John Pym and Hampden produced a document named the *Grand Remonstrance* detailing 240 points of objection to royal policy covering religious, financial, legal and foreign policy. This also called for the expulsion of bishops from Parliament, a purge of royal officials and Parliament having a veto over Crown appointments. The *Remonstrance* was put to the Commons on the very day that news arrived of a Catholic rebellion in Ulster which had resulted in the massacre of Protestant colonists. It was even rumoured that 30,000 Protestants had been put to death. Oliver was to describe it as: 'The most unheard of and the most barbarous massacre (without respect of sex or age) that ever sun behold'.[5] The great fear of papists, never far away, became uppermost in all protestant minds and many thought that there was a real danger of Irish papists invading England. In fact, although there had been an uprising, no Catholic massacre had actually taken place, but this fact did not stop the story of the brutal 'massacre' being accepted without question by Protestants for a generation to come.

At the time of the horrifying news from Ireland the king was away in Edinburgh, in the process of agreeing to the Covenanter peace terms. Parliament decided to disregard the absent king and voted for £50,000 to suppress the Irish rebellion and, on their own authority, place their appointees in charge of the Tower and other major citadels in the country. It was in this climate of anti-papist hysteria, and fear of a king who had Catholic sympathies, that the *Remonstrance* was passed. Charles returned to Whitehall having at last made peace with his Scottish subjects only to be presented with the *Remonstrance* on 21 December. Just before Christmas he gave his response, which, although expressed in moderate tones, set out why he could not accept the Remonstrance's demands.

Elizabeth and the family would have certainly heard about these great events in Ely. They would have also been directly updated by Oliver's letters and occasional visits, such as during the September-October recess. As to what part had her husband played in these historic actions, the answer was very little. Cromwell had gone to Parliament with religious zeal and had largely confined himself to religious and local matters. It had been Pym, Hampden, St John and Holles together with Sir Arthur Haselrig and William Strode who pressed forward with the opposition's major work in the Commons and were joined by Viscount Saye and Sele together with the earls of Manchester, Warwick and Essex in the House of Lords. Oliver was no orator and had seldom spoken in the chamber himself, but for all that he had been busy as a very active member on numerous committees. He did in fact work in close cooperation with Pym, Hampden and the other leaders and seems to have been seen by them as a valuable asset who was a dedicated and aggressive promoter of the cause.

His first committee action had been to take up the cause of John Liburne, an opposition pamphleteer who had been whipped for seditious libel. Sir Philip Warwick attended the committee and, in his Memoirs, gives the following picture of Oliver:

> 'very ordinary apparelled, for it was of plain cloth-suite, which seemed to have been made by an ill country tailor, his linen plain, and not very clean; and I remember a speck or two of blood upon his little band, which was not much larger than his collar, his hat was without a hatband, his stature was of good size, his sword stuck close to his side, his countenance swollen and reddish, his voice sharp and untunable, and his eloquence full of fervor.'[6]

Such then was Elizabeth's MP husband: a shabby, ill-kempt, graceless figure, full of sound and fury. And yet he had a certain presence, made more so by his piercing grey-green eyes. Even his total disregard for appearance among some of the best dressed men of the land showed a certain confidence. For the opposition leaders, his ardent un-parliamentary manner could also be employed to emphasise points that might be obscured by more moderate and diplomatic rhetoric.

Oliver busied himself on committees including the one on the Fens dispute, although his main work was on the religious committees and sub committees covering subjects such as the prevention of idolatry and drafting a 'Root and Branch' petition to abolish bishops, deans and chapters, indeed the whole church management. In fact, Oliver was to be an active member of some eighteen committees. One committee examined the Arminian conduct of his bishop, Matthew Wren, which led to Wren's impeachment and imprisonment in the Tower. One can only imagine the amazement in Ely at this turn of events. Often Oliver was carried away with his ardour for reform as he was when the chairman of a committee examining the episcopacy in Gloucester and Hereford forced him to apologise for using un-parliamentary language against an opposing speaker. In the committee on the Fens, of which Edward Hyde (later Earl of Clarendon) was chairman, Clarendon remembered Oliver speaking to Viscount Mandeville 'with so much indecency and rudeness, and in language so contrary and offensive, his whole carriage was tempestuous ... and his behaviour so insolent' that he threatened to report him to the House and Oliver was only saved by the intervention of Pym.[7]

Oliver earned a reputation for himself in parliament as a rather strange and impetuous Puritan zealot. Pym and Hampden would have recognised him as a loose cannon but appreciated that he worked exceptionally hard for their cause and got things done. Over the first year of what was to be named the 'Long Parliament' they had served alongside him as active members of the many new committees and witnessed his important contributions. As 1641 drew to a close, Oliver was by no means part of Pym's inner circle but was someone who was increasingly drawn into their plans.

Like most Puritans Oliver would have had serious reservations about celebrating Christmas but may have made the ninety-mile journey back to Ely anyway for the traditional holiday period to be with his family. It is unlikely that Elizabeth's husband had been back home since the end of the October parliamentary recess. As it was increasingly rare to have him and their eight children at home together this must have been a particularly special time for Elizabeth to have the whole family gathered in one place. Although her sons Richard and Henry would have themselves been away at Felsted School during term time, they probably returned home during breaks. As for young Oliver who had left Felsted in the summer, Elizabeth probably saw more of him given he had gone to study at St Catherine's College in Cambridge.

Although mostly absent from home, Oliver's activities in Parliament would have made themselves felt in Ely and nothing more so than the impeachment of Bishop Wren. The Isle of Ely was an area that generally subscribed to the Puritan ethos and many would have rejoiced at the fate of their bishop and check on the spread of Arminianism. This would not have been the case for those in Wren's immediate ecclesiastical entourage. The dean, William Fuller, had been in office for two years before Wren arrived so had not been appointed by him, but was a High Churchman and later investigated by Parliament for his 'popish innovation'.

Many of the cathedral chapter would have been appointed with Wren's agreement and would have been High Churchmen themselves and the cathedral and diocese's lay employers, such as those working for the Treasurer and Chancellor, probably supported the bishop to whom they owed their livelihood. The majority of what we may assume would have been Wren's supporters would have lived in or near the cathedral close, just a stone's throw from the Cromwell's house. Elizabeth and her mother-in-law surely knew these people and almost certainly the bishop himself and his wife, another Elizabeth. Also, Bridget, Elizabeth, Mary and even baby Frances would have known or played with their children. In such a small and inward-looking community, of which Oliver had once been an important part, the imprisonment of Wren must have come as a huge shock. That Elizabeth and her family had Puritan leanings would have been common gossip, but that her husband had taken part in the impeachment of the bishop must have placed a great strain on their relationships with Wren's supporters.

For all that, Oliver's mother and wife were strong characters who turned to God's grace in coping with resentment from their neighbours. Indeed, the family took some pride in Oliver's achievements. His parliamentary work had not made him a national figure but had made him of some prominence locally. The commoners of the Fens appreciated his championing of their cause and the Puritans of the area would have welcomed his part in the removal of Bishop Wren and his continued fight to purify the church of papist trappings. Oliver was no longer regarded as the man who had left Huntingdon with his tail between his legs, but rather as a person who had previously stood up to the Huntingdon Corporation, who also stood up for the Protestant religion and rights of ordinary people in the same manner as his cousin, the heroic Hampden. Growing local support that he received in Cambridge and the surrounding region stood him in very good stead in the challenging year ahead.

The momentous new year of 1642 began with even more turbulence than the last, with apprentices and other civilians rioting against popery and the bishops. There was a general fear for safety throughout the kingdom. The king nominated a new governor for the Tower, but then had to climb down on the insistence of the Commons. Charles had had enough; Parliament's demands were more than any monarch should have to accept. He decided to assert his authority and on 3 January gave a practical response to the *Grand Remonstrance*. He sent his attorney general to the bar of the House where he presented articles of high treason against Pym, Hampden, Holles, Hasilrig and Strode together with Viscount Manderville, the Earl of Manchester's son, in the Lords. Their crimes included subverting the law by depriving the king of his royal powers and encouraging the Scots to invade England. This was followed by the sergeant-at-arms arriving to demand the Commons surrender those charged.

The next day Charles arrived at the Commons with an armed guard and a large party of courtiers. The king entered the Chamber and requested that the speaker deliver those charged, only to discover that they had been tipped off about his visit and had gone into hiding. Charles had no option but to leave empty handed amid cries of 'Privilege! Privilege!' at the king's invasion of parliamentary privilege. Once the king left, the Commons decided to move to the City of London's Grocer's Hall for safety. The following day Charles went to the Guildhall and requested that the Lord Mayor hunt down and hand over the accused. This had no effect and was followed by serious demonstrations in which seamen and local mobs joined the apprentices. There seemed a danger that they might march on the Palace of Whitehall. Fearing for the safety of his family, on 10 January 1642, the king hurriedly left with them for Hampton Court, then on to Windsor. Neither he, nor anyone else, would have guessed that the next time Charles would enter his capital would be as a prisoner.

With the king gone, Pym and the other accused came out of hiding and returned to Westminster triumphant amid much popular rejoicing. The scene was set for civil wars that would cost thousands of lives across the three nations and lead to a dishevelled East Anglian farmer replacing the king as Head of State.

PART TWO

A Soldier's Family

Chapter 5

A Good Army Wife
1642–1643

'I had rather have a plain russet-coated captain that knows what he fights for and loves what he knows, than that which you call a gentleman and is nothing else. I honour a gentleman that is so indeed.'

Oliver Cromwell in August 1643

Almost exactly four months before the king left London, Elizabeth heard the Ely church bells ringing, as they were throughout the kingdom, celebrating peace with the Scots. By January 1642, that day of hope must have seemed a long time ago indeed. There had since been the Catholic rebellion in Ireland and government forces still not assembled to put it down. There were the rumours of the continued massacre of Protestants and fears that Irish Catholics might invade England, overturning the Reformation. Now, the rift between king and parliament had become so great no one knew where it was going to lead. Pessimists around the country surely wondered if the differences between them might only be resolved by war; but as England had been at peace for over 150 years, that possibility seemed unthinkable.

As it happened, war was not an impossibility to the king at Windsor or Pym and the opposition leaders in London. Neither side wanted war, but both began making preparations for what appeared an inevitable conflict ahead. The aim of both was to take possession of strongholds and arms stores and raise money for the recruitment and equipping of an army. Some of the king's courtiers took possession of the Kingston arms store and Parliament sent Sir John Hotham to take over the armoury at Hull. Hotham was an MP who had previously been governor of Hull, but who had been removed for refusing to pay Ship Money. In February Queen Henrietta Maria sailed from Dover to Holland ostensibly to accompany her ten-year-old daughter Mary for her wedding to Prince William of Orange. The more pressing purpose for her visit was to pawn royal jewels to raise money for an army. Parliament was just as busy raising money from the City. Both king and parliament soon began openly preparing to raise an army under the pretext of using it to put down the Irish Catholic revolt.

It should not be assumed that the whole of Parliament were members of the opposition. The *Grand Remonstrance* had only passed by eleven votes so there were members of the Commons and particularly the Lords who felt Pym's demands on the king had gone too far. People began to choose allegiances between king and parliament. Those sympathising with the king began absenting themselves from parliament and either returned home or travelled to join the king who had moved north to York, where he felt he had the most support. Areas such as the Midlands and East Anglia had a strong Puritan element and so tended to favour Parliament. This was not always the case even among MPs. For example, although Oliver and John Lowry, his co-burgess for Cambridge, and the two university MPs, Henry Lucas and Thomas Eden, supported parliament, as did Sir Dudley North the MP for the county, the other county MP, Thomas Critchley, was a royalist. The two MPs for the town of Huntingdon, George and Edward Montagu, were for parliament as was Oliver's brother-in-law Valentine Walton, the MP for the county, but Sir Sidney Montagu, the other county MP, was for the king. Just as the Montagu family had split loyalties, so did many families including the Cromwells where Oliver's uncle, Sir Oliver, remained an ardent royalist as did his eldest son Henry. His other son Oliver and his brother, Sir Philip's son, also an Oliver, supported parliament. In the months to come many families and most communities found themselves split by conflicting loyalties.

Like everyone in the country Elizabeth and the family tried to keep up with the fast moving and increasingly worrying events. She knew that her husband was deeply involved in the parliamentary opposition to the king, but probably had little idea of what role he actually played. In fact, Oliver worked for the opposition with continued vigour, but the emphasis of his work had changed from religious reform to preparations for war. He remained on many committees, the most important of which was the Council for Irish Affairs, but he was also engaged on more practical work for the re-conquest of Ireland. He became involved in the recruiting of captains for Irish service and arranging a loan of £100,000 for the relief of Munster from the Committee of Adventurers.[1]

Oliver even invested £205 of his own money towards raising the force to fight the Irish Catholics. Over the months Oliver's tireless contribution to the opposition brought him closer to Pym and Hampden's leadership, while king and parliament competed for military advantage. The Commons ordered all sheriffs to secure arms stores and the king sent out similar instructions and in April there was something of a watershed. The king went to Hull to take over the armoury which had been placed in the hands of Sir John Hotham, by parliament. When the king arrived outside Hull, Hotham refused his sovereign entry and Charles had to withdraw crestfallen and empty handed. The Commons were delighted with Hotham's defiance and ordered a payment of £2,000 to the Hull garrison.

It was Oliver who was chosen to take the order for payment to the Lords for their agreement, and in doing so began a new role as an intermediary between Commons and Lords. There followed many trips to the Lords mostly concerned with raising troops for Ireland; troops, which both Lords and Commons knew could also be used to defend parliament from being overawed by the king. By the end of May, Pym and the other leaders had agreed a document known as the *Nineteen Propositions* and sent it to the king. It was little more than a condensed version of the *Grand Remonstrance* calling for such things as parliamentary approval of royal councillors and the authorisation for parliament alone to carry out church reform. The king could not and did not accept the *Propositions*. It is hard to believe that Pym, Hampden and others like them and Oliver who supported the *Propositions* seriously thought that the king could agree to them. It is more likely that they were on a roll with garnering support and could not turn back in case the king later disavowed any settlement and they were tried for treason. The *Propositions* may have been no more than a propaganda gesture, but whatever they were, they were a force behind the increased pace to conflict.

In June the king moved to Newcastle which had been occupied for him by the Earl of Newcastle and sent out commissioners of array to raise the militia. In July parliament appointed the earls of Essex and Warwick as commanders of the army and navy respectively. Oliver was particularly busy with the rebellion in Ireland. The heads of the Catholic Church in Ireland had instituted the Oath of Kilkenny which drew all Catholics into a league to restore Catholicism to the country. The rebellion became a very serious matter and Oliver was engaged in such issues as moving forces from Ulster and Leinster to help with the siege of Limerick which had previously been taken by rebels. He raised troops and money for Ireland and Elizabeth must have been truly shaken at learning that over a number of instalments Oliver had invested just over £2,000 of his own money in the venture. It was an 'investment', but hardly a reliable one as those who invested were to be rewarded with land confiscated from Catholics. In fact, in July the treasurers of the fund handed over £100,000 to the Commons to be used for the defence of parliament. With Lord Goring having seized Portsmouth for the king, and militias sponsored by one side or the other carrying out their drills up and down the country, the pretence of raising forces purely for Ireland wore rather thin.

Oliver became more directly involved in overt measures directed against the king. As early as May he made a Commons motion that saddles being transported to the king at York should be seized. The next month he proposed that two ships be sent to guard the mouth of the River Tyne to prevent foreign aid from reaching the king. On 15 July he moved that Cambridge be authorised to raise an officer and two companies of volunteers. Slightly later he proposed that the Lord Lieutenant of Cambridge should permit the men of Cambridge to train and exercise in arms. Then, on his own initiative, he sent some arms to his constituents for which he was later reimbursed £100 by Sir Dudley North, the MP for the county.

As Oliver was extremely busy, it is unlikely that he returned to Ely to visit his family during this time. He and Elizabeth no doubt exchanged correspondence, but no record of it now exists. Any correspondence on Elizabeth's side probably concerned such matters as the health of the family, relations with neighbours and updating her husband of the management of such property they had left in their possession. It is likely that Oliver's letters enquired about the family and described his general way of life but offered little precious detail about his work or where it all would lead. Like most of the country, the Elizabeths, both wife and mother, and the girls, must have felt very much in the dark.

The main action of the time was occurring in York where the king was residing or in Westminster with parliament. Ely was far away from both. The family may have heard more about Oliver's activities, such as the arming of the militia, as they manifested in nearby Cambridge. Friends in Cambridge, such as Thomas French, the mayor and a possible relation of Elizabeth's son-in-law, probably kept them abreast of developments. However, not only would Oliver's actions be the talk of the county and he would soon be back with his family to speak to them directly at last.

Oliver's energy and dedication to reform moved him closer to Pym's inner circle, which included Hampden, Holles, Haslerig, St John and Strode. He would certainly have stood out as a badly dressed, unkempt figure striding across from the Commons to the Lords with a glint of determination in his eyes. There were others who, like Oliver, also rose in prominence because of their service to the opposition, such as Erle, Pickering, Hayden and Rouse. Yet, they were all to become no more than footnotes in history. What marked Oliver for greatness was about to begin and was an event that changed the direction of his life and turned him into a supreme man of action.

The king requested that both Oxford and Cambridge universities send their college silver plate to him in York for 'safekeeping' from the rebels. Oxford eventually did some weeks later, but it took even longer for Cambridge to respond. In the second week of August news arrived at Westminster that the colleges were collecting their plate to send under convoy to York. With his usual impetuosity Oliver decided to take action to prevent this from occurring. Valentine Walton, the county MP for Huntingdonshire and the husband of Oliver's sister Margaret, felt the same. Both men rode off to west Cambridgeshire to gather supporters including those of a like-minded friend, Sir Francis Russell of Chippenham Hall. Meanwhile the first consignment of college plates had assembled at St John's College with active assistance from the sheriff of Huntingdon and passive consent of the sheriff of Cambridge. A fellow of St John's formed a party of horse from members of the college to act as escort. This escort left Cambridge and successfully delivered the first consignment to the king at Nottingham.

Cromwell learned that they had arrived too late to intercept the first consignment, but he heard that there was a second consignment being assembled at King's College. He led his band of supporters to King's College but stopped *en route* to place men with muskets in the fields covering the road out of Cambridge. When Oliver and his men arrived, he found the convoy about to depart, with drums beating, flags waving, the captain of the Cambridge militia providing protection and the sheriff and undersheriff in attendance. It looked as though Oliver was again too late, especially when it was learned that his cousin, Sir Oliver's son Henry, was on his way with fifty armed horsemen to escort the plate.

What happened next is not fully recorded. It is known that Valentine Walton sent out warrants for 200 men to join Oliver and many of the citizens came out to watch the outcome. The final showdown is thought to have occurred on the Great North Road leading out of Cambridge where Oliver had deployed his musketeers. However it happened, there seems to have been little or no bloodshed and the end result was that Oliver and his men took possession of the plate and then went on to seize the magazine and arms in Cambridge Castle. Oliver, a man with no previous military experience, had suddenly transformed himself into not just a soldier, but a military leader, albeit of a small band of followers. He was able to send a report to a grateful parliament that the plate he had seized on their behalf had a value of £20,000 and they granted him immunity for his 'illegal' action. Parliament now took Oliver's quasi-military status for granted and ordered him to: 'set strong watches upon several bridges between Cambridge and King's Lynn to apprehend all horses of service for the wars, arms, ammunition, or plate to His Majesty'.[2]

For the citizens of Cambridge this must have been an astounding turn of events. One of their burgess MPs was now effectively in military control of the town; a town, like anywhere else, divided in its loyalty. As we have seen, the mayor and most of the corporation were Puritans and favoured parliament, whereas the sheriff, undersheriff and head of the militia supported the king. It was also something of a town versus gown divide with the university largely supporting the king and the puritan-minded citizens leaning towards parliament. Of course, not everyone at the university supported the king. Oliver's son, Oliver junior, was an undergraduate at St Catherine's and would have been one of the spectators who witnessed his father's demands for the plate. We do not know if he joined his father's group to provide such assistance as he could. If he had, he certainly would have alienated himself from the majority of his fellow undergraduates whose natural inclinations were of support to the king.

Eighteen miles away in Ely there must have been almost equal surprise over the events in Cambridge. It would have been a major shock to Elizabeth to hear that her husband had led what was in effect a highway robbery and shown himself to be in open rebellion against his sovereign. She was well aware of Oliver's strong opposition to the king's policies, but he had now gone too far. As King Charles had pronounced Sir John Hotham a traitor for defying him at Hull and Oliver could expect little less, it must have been a time of great anguish for the whole family. They were Puritan and fully approved of Oliver's efforts in parliament to put pressure on the king to purify the church from all traces of Catholicism. This did not mean, however, that they were not loyal subjects of His Majesty. To go into what amounted to be rebellion against the king was beyond comprehension and could only end badly. Elizabeth's mind must have worked overtime imaging the worst—Oliver ending up being executed or, at the very least, imprisoned and the family ruined.

Cromwell was of course very busy but being so close he must have returned home if only for a brief visit. As a strong family man and having been absent so long, he would have longed to see his wife and mother and his daughters who he called 'his little wenches'. Whenever it was that Oliver returned home there would have been two urgent topics of conversation. The first would have been 'where will it all end?' and the second, family finances. Of the first, Oliver probably did not know himself. He knew he was opposed to most of the king's policies and actions, but not yet sure what he wanted instead. He had wholeheartedly supported the *Grand Remonstrance* and the *Nineteen Propositions*, but if the king had caved in and agreed to all the reforms, then what form of government did he want for the future? As Oliver said to Sir Philip Warwick and others a year before: 'I can tell you, Sirs what I would not have; tho' I cannot what I would.'[3] For Cromwell the future was in God's hands and as an instrument of the Almighty answers would be revealed to him in time while he accomplished God's designs. His success in Cambridge, against all odds, was a clear manifestation of God's support for him and was enough for Oliver who had no doubts about the justice of his cause or the divine direction of his own actions. Whether Elizabeth and the family would have been totally reassured by Oliver's convictions is not recorded.

The other matter of family concern was money. As a dutiful wife Elizabeth may not have thought it her place to question the family finances. Oliver's mother, on the other hand, would have had no such inhibitions. After all it had been her brother's legacy which had put the family back on its feet after the depressing period in St Ives. Oliver and Elizabeth's eldest daughter Bridget was 18 and, as such, it would not be long before a dowry would have had to be found for her. There was also the cost of the boys' education, as well as the additional expenses that Oliver's position as MP incurred, including having to pay for his lodgings in London. Never mind the ordinary living expenses of a large family.

Financial matters were never Oliver's strong point, but there can be little doubt that they were a matter of importance to his wife and mother. The cathedral revenues and tithes had provided a good steady income, but these had been sold—at much the same time as when the dowry had to be provided for Oliver's sister Robina's marriage to Peter French. We do not know what Oliver did with the £3,000 or so payment he received for selling his cathedral interests, but he may have invested some or all of it in the Providence Island Fund of which Pym was treasurer. This seems likely as we do know was that he had recently invested about £2,000 of it into parliament's Irish fund. Although a noble gesture, it was at best a long-term investment with no prospect of any return to help pay the bills for many years to come or more probably, ever.

In the weeks after Oliver seized the Cambridge silver plate, the political situation clarified. On 22 August the king raised his standard at Nottingham and proclaimed war on the rebels. It was unfortunate that the huge standard which had taken twenty men to raise, blew down that night and had to be replaced by a smaller one the next day. Nevertheless, the fact remained that it signalled that the monarch, as the country's feudal leader, was summoning all loyal subjects to his side. Civil war had officially begun. Oliver was a rebel, but no longer one who worked on his own initiative with the backing of a small group of local activists. He was a soldier employed under the authority of parliament which had issued the Militia Ordnance to raise troops and stated that it took the arms 'for the safety of His Majesty's Person, the Parliament and the Kingdom against the bloody councils of papist and other ill effected persons'. Elizabeth, and the family, may have taken some comfort that her husband had thus been formally employed in a legitimate undertaking to help rid the king of his evil advisers.

As soon as Oliver received news of the king's declaration at Nottingham he lost no time in going to the Huntingdon Market House where he formally raised a troop of horse. Parliament had formed a Committee of Safety to run the war and had given Oliver a lieutenant's commission. For those with no previous military experience the ranks allocated were based on their importance to the opposition's cause and Oliver's rank of lieutenant contrasted with his more eminent parliamentary relations, Hampden and St John, who were made colonels. This was of no consequence to Cromwell who just threw himself into the job and went to Cambridge to raise more recruits for his troop. He contracted his sister Jane's brother, John Desborough, to be quartermaster and soon received £1,104 'mounting money' from parliament for pay for the troop's formation. Elizabeth was no doubt relieved to find that Oliver had not tried to cover the cost of equipping the troop himself as a number of other land owners did. Better yet, there was even a chance that Oliver would receive lieutenant's pay. Although 8s a day was not a lot and had to cover his horse's fodder and other expenses, it would amount to £140 a year and make some contribution to the family budget. That is if it was ever paid and the war lasted that long.

Among the officers appointed by Cromwell was his son, young Oliver, who had abandoned his Cambridge studies to join his father. Within a matter of days there were a total of sixty troopers under command. Virtually all these troopers were small holders of the Puritan persuasion who may have never fought before but were good horsemen and dedicated to the Protestant cause. At the same time Oliver's brother-in-law Walton had been commissioned as a captain, probably to mark that as a county MP he was a 'knight of the shire' and therefore considered senior to a burgess MP like Oliver. Walton also soon raised a troop in which his own son, named Valentine after him, received a commission. East Anglia was on its way to supporting the parliamentary cause.

No sooner than he had formed the troop than Oliver was off again to Westminster for a brief visit. It would be a worry which would be experienced by countless wives and mothers during the next few years, but Elizabeth surely must have been one of the first in England to worry that not only her husband, but also her son was to be exposed to the dangers of battle and if the king succeeded, likely executed. However, in late August there seemed a chance that good sense would prevail, and a peaceful solution found. Three days after the king raised his standard he sent a message to parliament requesting the appointment of a peace commission. Pym refused to consider this until the king took down his standard and recalled his proclamation of treason against Members of Parliament. Charles agreed and sent his secretary to London to say he would do as requested if parliament itself would disband the armed force it had raised. Importantly, the king also consented to a thorough reform of religion.

It looked as though war would be averted. That is until Pym replied that parliament would never lay down arms until the king ceased to protect those Crown servants it had declared as 'delinquents'. Furthermore, Pym demanded that all who had advanced money to support parliament should be repaid from the confiscated estates of those delinquents. Naturally the king could not agree such terms. As the parliamentary force called on the trainbands of London, Pym was probably anticipated that the Earl of Essex would gain a quick victory over Royalist troops and so enable parliament to dictate terms. When news of Pym's rejection became known, it would have become clear to Elizabeth that her husband and son would very probably have to risk their lives in combat before there would be any chance of a settlement.

The efforts of both king and parliament concentrated on bringing a strong enough force to battle against their opponent. There was intensive recruiting by both sides and often in the same towns as was the case in Cambridge. A certain Mr Russell came to Cambridge to read the king's commission of array calling for volunteers at the same time as the county MP, Sir Dudley North, was raising volunteers with parliament's militia ordnance. The same situation probably occurred in Ely. The citizens of towns and villages across the country were divided and indeed confused over which, if any, side they should support. Many of those who did volunteer to serve in the forces of king or parliament did so out of conviction, but most probably because they followed the lead of their local land owner or employer—and a few out of simple bravado probably having drunk too much ale at the recruitment fair.

Oliver returned to his troop, which had risen in number to eighty, and was ordered to take them to join the field army assembled by the Parliamentary lord general, the Earl of Essex, which was thought to be advancing on Worcester. Young Oliver had since moved to take up the commission of a cornet in a troop under the command of Lord St John. This was Baron St John of Bletso, the cousin of Oliver St John, who had been MP for Bedfordshire before inheriting his title. Lord St John had used credit to raise a troop of horse and a regiment of foot for parliament.

Quite why Oliver junior joined Lord St John's troop is not known. There was an obscure family connection and Oliver senior may well have known Lord St John as a fellow Puritan MP and one who, like him, had been involved in the drainage of the fens. For whatever reason, Oliver junior joined Lord St John's force which had also received orders to join Essex's field army.

Locating the lord general's army was easier said than done in an age with no modern communications. Essex had entered Northampton to muster an additional 20,000 volunteers and then moved to Worcester. The king had taken his army to Chester and then Shrewsbury where he had gained a number of recruits from the Welsh borders. It is probable that Lord St John and young Oliver managed to make contact with Essex's field army south of Worcester and were given the task of occupying Hereford for parliament. The king had also made for Worcester and on 23 September the first engagement of the Civil War took place south-west of the city at Powick Bridge. This occurred when a Royalist cavalry unexpectedly found themselves camped in almost adjacent fields to an element of the parliamentary vanguard. The Royalists under the king's nephew, Prince Rupert, charged the parliamentary vanguard and put them to flight. It was more a skirmish than a battle, but it did launch Rupert's reputation as an invincible cavalry leader.

Both armies looked for a decisive battle and the knockout blow to win the war. The king's force of 13,500 concentrated at Shewsbury and then advanced towards London knowing that Essex would intercept them on their way. Essex heard of the Royalist advance towards Banbury but did not know their exact location. On 22 October elements of the two armies happened to bump into each other at Edgehill and the next day drew up for battle. At this point Lord St John and young Oliver arrived from Hereford and joined Essex's 12,500 strong force. Some 3,500 of Essex's field army, including Cromwell's troops and Hampden's regiment, had not yet arrived. The battle began and the Royalist cavalry under Rupert drove the cavalry on Essex's left wing off the field and then busied themselves plundering the parliamentary wagon train. The Royalist cavalry did the same to the Essex's right wing, but the infantry of the Parliamentary centre held their ground. The fighting continued with no clear advantage until failing light and lack of ammunition on both sides brought the battle to an end. Having lost hundreds dead and wounded, neither Essex nor the king wished to renew the bloody contest and after a bitterly cold night both armies withdrew; Essex toward Warwick and the king towards Oxford.

But what of the two Olivers involvement in this first major battle? Oliver senior did not arrive with his troop until the battle had begun and the left wing had been pushed back. He may have either missed taking part in the battle completely or arrived just in time to join a counter attack against Rupert's cavalry around Kineton which helped to stabilise the parliamentary left. For young Oliver it was a different matter. It seems he was in the unit under Lord St John which was part of the left wing driven from the field by Rupert. Fortunately, he survived the attack unscathed, but would certainly have been in some danger as Lord St John was seriously wounded in the fighting, then captured. He was to die of his wounds the next day.

Back in Ely, Elizabeth would have had no idea that the battle had taken place until sometime after, let alone known that her husband and son were involved. The first the Cromwell family would have heard about the battle was as a victory for parliament. Had they lived in Royalist York they would have heard that it was a victory for the king as both sides had claimed victory; the war propaganda officially commenced. The reality was that it had been a messy battle between largely untrained and ill-disciplined volunteers, most of whom had not eaten for at least twenty-four hours before the fight began. As they were unprepared for the ghastly reality of combat, quite a number of them fled amid the smoke of cannon and musket fire. Others, such as the successful Royalist cavalry, were so carried away with enthusiasm that their plundering was almost impossible to control. Well over 1,000 Englishmen were killed at Edgehill and 2,000 to 3,000 were wounded. It would be some time before Elizabeth would hear whether the two Olivers in her life were included in these categories. A trying time, indeed, for her and the family.

Following the battle, the Royalists occupied Oxford and Rupert captured towns along the Thames Valley. The king decided to march on London, but the slow progress of the army and pauses during which he tried to negotiate with parliament, meant that Essex's army reached London first. Essex himself decided to block the Royalist advance by taking up a defensive position at Turnham Green. Rupert had just sacked Brentford and the citizens of London were so incensed by this move that they joined Essex, raising his force to 24,000. When the king arrived at Turnham Green on 13 November with his 13,000 strong army, it was clear that it was not sensible to launch an attack against such a strongly defended position. After a short cannonade the king withdrew and returned to Oxford to take up winter quarters. The campaign season was over, and Essex moved his army to their winter quarters at Windsor. As Ely is about 100 miles from Windsor it is likely that during this period of military inactivity Oliver made at least one visit home to give his family a first-hand account of what he and young Oliver had been through.

It might have been expected that a husband returning on leave from war was changed in appearance. However, Elizabeth found Oliver looking much the same as he had as a civilian. Although he would have been wearing his buff jacket, he would not have been in uniform as uniform was not worn by cavalry of either side. Indeed, although those landowners and others who raised volunteers provided their men with coats, they could be of whatever colour they chose, or the tailor provided. With no standard uniform on either side to distinguish friend from foe, this was done by wearing something in their hats or helmets such as a sprig of gorse or piece of paper. The cavalry did wear sashes, orange for parliament and red for the king, but Oliver would not have donned his sash at home as wear of it was reserved for battle. It would have been a relief for Elizabeth that when Oliver arrived back for the first time after Edgehill, he was uninjured and looked his old, familiar, scruffy self. She would have been praying that young Oliver would soon also return home unscathed.

In January 1643 parliament promoted Oliver to captain and ordered him to leave the field army and return to his home area, specifically to East Anglia to assist Lord Grey of Warke who had been directed to form what was to be called the 'Eastern Association'. This organisation was to recruit and train parliamentary supporters in Norfolk, Suffolk, Essex, Cambridgeshire and Hertfordshire and Oliver turned himself in to the hub and driving force for the newly created Eastern Association. He was based in Cambridge, and although in charge of overseeing a large region, he had opportunities to visit Ely and even stay with his family. In February he was promoted to Colonel and given formal command of the regiment of horse that he had recently raised. His pay went up to at least £1 10s a day and possibly even £2 5s.[4] Either way it was a welcome contribution to the family finances.

His work was more than recruitment and recruit training. The Cambridge area faced raids from the Royalist garrison in Newark under Lord Capel and Oliver set about improving the fortifications of Cambridge castle and the town walls and turning the town into a parliamentary garrison. The citizens of Cambridge would have welcomed concern for their safety, but others in places such as Ely may have felt that their safety had been neglected. Added upset was caused when they were made to contribute to the cost of the defences for another town as Oliver had decided to raise money from towns and villages in the surrounding area through forced donations. A letter survives, signed by him, addressed to the small village of Fen Drayton saying 'we do therefore desire what shall be by you freely given and collected may with all convenient speed be sent to the Commissioners in Cambridge'.[5]

The village of Fen Drayton reluctantly coughed up £1 18s 2d and presumably the far larger cathedral city of Ely contributed considerably more. Some citizens may have drawn the comparison between Oliver's levy and the forced loans and Ship Money that had been one of the reasons that led to opposition of the king. Elizabeth and her family could take pride that Oliver was an MP, a colonel and an increasing important local figure. But with his extra responsibility came the need to make decisions which were sometimes unpopular, and this was to be the first time that Cromwell enforced something that many people had objections to. His future career provided many more such occasions and Elizabeth would have had to gradually become used to being married to a man who was not universally liked, even among those who shared his Puritan beliefs.

One man who did not welcome Oliver's return was Robert Barnard the recorder of Huntingdon, and the man who had been the cause of so much trouble to Oliver thirteen years earlier. Barnard was on the parliamentary committee for Huntingdon and Cromwell believed he had Royalist sympathies so dispatched some of his troopers to Huntingdon to investigate him. Barnard sent a letter of protest to which Oliver replied that he would not 'hurt him,' adding rather menacingly: 'I hope you will give me no cause.'[6] A short time later Barnard fled to London scared that Oliver would arrest him as a Royalist delinquent. As unpleasant as the incident may have been for Barnard, it probably provided satisfactory closure for Oliver and Elizabeth concerning the unhappy circumstances that led to their departure from Huntingdon.

In April preparations were made for the new campaign season and Essex was told to take his army into the Thames Valley. Lord Grey was instructed to join him with 5,000 men from his Eastern Association. Oliver was left responsible for the rest of the Association in Lord Grey's absence. The parliamentary strategy for the year was to take the towns defending Oxford and then attack the city itself. The king's strategy was to remain with his army in Oxford while a northern force under the Earl of Newcastle and a south-western force under Sir Ralph Hopton fought their way towards London whilst Essex was pinned down in the Thames Valley. This is indeed how the main action of the year turned out. The principal fighting was between Newcastle and the parliamentary leader Lord Fairfax in the north and Hopton and Sir William Waller in the south-west.

While the main military activity occurred elsewhere, Cromwell continued with his recruiting and training, but became increasingly active in the field, defending the borders of the Association and dealing with any pockets of Royalist 'malignants' within those borders. In March he and his regiment swept through Norfolk via Norwich, Lowestoft and King's Lynn. In April he besieged and captured Crowland Abbey near Peterborough which had been fortified as a Royalist stronghold. A little later he visited his Royalist uncle Sir Oliver Cromwell at Ramsey with a party of horse to search for arms and valuables. He approached his uncle respectfully, removed his hat and then asked for his blessing to do so. It was not forthcoming, and Oliver left his uncle, after whom he had been named, having confiscated his plate for the parliamentary cause. Following this brief family 'reunion', in May he took part in a successful skirmish at Grantham.

In July Cromwell won another skirmish at Gainsborough, then went on to take Burleigh House near Stamford. From there he joined forces with a Northamptonshire contingent of 3,000 horse and dragoons to relieve Gainsborough. No sooner than he had defeated the Royalist besiegers than he found that Newcastle's full army had arrived and so was forced to retreat to Huntingdon. Oliver had built up his military experience, but his achievements were minor and seemingly had no impact on the progress of the war. Despite this, as the main parliamentary forces received setbacks on all fronts, Oliver's successes were seized on for parliamentary propaganda in papers such as the *Parliamentary Scout*. As early as May 1643 the news sheet *Special Passages* extolled Oliver for his leadership and discipline, describing how 'no man swears but he pay his twelve pence, if he be drunk, he be set in the stocks or worse'.[7]

Young Oliver too had returned to Cambridge and commanded a troop in his father's regiment. This must have been a joy for his mother and sisters, but with so much going on they probably saw little of either father or son and probably found themselves relying on papers like the *Scout* for news about them. Ely was a largely Puritan town deep in the parliamentary dominated Eastern Association, so Elizabeth and the family were fortunate to be some distance from hostilities, or so they thought. It must have been a particular shock to them when a sudden Royalist uprising happened in their town. Their position as the family of the leading Parliamentarians in the area would have made them a particular target for Royalist revenge and fortunately for them the uprising was quelled by parliamentary soldiers in the area. However, the unrest clearly posed a real threat because parliament were sufficiently concerned to appoint Cromwell as Governor of the Isle of Ely. For Elizabeth, worries about the uprising had been worthwhile as the result meant that she would at last see more of her husband and, hopefully, young Oliver.

Cromwell returned to Ely to ensure the town was purged of Royalist malignants. With him were some of his troop commanders including young

Oliver and others well known to Elizabeth, such as her brother-in-law Captain John Desborough, Oliver's nephew Valentine Walton and Oliver's cousin, Edward Walley. There were also some new faces who would become familiar with time, two deeply religious young men, Charles Fleetwood and Henry Ireton. Fleetwood was the 35-year-old younger son of a Northamptonshire knight who had been educated at Cambridge then admitted to Gray's Inn, and who, like many young lawyers, had joined Essex's Life Guard at the start of the Civil War. Ireton was three years younger, also from Northamptonshire and had a similar background having been educated at Oxford then moved on to the Middle Temple before gathering a troop and also joining Essex's Life Guard. He had fought at Edgehill and had been promoted to the rank of major. These two officers were part of the Northamptonshire detachment that had linked up with Oliver at Gainsborough and remained with him having been cut off from returning to their unit.[8]

As a family man, Oliver would have delighted in spending more time in Ely with his family, even if he was unfortunately kept busy running the Cambridge garrison, leading his regiment against Royalist incursions and carrying out his tasks as an MP. Of most immediate concern was the news that Newcastle had taken Gainsborough and then Lincoln and had become a major threat to the Association's north flank. Cromwell decided to make Ireton the Deputy Governor of Ely so he could attend to his other duties. Ireton, who took up quarters in Ely with his troop, naturally became friends with Oliver's family. No one ever described Oliver as being handsome and it must be said that Elizabeth was slightly plain, but they had two pretty daughters. Mary and Frances were only aged 7 and 4 at the time, but Bridget and Elizabeth were 19 and 14. Bridget was a serious and devout young lady and was attracted to the tall, rather handsome, equally serious and devout young Deputy Governor. The feeling was reciprocated and grew with time, but urgent military duties prevented the immediate full blossoming of romance.

By this time the situation for parliament was grave. Essex had captured Reading, but then remained inactive as his army began to waste away with disease. Waller had received major defeats at the Battles of Lansdowne and Roundway Down as a result of which Hopton's Royalist army had advanced to the borders of Sussex and opened the way for Rupert to take Bristol. In the north, Newcastle had secured Yorkshire for the Crown after winning the battle of Aldwalton Moor and Fairfax had to fall back to Hull. The queen had landed in Bridlington with supplies from Holland and managed to bring them by convoy to Oxford. The king marched to besiege the parliamentary stronghold of Gloucester, there were peace riots in London and to cap it all,

Cromwell's cousin, the inspiring parliamentary leader John Hampden, died of his wounds after a skirmish at Chalgrove Field on 18 July.

It was against this bleak background that parliament decided to remove the ineffective Lord Grey from the Easter Association and place it under the command of Edward Montague, Earl of Manchester, with the authority to conscript 20,000 men. Manchester was made a major general with four colonels under his command, one of which was Oliver. Manchester had impeccable parliamentary credentials. Prior to inheriting his title, the year before he had been Viscount Manderville, the only member of the opposition in the House of Lords that Charles had tried to arrest with the five members of the Commons. He was also the son-in-law of the Earl of Warwick, the main opposition leader in the Lords and now the parliamentary admiral. He had been made the colonel of an infantry regiment under the Earl of Essex. He had taken part in Edgehill, but when battle was joined most of his unit of raw recruits left the field in unseemly haste. After the battle, his regiment was disbanded and he returned to London as a parliamentary leader in the Lords.

Manchester and Oliver had much in common, they had both been at Sidney Sussex College and sat as MPs, with Manchester being MP for Huntingdonshire in the 1625–6 parliament. Another thing they had in common was Hinchingbrooke House, now Manchester's family seat after the Cromwell family had been ousted by his father. Oliver was just three years older than Manchester but had acquired some wide military experience and was very used to being *de facto* commander of the Eastern Association. It was of interest to see how the urbane aristocrat and the worst dressed man in the House of Commons would work together at this perilous time. The result could have major repercussions on Elizabeth and the family.

Chapter 6

A General's Family
1643–1644

'God have made them as stubble to our swords, we charged their regiments of foot with our horse, routed all we charged.'

Oliver Cromwell, 4 July 1644

On the brief occasions that Oliver visited home during the summer of 1642 Elizabeth probably found him much troubled. On the one hand he had no doubts about the justice of his cause. Having had eight small, but successful military engagements it was clear that he was blessed by God and was operating as one of His instruments on earth. On the other hand, the main parliamentary armies had suffered major setbacks and the soldiers of the Eastern Association were so starved of resources there was a chance of mutiny even in his own godly and disciplined regiment. The soldiers had not received pay and the supplies of equipment had dried up. Cromwell resorted to paying for shoes and stockings for some of the men out of his own meagre funds.

If the financial situation was bad for the Eastern Association, it was equally bad for the Cromwell family. It was fine that Oliver was on a colonel's pay scale, but of little use when that pay was not received. The family finances were in a crisis. No doubt Elizabeth tried to do her best to reduce household expenditure to a minimum and tried to raise any money she could. Oliver's redoubtable mother, Elizabeth, now 78, had swallowed her pride and sent a 'begging letter' to one of her cousins: 'I wish there might be care to spare some monies for my son who I fear been too long and much neglected.'[1] Elizabeth had requested £50. If she did receive that sum, it may have been just enough to see them through.

For Oliver there was a brief lull in fighting in August as both sides had to concentrate on bringing in the harvest. It was also the time to start work with Manchester to reorganise the Association and begin conscription. Manchester was later described by Bishop Burnet as: 'Of soft and obliging temper, of no great depth, but universally beloved, being a virtuous and generous gentleman.'[2] He is unlikely to have forgotten that Oliver had savagely attacked him in committee over his enclosure of the Fens, but it was not in his nature to bear grudges. Despite the potential areas of conflict between the two men they worked well together. Indeed, they complimented each other. Manchester was an able organiser and administrator and Oliver was a man of action with greater military experience. Manchester recognised the central role Oliver had had in the Association and took his advice making him his *de facto* deputy. Despite Oliver sending letters pleading funding for the Association to St John and others, none came through, but notwithstanding this, the Association returned to the field in September. Oliver's regiment of his specially selected and trained godly men had grown to ten troops with about eighty men in each. Remarkably, just over a year before, Oliver had been a man with no military experience who had gathered a few supporters to capture the Cambridge plate. In time his strength as a commander would lead to him being nicknamed 'Old Ironsides' and the regiment that set out with him that September were to become known as the 'Ironsides'.

The expedition began well. Manchester took King's Lynn after which he joined Oliver to attempt to relieve Hull where Lord Fairfax was besieged by Newcastle. Lord Fairfax's son, Sir Thomas Fairfax, took his cavalry from Hull by boat and after landing was then joined by Oliver and his cavalry at Spilsby. The Royalist governor of Newark took a force of 1,500 to counter the Association's advance, but was defeated by Oliver and Fairfax's cavalry at Winceby on 4 October. Oliver's horse had been shot under him in the fighting, but he had grabbed another and resumed the attack. On the same day Lord Fairfax ventured out of Hull to successfully attack Newcastle's besieging force, which suffered casualties and gave up the siege. Winceby had been only a minor battle with the Royalists losing 300 killed and 800 prisoners, but it led to the surrender of Lincoln and Gainsborough and the whole of Lincolnshire coming under the control of the Eastern Association.

Meanwhile parliamentary military fortunes improved elsewhere. Essex at last stirred himself and relieved Gloucester, which had been besieged by the king. The king had then caught up with Essex's army at Newbury as it made the return journey to London. The armies were each about 14,000 strong and the battle ended in stalemate with the Royalists having lost 1,300 dead and parliament 1,200. Both armies disengaged with the king moving back to Oxford and Essex to London where he received a hero's welcome.

Elizabeth and the family would have been delighted to hear of the Association's success in Lincolnshire and relieved to find that Oliver had not been seriously hurt despite having his horse shot from under him at Winceby. They would have also joined Londoners in rejoicing in Essex's success at Gloucester and Newbury. What they would not have known was that Newbury was to lead to a major change in the civil war. The stalemate of the battle made it clear to Charles that he was not strong enough to have an outright victory. He therefore made a truce with the Catholic rebels of Kilkenny so that he could bring the Royalist army who had been fighting them over to support his army in England. On the face of it this seemed a sensible idea, but to many Protestants it looked as though the king was bringing an army of Irish Papists to invade England and overturn the Reformation. Pym seized the opportunity and made a pact with the Presbyterian Scots. He persuaded parliament to sign the Solomon League and Covenant and got the Scots to come to parliament's aid. Within a matter of weeks, the English Civil War was to be transformed into a war that was to encompass the three kingdoms of England, Ireland and Scotland.

With the main campaigning season over, Manchester and Oliver returned to Cambridge, and the family in Ely would have seen more of him. The autumn in Ely was interspersed with Oliver returning to the Commons, but for the most part it provided a welcome break for the family to be together. It also enabled Oliver to come to know his deputy as Governor, Henry Ireton. Oliver had increased respect for this serious, intelligent, hard-working and very godly young man, and a strong bond of friendship grew between them that would last for Henry's lifetime. A bond had also begun to grow between Henry and Oliver's daughter Bridget, but Henry's mind was more focused on carrying out God's work than thoughts of romance. To Oliver's approval Henry did his best to purify the churches in Ely to the extent that his more devout soldiers took up the practice of delivering sermons, leaving the parson sitting in the pews. Locals claimed the town had become a Calvinist Geneva.

In January 1644 parliament issued an ordnance stating: 'meanwhile let all Churches, especially all cathedrals, be strip of whatever the general soul so much as suspects to be stage-popery and prayer by machinery, — a thing we justly hold in terror and horror and dare not live beside'.[3] Oliver also did his bit to help purify the church in the Isle of Ely. He heard that choir services were conducted in Ely Cathedral under the Precentor, Rev Hitch, and though Oliver loved music and singing, he did not approve of it in church so sent the following stern letter to Rev Hitch:

> 'I require you to forbear altogether your choir service, so unedifying and offensive; and this as you will answer it, if any discord should arise thereupon. I advise you to catechise, and read and expound the Scriptures to the people, not doubting but Parliament, with the advice of the Assembly of Divines, will in due time direct you farther, I desire the sermons may be where usually they have been,— but more frequent.'[4]

Rev Hitch took no notice and continued to hold choir services so Cromwell entered the cathedral with troopers and commanded them to dismiss and the whole congregation was escorted out of the building. Choir services did not take place again for almost another twenty years.

Oliver had signed his letter to Rev Hitch: 'Your loving friend, Oliver Cromwell'. This was not written ironically, but because it was a fact. Hitch would have been a neighbour of Oliver's in the cathedral close and given Oliver's close association with the cathedral they knew each other quite well. This incident emphasises the difficulties when religious or political differences come to divide a community, especially as Elizabeth and the family surely knew Hitch and his wife. Such incidents occurred all over England, but we should spare a thought for Elizabeth and her family having had to live in these circumstances. The more Oliver gained prominence and respect for his allegiance to parliament and the Puritan cause, the more he gained the scorn and dislike of those who remained loyal to the king and his established church. Some of that scorn and dislike had been bound to rub off on Oliver's relatives in Ely, where not long before there had been a Royalist uprising.

To Oliver's increased dismay, by the start of the new year there was still no money from parliament for either the Association or the Cromwell family. For the parliamentary leadership in London, January 1644 was a time of soul searching. The leadership had been dominated by Pym, the busy high-pressure man of business, Hampden the quiet ascetic Puritan, and Essex the haughty, self-willed Lord General. Yet, the inspiring Hampden was dead and in December Pym died of cancer. Essex believed there was no hope of victory and felt it was time to make peace with the king. Another leading figure and aristocrat, Denzil Holles, the younger son of the Earl of Clare, also wanted peace, based on a Presbyterian settlement while other leaders such as Oliver St John, Sir Harry Vane, Lord Say and Sele and the Earl of Warwick supported continuing hostilities.

With the parliamentary leadership at odds, Manchester went to London to take a full part in the decision-making process and took Oliver with him. They arrived in London on 18 January 1644 and the very next day the Scots answered the call from the now dead Pym. Alexander Leslie had been made Earl of Leven by Charles as part of his settlement of the Bishop's Wars and had gathered a Scottish Covenanter army of 21,000 which crossed the border at Berwick and began to advance against Newcastle. When this news reached London, it must have greatly encouraged the war faction. Oliver was busy in the Commons pressing for increasing payments from counties in the Eastern Association to finance the war and generally doing what he could to promote the continuation of opposition to the king. Oliver and other members of the war faction were successful in their efforts and he and Manchester obtained the support they needed.

Parliament decided to provide funding to the Eastern Association and to recognise Oliver as its official second-in-command, with the rank of lieutenant general. A new joint committee was set up with the Scots to direct the war called the Committee of Both Kingdoms. It was made up of four Scottish commissioners and an English contingent of seven peers and fourteen commoners. Those included on it were the earls of Essex and Warwick, Viscount Saye and Sele, Sir William Waller, Sir Henry Vane, Sir Arthur Haselrig and Oliver St John together with Manchester and Cromwell. A slightly unwieldy number of members, but Oliver had finally made it to the top table for the direction of the war.

He returned to Ely in mid-February having been away for a month. Elizabeth was probably rather proud that her husband was a lieutenant general. His official pay was in the region of £5 per day and a further £2/1s a day for commanding his cavalry regiment. This was a considerable sum but was largely theoretical as pay was still not being issued. Nevertheless, in the worst case, it proved a useful collateral for obtaining credit for the family although they could not live off fresh air indefinitely. All too soon Cromwell left again, this time to carry out raids in Oxfordshire where he stormed Hillesdon House. It may be about this time that Oliver and Elizabeth were to receive another 'dagger to the heart'. News arrived that their son Oliver had died of smallpox at Newport Pagnell.

Why young Oliver was at Newport Pagnell is not known. The town had been taken from the Royalists a few months earlier and turned into a fortified parliamentary garrison. As such it would have become important to the Eastern Associations as a depot in its supply train. It could be that Oliver and his troop had been sent there to provide defence in case the Royalists attempted to take it back and, at the same time, keep an eye on any supplies destined for the Eastern Association. Whatever the circumstances, the end result was that a promising young man was dead. Little is known about Oliver, but he was described as 'a civil gentleman and joy to his father'.[5] And with good reason, as at just 21 he had been a captain who commanded a troop of eighty men who had fought at Edgehill and taken part in several of his father's skirmishes. He was also known to have been a strong disciplinarian who ensured that his troop only consisted of godly men.

Above all young Oliver was Oliver and Elizabeth's heir and all the dearer to them following the tragic loss of his elder brother Robert four years before. As Frances was only 4 she was probably too young to fully realise the loss, but Oliver's death would have been a great shock to his other brothers and sisters, who would have looked up to their elder brother. Young Oliver's grandmother naturally would have been distressed at the death, but the full brunt of the grief would have been felt by Elizabeth. Oliver shared in the grief, but urgent military service called him away, perhaps helping to take his mind off his own bereavement as he left his mourning family in Ely.

Lord Leven's Covenanter Scottish army had reached Durham by this time. Having failed to stop the Scots advance, the Marquis of Newcastle had pulled back to York. Lord Fairfax and his son, Sir Thomas, advanced to York with the intention of linking up with the Scots to besiege the town. The Earl of Manchester was ordered to take his Eastern Association force north to join with Leven and the Fairfax's troops to support the siege and it was to take part in this important task that Oliver had left Ely. On 22 April Leven and Fairfax had joined forces at Wetherby and began organising the siege. On 3 June they were joined by Manchester and Oliver and it was agreed that Leven should be the overall commander. Meanwhile, the king in Oxford dispatched Prince Rupert to relieve York. Rupert moved north, capturing parliamentary strongholds as he went and increasing his army to 14,000 before arriving at the Royalist garrison of Knaresborough Castle fourteen miles from York on 30 June. Leven ordered the joint force to abandon their siege positions and concentrate on blocking Rupert, but Rupert outmanoeuvred them and entered York anyway.

With brilliant tactics Rupert had relieved York, but he wanted to seal a victory. He therefore instructed Newcastle to join him the next day to attack Leven's combined army, which had formed up at Long Marston. Rupert had hoped to bring his total army of 19,000 in the field before the joint Scots/Parliamentarian army had organised its 27,000 strong force. However, this did not work out as planned as the Marquis of Newcastle failed to arrive till lunch time. Both armies had their infantry in the centre and cavalry on each wing. Oliver was on the parliamentary left facing Lord Byron, with Rupert in reserve behind, and Sir Thomas Fairfax on the right facing Lord Goring. In the late afternoon both armies stood looking at each other, neither wanting to advance to cross the ditch dividing them. It was clear that there would be no battle that night so the Royalist officers went to their coaches for supper. At 7.30 pm, amid heavy rain, Leslie saw an opportunity to attack. The biggest battle ever to be fought on English soil had commenced.

The Scots/parliamentary left wing advanced with Oliver's cavalry in the lead, followed by Leslie's dragoons and lancers and were met head on by Byron's charging cavalry. Byron's cavalry masked their supporting musketeers, broke up against Oliver's cavalry and fled. During this, Oliver was wounded by a pistol ball in the neck. This was swiftly dressed and he returned to command just in time to successfully drive off Rupert's reserve cavalry after Rupert had been unhorsed. On the right wing, Fairfax's horse had been pushed back by Goring, but the Royalist cavalry had become distracted by pursuit and pillage. Goring's dragoons caused heavy parliamentary casualties and it looked as though the Royalists would win. At this point Oliver took his cavalry, still in correct formation, to the threatened right wing and drove off Goring's returning cavalry. With the Royalist horse scattered, Oliver and his cavalry concentrated on the infantry. By the time night fell the Royalist infantry were defeated and the Scots/parliamentary army had won the day. Four thousand Royalists lay dead and 1,500 were taken prisoner. Parliament had lost 300 dead.

A few hours had transformed the military situation. Rupert retreated to York and then departed with just 5,000 cavalry and 200 infantry to re-join the king; his invincible reputation forever tarnished. York soon surrendered and a little later the Scots took Newcastle. The Marquis of Newcastle left for Hamburg and other Royalist grandees forsook the north leaving it leaderless and in parliamentary hands. This had been Cromwell's first major battle in a position of command and he and his disciplined Ironsides had been the decisive factor in achieving victory. For Oliver, credit for the victory had been God's alone, but he was able to exalt that he had been God's instrument in helping it come to pass. Oliver had not only shown his worth as a second in command of the Association but made his name as a general in action. But what of the senior generals in the battle? Manchester had been with his infantry as they pushed forward to victory on the centre left. On the centre right there had been a bleaker picture. Lord Fairfax's raw levies suffered severe casualties against Newcastle's foot and were attacked by Goring's horse. When, in the chaos of battle, it looked as though Goring's cavalry had won the day, both Lord Leven and Lord Fairfax decided the battle was lost and fled the field. Lord Fairfax had returned to Hull and Leslie was said to be in bed in Leeds when they eventually heard the news of the victory.

After the battle Oliver was elated and wrote: 'God have made them as stubble to our swords, we charged their regiments of foot with our horse, routed all we charged.'[6] But with the elation there was also deep sadness. His nephew Valentine Walton, son of his sister Margaret and Oliver's close friend Colonel Wanton, had been hit in the leg by shot and Oliver had been there when the surgeons decided to amputate his leg. A major operation but not life threatening today, however, a different matter at a time of no antiseptic and just the use of an unsterilized saw. The boy died and Oliver had to write to his father with the chilling news: 'Sir, God hath taken away your eldest son by cannonshot ... There is your precious child full of glory, to know sin nor sorrow more. He was a gallant young man, exceedingly gracious. God give you his comfort.'[7]

Back in Ely they most likely heard of the battle by letter from Oliver, but any rejoicing in the victory would have been tempered by the sad news of Valentine Walton's death. As Valentine was both a nephew and a captain in Oliver's own regiment, Elizabeth had known him well since he was a little boy. No doubt she tried to console Oliver's sister Margaret, who was probably still at Great Staughton;[8] after her own recent loss of young Oliver, and Robert before that, she would certainly have known what Margaret was going through. It was some small consolation that both women had other children. Elizabeth was fortunate because as well as her four daughters, she still had two sons. Richard, who was now the heir, had reached 18 and Henry was 16. They had both left Felsted School and Henry was about to begin at Emanuel College Cambridge. As there is no record of Richard studying at Cambridge, we must presume he was back home in Ely. Of one thing we may be certain, that Elizabeth would have been in no rush to encourage Richard to join his father at war.

The growth of the family in Ely meant a growth in expenses, not least money for Cambridge fees and horses for the two young men. The family members numbered eleven, counting Oliver's mother and two sisters; a fair number to feed, clothe and generally try to maintain some semblance of gentry standards. Fortunately, Oliver was at last in receipt of his pay as a lieutenant–general in command. This pay was intermittent, but as it came through it must have been a huge relief to Elizabeth. The pay in general was sent to Oliver, but in April he arranged for £5 a week to be sent to Elizabeth to run the household.[9] This meant that however intermittently Oliver received his pay, Elizabeth could at least count on a steady weekly income. If this system worked as planned it meant Elizabeth received £260 a year for household expenditure. Assuming Oliver used his pay to finance extra expenditure, such as university fees, then Elizabeth had sufficient money to get by on—if she was careful. And careful she certainly was as later in life she would be accused of being parsimonious. In truth, Elizabeth was no more than a good and efficient Puritan wife who had known financial hardship and who had learned to manage family finances by herself during long absences by her husband.

Oliver was to be absent from home for about two months following the Marston Moor victory. Much to his frustration, Manchester did not attempt to pursue Rupert, but slowly moved his army back to Eastern Association territory without attempting to capture any Royalist strong holds such as Belvoir Castle on the way. As such, friction between Oliver and Manchester began, while sparks had already been flying between Oliver and Manchester's Major-General, Lawrence Crawford. Manchester was a Presbyterian and Crawford was a strict Scottish Presbyterian; neither were happy that most of Oliver's Ironsides were Congregationalists, Baptists and other such Independent sects. Crawford wanted to remove what he regarded as Anabaptists from the Eastern Association Army and require all officers to sign the Covenant. Oliver was furious when a Baptist officer he knew was arrested by Crawford and had insisted that he was released because, Baptist or not, he was a godly man and a good soldier. Relations were not improved when it appeared to Cromwell that Manchester was using Crawford as his main military advisor and it was Crawford's advice that had led Manchester to avoid combat.

When Oliver next returned to Ely in September, Elizabeth found him bursting with frustration. Manchester's inactivity appeared to have helped squander the success of Marston Moor. While the Eastern Association had made its leisurely way back, he learned that the two other parliamentary armies had suffered major defeats. Just before Marston Moor, Sir William Waller had been defeated by the king at Cropredy Bridge north of Banbury, after which many of the unpaid and disheartened remnants of his army deserted. This Royalist success emboldened the king to seek out Essex's army, which was trying to subdue the South-West. Essex had occupied Lostwithiel in Cornwall with 10,000 men and was resupplied by the parliamentary fleet through the port of Fowey. The king's army of 14,000 joined a local Royalist contingent of 2,400 and surrounded Essex's position, cutting it off from Fowey. On 13 August the fighting began then continued until 3 August, resulting in a major Royalist victory. Most of the parliamentary army surrendered, but a few fled to the east. Essex himself managed to escape by fishing boat, but he left behind all his cannon and train, over 1,000 dead and 6,000 men prisoners. There remained no parliamentary army between the king and London.

Oliver did his best to persuade Manchester to block the king's route to London, but to no avail. He blamed Crawford for this and told Manchester that all his colonels would resign if Crawford was not replaced. This clash was finally resolved when Oliver took the matter to the Committee of Both Kingdoms. There a compromise was agreed in which Manchester would take his Association army west to support the remnants of Essex and Waller's armies to block the king, and Crawford would continue as his major-general. It should have been a pleasant time for the family to have Oliver based in Ely even though he was not there that often, what with trips to Cambridge and the region generally and stays up in London. On the other hand, Oliver's mounting frustration and anger with Manchester may not have made him very congenial company for those nearest to him and in some ways, it may have been a relief for Elizabeth to see her husband depart with the Association. For Oliver, his departure meant being able to fulfil what he had been longing for, to be God's instrument in helping to defeat the king.

Oliver's enthusiasm was soon dampened when he noted that Manchester seemed to be advancing without any urgency, indeed moving deliberately slowly. The king had captured Donnington Castle near Newbury and by 28 October the Eastern Association had joined forces with those of Waller and Essex, ready to attack the king's positions round Newbury. As Essex had been taken ill and remained in Reading, Waller and Manchester decided the battle tactics. These were for a coordinated, simultaneous attack on Royalist defensive positions in the village of Speen and at Shaw House. Manchester and his infantry were to attack Shaw House once Waller, with the cavalry and the remains of the infantry, began to attack Speen. Manchester was to begin his assault on Shaw House as soon as he heard Waller's cannon firing. Waller brought his troops round and after heavy fighting captured Speen. Oliver had been uncharacteristically slow in bringing his cavalry into action and his wing had been mauled by Royalist cavalry under Lord Goring. Nevertheless, Speen was captured, but it was no thanks to Manchester who had remained inactive all day, apparently not hearing Waller's cannon and unaware the attack on Speen had begun. At 4pm Manchester at last attacked Shaw House but was repulsed and he then retreated because of failing light. With darkness having fallen, this messy and inconclusive battle came to a close. Having lost Speen and being outnumbered, the king decided to withdraw to the north, leaving his cannon behind at Donnington Castle.

As soon as it was realised that the king was withdrawing, Oliver and Waller rushed to Manchester to request that they pursue the retreating Royalist army, but Manchester opposed the idea. It was not until late the next day that he reluctantly agreed to a pursuit and Oliver set off with his cavalry, only to find that the Royalists had already reached the security of their fortifications around Oxford. Equally unfortunate was that Manchester then made only a half-hearted attempt to besiege Donnington Castle. This resulted in a force under Rupert having time to arrive and relieve it on 9 November, right under the noses of Manchester's army. To add insult to injury, Rupert then managed to ride out taking the king's abandoned cannon with him.

Having been reinforced by the arrival of Rupert, Charles was again prepared to do battle, but Manchester had lost heart and so the two armies pulled back. Manchester had come to the conclusion that there was no hope of victory against the king and made the remark: 'King need not care how oft he fights ... If we fight a hundred times and beat him ninety-nine he will be King still, but if he beats us but once, or the last time, we shall be hanged, we shall lose our estates, and our posterities be undone.' To this Oliver made his famous rejoinder: 'If this be so, why did we take up arms at first? This [Manchester's remark] is against fighting ever hereafter. If so, let us make peace, be it never so base.'[10] It was probably at this moment that Oliver realized that the whole parliamentary military leadership would have to be removed and replaced by those who had the determination to achieve victory.

Oliver was not alone in his conviction that generals such as Manchester must be replaced. Henry Ireton, who had become quartermaster-general of the Eastern Association, was equally furious with Manchester. As Royalists and Parliamentarians pulled back at the end of the campaigning season, Oliver began a different campaign of his own, which would prove just as bloody in its own way. This was a campaign to challenge Manchester's fitness to be a general. Manchester was well aware that Cromwell wanted to destroy his reputation and did not take it lying down. It was with this raw, bad feeling that both men returned to London to seek support and thrash the matter out in parliament and in the Committee of Both Kingdoms.

Parliament was aware that all was not well with the army leadership. The army was ordered to take up winter quarters in Reading, and Manchester, Waller and Oliver were directed to give an account of their actions at Newbury. At the request of the Commons, on 25 November Oliver presented his case against Manchester to the House. In a long and articulate speech, he attacked his superior officer saying such things as: 'the Earl hath always been indisposed and backward to engagements, and ending the war be the sword, and always for such a Peace as a thorough victory would be a disadvantage to'.[11] Sir William Waller, like Oliver both a general and an MP, supported the attack on Manchester.

In the House of Lords Manchester made his own accusations against Oliver, such as that he was against the nobility: 'he [Cromwell] hoped to see never a nobleman in England'; that he was an religious extremist: 'He desires to have none in the army but such as were of the independent judgement'; that he hated the Scots: 'He would as soon draw his sword against them as any of the king's enemies;' and that he was disloyal and disruptive to his commander and was 'attributing all praise to himself of other men's actions'.[12] For good measure Manchester even accused Oliver of misappropriating army funds by having the £5 a week sent to his family in Ely. The contest went well past the gentlemanly stage. Essex also spoke in the Lords giving his firm support to Manchester and the majority of the house rallied around the general as one of their own, compared to the scruffy Cromwell who seemed to be little better than a disruptive Anabaptist.

There was no time for Oliver to return to Ely after Newbury and so the family most likely heard about this vitriolic contest largely from news sheets and occasional letters from Oliver when he found time to write. Although Ireton stood firmly with Oliver, he probably had at least occasionally to visit Ely in his capacity as deputy governor and would have given Elizabeth and the family a first-hand account of the situation. The clash between her husband and Manchester would hardly have been a surprise to Elizabeth, but that it had become public and a matter that needed parliament to resolve, was very worrying indeed. There seemed every likelihood that Oliver, who was a subordinate officer, would come off worse in any contest between him and a popular Presbyterian earl who commanded the Eastern Association. The gloom of the situation would have at least been lifted for Bridget if she had been able to see Henry Ireton. Some of the officers she knew in her father's regiment had been wounded at Newbury such as Charles Fleetwood and it would have been a relief to see Henry alive and unharmed. It would have also been encouraging to hear that Oliver received whole-hearted support from his cousin Oliver St John and many of the parliamentary leaders in the Commons, such as Sir Henry Vane.

The vitriolic arguments between Oliver and Manchester opened up serious divisions within the parliamentary leadership. The majority of them were Presbyterians who were suspicious of Cromwell who himself seemed to favour Independents. This was particularly so of the Covenanter Scots on the Committee of Both Kingdoms, who as unbending Presbyterians, had no time for those with Independent sympathies. Then there was the traditional rivalry between the Commons and the Lords, each wanting to support their own man. On top of that there were those like Holles who agreed with Manchester that a peaceful solution should be found to the war, a policy which was bitterly opposed by Vane's war faction. The tide for peace seemed to move Manchester's way and was supported by Essex. In fact, there was so much support for a peaceful outcome among both the Royalists and parliament that negotiations were planned to start in January.

The king was of course delighted to see such discord amongst the opposition and felt the series of victories by Montrose against the Covenanters in Scotland had strengthened his bargaining position. It was against this background that the parliamentary leadership, which really boiled down to the Committee of Both Kingdoms, found themselves divided; so divided that they could not decide how to proceed regarding the important matter of Manchester and his lieutenant-general of horse. Out of the blue Oliver offered them a solution to the impasse.

In a speech to the Commons Oliver said: 'And I hope we have such true English hearts, and zealous affections towards the general weal of our Mother Country as no Member of either House will scruple to deny themselves, and their own private interests, for the public good.' This was rapidly turned into a motion, probably drafted with the help of St John and Vane, called the *Self-denying Ordnance*. By this measure no member of either house of parliament could hold an office in the army from forty days after it had been passed. This meant that both Manchester and Oliver had to give up their commissions. As neither side could claim victory over the other, a compromised solution had to be found. The Commons passed the *Ordnance*, but the Lords had severe doubts when it was sent to them on 19 December as it meant that, as well as Manchester, other lords had to surrender their commissions, most notably Essex the Lord General himself. Similarly, parliament would lose the services of some good generals who were MPs, such as Waller. It took some time before this bill was to be finally accepted or rejected.

The year came to a close with peace negotiations having begun with the king and the Lords and Commons at loggerheads over the *Ordnance*. Oliver was more interested in a project that could not have been closer to his heart having been placed on a sub-committee of the Committee of Both Kingdoms to make recommendations on the restructuring of the army. He set to work with huge enthusiasm to design a New Model Army. This was to be an army strong enough to defeat the king and so had to be provided with the necessary funding for pay, stores and equipment and to have the same standards of training and discipline of his own Ironsides.

With Oliver this busy in Westminster, interrupted only by occasional visits to his troops in Reading, there was little or no time for him to return to his constituency of Cambridge, let alone Ely. Elizabeth probably had not seen him since September and was not likely to see him for some time to come and as a good army wife just continued on with things in his absence. At least there was the help of £5 a week family income and probably advice and encouragement from Oliver in letters that are now lost. Two hopes may have occupied Elizabeth's mind. The first was that the forthcoming negotiations, which were to be held at Uxbridge, would lead to a lasting peace. The second was that if the *Self-denying Ordnance* was agreed upon, then Oliver would have to give up his command. In both scenarios, her husband might be able to return home as a civilian before too long.

Chapter 7

Two War Brides
1645–1647

'This is none other than the hand of God and to Him alone belongs the glory.'

Oliver Cromwell, after the Battle of Naseby.

Some like Elizabeth might have been hoping for a peace settlement to come from the talks that were to begin in early 1646. This was not the case for Oliver who was fully focussed on designing what was generally referred to as the 'New Model Army'. Although Oliver was busy in London, it was some compensation for the family to have Henry Ireton return to them. This was not just a brief visit as deputy governor but lasted about a month while he used Ely as a base for recruiting the army Oliver was engaged in designing. By 27 January Oliver's plans for the New Model Army were complete and put to the Commons. It would have eleven regiments of horse each 600 men strong, twelve regiments of foot with 1,200 men and 1,000 dragoons, making a total of 21,400. The cost for this new properly equipped and paid army would be raised by taxing districts under parliamentary control £56,000 a month. This dramatic proposal was agreed by the Commons and sent to the Lords who were still unconvinced by the *Self-denying Ordnance*.

The day after the Commons agreed the New Model Army, peace negotiations began in Uxbridge. The negotiations dragged on for nearly a month, but as parliament made its old demands, such as that the king take the covenant, abolish the episcopacy and put the army and navy under parliamentary control, there was no middle ground. It soon became clear that peace was impossible and the Lords passed the New Model Ordnance. After much wrangling between Lords and Commons on appointment of officers, on 15 February it was agreed that Sir Thomas Fairfax should be the Commander in Chief and be able to appoint officers of his choice.

Sir Thomas Fairfax was the ideal political choice as Commander in Chief because he did not have a seat in either house and, being the son of Lord Fairfax, was an aristocrat and therefore acceptable to the Lords.

Fairfax was also a brave and successful cavalry leader who Cromwell had already served with and fully respected. Oliver was thus poised to retire having completed his task of designing the new army in which he would take no part. However, it was one thing to have a blueprint for an army and a theoretical way of raising money to pay for it, quite another to put them into practice. While the implementation of creating the New Model Army was still work in progress, there was the matter of conducting the war with what resources parliament currently had available. This became urgent when Lord Goring made headway for the Royalists in the south-west and on 27 February captured Melcombe Regis. The Committee of Both Kingdoms decided that Sir William Waller should be sent with the remnants of his army to counter Goring.

Waller's army was in a bad shape; its troops had not been paid for nearly two years and his cavalry had deserted. It was therefore decided that Oliver should take his cavalry to join Waller as his lieutenant-general. Both men were MPs, but as the *Self-denying Ordnance* had still not passed the Lords, they continued to be employed. Oliver returned to the war on 4 March having gathered 5,000 horse and appointed Ireton as his quartermaster. This turn of events must have been a disappointment for both Elizabeth and Bridget who had been expecting their menfolk back home once again rather than facing the dangers of combat. For the next month Waller and Oliver carried out a number of minor skirmishes, which achieved the objective of not allowing Goring to advance further. By the beginning of April as it was clear that the Lords would sign the Ordnance, Waller returned with the army to Salisbury to deliver up his commission to Fairfax. Essex and Manchester had resigned their commissions on 3 April, the day the *Self-denying Ordnance* was formally passed and Oliver went to Fairfax to surrender his. Although the Ordnance took effect, in Oliver's case there was a postponement.

The Committee of Both Kingdoms had been concerned that the king's 10,000 strong force in Oxford would receive men and cannon from Royalists in Hertfordshire. Oliver was ordered to take two regiments of horse to prevent this. Ireton accompanied Oliver as quartermaster and they won a large skirmish to capture the bridge at Islip, taking 200 prisoners. They then went on to capture Bletchingdon House, one of the Royalist strong points protecting Oxford. The Ordnance stated that MPs had to give up their commissions within forty days of it being passed, but Oliver was then granted an extension in order to harass the Royalists in south Oxfordshire and shadow any movement of the king's army. He was then ordered to defend the Eastern Association area in case Montrose and his Scottish Royalists should advance south. On 31 May Oliver returned to Cambridge where he recruited 3,000 more horse and then moved to Huntingdon for further recruiting on 4 July. We must assume that he at least spent a little time with his family in Ely who he had not seen for many months.

Any hopes that Oliver might at last be about to have to resign his commission and return home for good were almost immediately dispelled. On 1 June Prince Rupert captured and sacked Leicester. Following this major setback Fairfax urgently petitioned parliament to allow him to appoint Cromwell as his lieutenant-general. There were many who were suspicious of Oliver as a supporter of the Independents, but he was the obvious choice to command the New Model Army cavalry. On 10 June the Commons approved continuation of his commission for forty-two days, to be renewed on a rolling basis subject to parliamentary approval. Whereas the senior posts in the New Model Army, such as major-general of foot, had been filled for some time, the post of lieutenant-general had been left vacant. Oliver would have known that his friends in the Commons tried to have him appointed, but however good his credentials, they were easily thwarted by the Presbyterians. His appointment as lieutenant-general would have come to him as a relief rather than a surprise. For Elizabeth, however, the news was double-edged. How far her pride in her husband's achievements, and rise in family income, were tempered by her desire and expectation simply to have him home, we can only imagine. A sense of disappointment would have been shared by Bridget who found herself having to wait longer to be with Henry Ireton as he had been made colonel of a regiment of horse in the New Model Army.

The war was obviously going to drag on until king or parliament secured sufficiently resounding victories and imposed surrender. The consequences of losing the war would have been disastrous to the families of the rebel leaders. Even if the war was to be won, it would be at the cost of considerable bloodshed to come. Bloodshed that could well have included that of Oliver and Henry Ireton, both of whom found themselves in the highly vulnerable position of leading cavalry charges. As if this was not enough, Elizabeth and Oliver's second surviving son, Henry, decided to leave Cambridge and join the New Model Army as a lieutenant in Thomas Harrison's regiment of Horse.

Oliver lost no time in taking his cavalry to join Fairfax near Bedford. The king's army was at Market Harborough en route to Newark and on 13 June Ireton, with a body of cavalry, overran one of the Royalist outposts at the village of Naseby. The next day both sides battled, although the king had only 9,000 men compared with Fairfax's 14,000. There was the usual deployment for battle with infantry in the centre and cavalry on each wing.

Fairfax had agreed to Oliver's request that Ireton should command the cavalry on the left supported by some dragoons and opposed by the Royalist cavalry under Rupert. Oliver was on the right wing facing Sir Marmaduke Langdale's Northern Horse.

The battle began with a charge by Rupert, which was met by a rather ragged one by Ireton with savage horse to horse fighting. Ireton's horse was shot under him, but he fought bravely on, receiving a wound in the thigh from a pike and a hit to the face with a halberd before being taken prisoner. Rupert's cavalry won the engagement and set off in pursuit and in the pillaging of the parliamentary baggage train four miles to the south. Much of the parliamentary centre was then pushed back, but Oliver charged on the right wing and put the Northern Horse to flight. He ordered some of his men to pursue but wheeled the rest round to attack the exposed flank of the Royalist infantry. The Dragoons then repositioned themselves to attack the Royalist infantry from the other side and before long the Royalist army broke and fled back towards Market Harborough. The king's army was destroyed with 6,000 killed or captured and all baggage and artillery lost. Oliver had once again won the day.

Bridget Cromwell was relieved to hear news of the battle victory once it reached Ely. Although Ireton had been wounded and taken prisoner, he had managed to escape at the end of the fighting and was alive. As for Elizabeth, again, her sense of pride in her husband's accolades as an acclaimed hero was tempered by the reality that Oliver would not be coming home until parliament had dispensed with his services and that was only going to happen when the war was over. Certainly, there was no let up for Oliver after the battle because, with Fairfax, he took Leicester four days later, then set off to deal with Lord Goring in the south-west. Having taken Taunton and Yeovil, Goring was cornered at Langport on 10 July and the last Royalist field army was defeated largely thanks to cavalry charges led by Oliver and his brother-in-law Desborough. Other towns surrendered and then Fairfax besieged Rupert in Bristol by which time he was re-joined by a recovered Henry Ireton. After an initial assault on the city Rupert surrendered and the main city in the West Country was lost to the king. Devizes and Winchester soon surrendered and the stronghold of Basing House was stormed by Oliver in October. This was followed by a brief spell in Axminster for winter quarters when, afterwards, Oliver at last had the chance to visit home.

In January 1646 parliament was so appreciative of Fairfax and Cromwell that they voted them large sums of money as a reward for their service, which in the case of Oliver came from confiscated Royalist estates worth £2,500 a year and a lump sum of £500.[1] The payment for Oliver's triumphs could not have come at a better time for Elizabeth who was planning for a forthcoming family wedding, for which a dowry would be needed. She and Oliver's favourite daughter, the carefree Bettie, now 16, was to marry the 22-year-old John Claypole. It seems to have been a love match. Bettie was a Puritan in her faith, but cheerful and fun loving in her personality. John had a light-hearted disposition and although a parliamentary supporter, had a lifestyle of a cavalier gentleman. The marriage was also a good match for the Cromwell family as John was the eldest son of John Claypole senior, a member of an old established gentry family with estates in several counties and a country seat in Northborough, just thirty miles from Ely. John senior had refused to pay Ship Money and was an old friend and neighbour of Oliver and Elizabeth. The betrothal of their children was a happy outcome further strengthening their long friendship. A dowry of £1,250 was agreed upon and the marriage took place at Holy Trinity Church Ely on 13 September.

It must have been a joyous occasion for Elizabeth and the family but marred by Oliver's absence as he had returned with Fairfax and the army to complete operations in the West Country—which lead to the capturing of more towns for the Parliamentary cause and included the surrender of Hopton's remaining army at Exeter on 14 March. While the loss of the king's army meant that in April Oliver returned to London to attend the Commons, who were considering a peace settlement, and Ireton and the army moved to blockade the king's headquarters at Oxford, out of the blue, on 27 April the king escaped Oxford in disguise and made his way to Newark to surrender to the rather surprised Scots army on 5 May. Fairfax and Oliver returned to Oxford themselves to capture the town or force its surrender.

As the war appeared to be almost over and it was only appropriate that Ireton and Bridget's long courtship was, at last, brought to a happy conclusion. Bridget was a rather shy and devout 22-year-old Puritan maid and Henry was a serious, conscientious and godly man of 32. Although the happy couple were not by nature of a cheerful disposition, they were in their way a good match. Their marriage took place on 15 June at Fairfax's headquarters in Lady Whorton's fortified manor house at Holton to the east of Oxford and was conducted by Fairfax's chaplain with Sir Thomas and Lady Fairfax present. Elizabeth no doubt accompanied Bridget to Holtam, allowing her and Oliver to enjoy one of their daughters' weddings together for a change. Financially, it was not a good match for the Cromwells. Henry was the eldest of five sons of German Ireton, a wealthy member of the gentry living in Attenborough, Nottinghamshire, who had died in 1624. They do things differently in Nottinghamshire and it was the practice to have ultrageniture, that is to say the youngest rather than the oldest son inherited.[2] In Henry's case it was his youngest brother William who inherited the estate and Henry received next to nothing. For all that, Oliver had become very attached to Henry as an equally devout Puritan and a cavalry officer who had fought bravely alongside him from the start of the war. His legal training and natural aptitude made him a deep thinker, clear writer and excellent administrator as he had demonstrated both as a quartermaster and a negotiator. In fact, towards the end of the previous year there had been elections for vacant seats in the Commons and Ireton had become MP for Appleton. There had been little time for him to attend the House, but there was every reason to believe his political acumen would eventually be put to good use. In short, the Cromwells were pleased with their new son-in-law and provided as a dowry the leases of some lands in Ely.[3]

There was just the matter of the surrender of Oxford and a settlement with the defeated king and then Henry and Bridget would be able to settle down in London with him as an MP and working as a lawyer. Henry negotiated the surrender of Oxford and it came into effect five days after his wedding. Elizabeth returned to the family in Ely and Oliver decided to base himself in London so he could be near the seat of decision making for negotiating a settlement with the king. He had received a six-month extension of his commission in January which had expired and was close to finally being a civilian. The good pension he received as a lieutenant-general was sufficient enough to move the whole family to a house in London big enough to accommodate them all.

Oliver decided to set up home in Drury Lane, which was just off the fashionable area of Holborn, with its pretty gardens, horse-chestnuts and mulberries. Departing Ely was a major move for the family consisting as it did of Elizabeth, Oliver's mother, Richard and the two unmarried girls, Mary and Frances, with Henry likely to be based there once his military duties were over. One person who did not want to join the move was Oliver's unmarried Aunt Elizabeth who at 56 preferred to stay put in Ely and went to live with friends. For the family there would have been regrets leaving their friends and the familiar life of Ely where they had established roots after being there so long, but these were at least compensated by the knowledge they would be united at last with Oliver.

Moving to London was a mixed bag for the family. Although some twenty-six years before, Elizabeth would have been reasonably familiar with London having sometimes stayed with her father's residence near Tower Hill, times had changed. For Oliver's 81-year-old mother who had probably never moved out of the county in her life, the relocation would not have been welcome. As for Oliver and Elizabeth's children, they very probably welcomed the move and exchanging the humdrum existence in a small cathedral town for the excitements and opportunities of the capital.

As a strong family man, no doubt Cromwell was very happy to at last be able to spend time with his loved ones. The family had no sooner moved into Drury Lane than it increased in number. Oliver's sister, Anna Sewster, died in November and it seems her daughter Robina came to live part of the time with them and partly with her father at his home in the Fens. Robina fitted in well and Oliver and Elizabeth were to become particularly fond of her. Cromwell did not forget his married daughters and wrote to Bridget with fatherly advice of a type typical of him: 'Dear Heart, Press on; let not husband, let not anything cool thy affections for Christ. I hope he will be an occasion to inflame them. That which is best worthy of love in thy husband is that of the image of Christ he bears. Look at that, and love it best, and all the rest for that. I pray for thee and him, do so for me.'[4] Although content to be with the family, Elizabeth probably noticed that in other respects he was far from happy. Until recently he had been a man of action carrying out his military duties with great success to the obvious approval of God. Being a politician was a different matter where successes were more complex, time consuming and often harder to achieve than victory on the battlefield.

The war had been won, but Oliver felt driven to complete his divinely appointed task and win a godly peace. In his view, that peace was the traditional form of government of king, lords and commons with regular parliaments and the king's powers strictly limited particularly over control of the army and navy. As far as religion was concerned, he wanted to end the episcopacy and all Popish practices, but allow for freedom of worship for all Puritan sects. This was much the same as Oliver's fellow Members of Parliament, but it did differ in some important respects. Firstly, Holles, Essex and the Presbyterian majority could not abide freedom of worship for Independent Nonconformists. Secondly, they also wanted only minimum reductions in royal power. Finally, they distrusted the army, many of whom were Independents, and wanted it disbanded as soon as possible by the war's end. Oliver wanted cast iron limitations to the king's powers before the army should be disbanded and any disbandment accompanied by soldiers being given the pay they were owed in full. Oliver's views were shared by others, principally Vane, St John, Saye and Sele, Ireton and other officers like Fleetwood who had become MPs. This group formed a minority and were disregarded by the parliamentary majority who opened new negotiations with the king in Newcastle upon Tyne where he was then being held by the Scots.

In December parliament reached agreement with the Scots that for the sum of £400,000 they would withdraw to Scotland and hand the king over to parliament. The king was duly handed over and on 16 February 1647 taken to Holdenbry Hall in Northamptonshire to be held in honourable captivity while negotiations continued. Oliver had been becoming increasingly frustrated and depressed about the settlement the Presbyterian dominated parliament might make with the king. On top of everything, they also intended to disband the majority of the army and send the rest to Ireland under Presbyterian officers. At the time Charles arrived at Holdenbry Oliver fell seriously ill with 'an impostume of the head', which was some form of infected abscess. Although this was not psychosomatic, it may have been that his state of depression made him more susceptible to infection. This was a worrying time for Elizabeth and the family, but by the end of March he had recovered from his illness and was back sitting on numerous Commons committees.

What Oliver had not recovered from was being depressed about the peace settlement which appeared to be going nowhere, or if anything in the wrong direction. Throughout this period Elizabeth must have been concerned that this might indicate a return of his clinical depression, but fortunately it did not materialise. Other problems occupied his mind, such as the army he loved so dearly being near to the point of mutiny. Infantry regiments were eighteen weeks in arrears of pay and cavalry regiments forty-two days but had been offered only seven weeks of back pay to disband.[5] In addition, new and dangerous movements were at work within the army itself. Those who had decided to oppose parliament organised themselves into what were termed 'Agitators' and others joined the sect called Levellers who regarded God alone as ruler and who wanted to dispense with human authority of all sorts.

The Commons dispatched Oliver, Ireton and Fleetwood to try to quieten the army which was concentrated at Saffron Walden. Oliver found himself the go-between with parliament and the army, somewhat distrusted by both sides and with little hope of a compromise as parliament refused to pay off the army before its disbandment. On 3 June a junior officer and Agitator called Cornet Joyce transformed the situation. He took some troopers to Holdenbury Hall, arrested the king and took him to Newmarket. Oliver seems to have been visited by Joyce a few days earlier and probably agreed to at least putting the king under army guard. Joyce's action meant that the king was suddenly under the control of the army rather than parliament. The army had become a political power in the land.

The next month there were riots in London with people calling for the return of the king and the House of Commons was occupied. Fairfax, who was not well and who had been thinking of resigning his post as Commander-in-Chief, decided to march on London to restore order. If there was ever an outward and visible sign of the army's new power it was this. A large portion of it entered London in a triumphal parade on 6 August with Oliver leading his regiments of horse and Fairfax behind leading the main body of cavalry. They were welcomed by the Lord Mayor and Aldermen at Hyde Park and then by the Common Council at Charing Cross. They then travelled to parliament and the Tower of London. The next day Fairfax was too ill to ride and Oliver led the 18,000 strong army over London Bridge into Kent.[6] This military demonstration had taken the heart out of any thoughts of rioting or resistance.

Oliver's dramatic parade had not only been witnessed by Elizabeth, but she had participated in it by travelling with Lady Fairfax and her ailing husband in the same coach. The two wives probably previously met at Bridget's wedding and would have certainly become better acquainted on this journey. Anne Fairfax was the daughter of Baron Vere and a strong and attractive personality, liked and respected by Oliver who had written to Bridget on 25 October the previous year stating that: 'My service and dear affections to the general and generaless; I hear she is very kind to thee; it all adds to other obligations.' Anne seems to have taken Bridget under her wing when they were both quartered near Devizes and no doubt Elizabeth would have wanted to thank her for that.

Elizabeth, in particular, must have marvelled how her life had changed since the hard times in St Ives as her husband led the triumphal procession through London and received greetings from its leading citizens. She had been brought up the daughter of a knight, spent most of her life as the small-town housewife of a minor landowner, yet found herself seated in a fine coach with the commander-in-chief and his wife. Given her past experiences, she must have wondered in such unsettled times where life and God's Providence would lead. For the time being, however, it was clear that the Cromwell family was flourishing. At last they had sufficient amounts of money and Mary and Frances appeared happy in London. Richard, nearing 21, seemed to be settling down and had recently enrolled at Lincoln's Inn and Oliver had put feelers out about finding him a wealthy heiress in the form of Dorothy Mayor from Hampshire.[7] Bridget and Bettie were happily married and one of Cromwell's sons-in-law, Henry, proudly led his regiments of horse in the parade. God was indeed smiling on the Cromwell family.

Although the army's march through London had restored order to the city, parliament was still faced with the major problem of achieving a successful settlement with the king. In September it was agreed that

Cromwell could begin negotiations with Charles based on a document called *Heads of Proposals* drafted by Ireton, which listed religious and constitutional demands. In October the matter of dissenters in the army was dealt with in a series of debates organised in Putney that considered the Agitators' grievances and the political objections of the Levellers. Ordinary soldiers were elected to debate with senior officers on wide ranging matters, such as whether there should be any further negotiation with the defeated king, whether there should even be a king or lords for that matter and whether the right to vote should stop being limited to property owners and extended to all men. With Fairfax still unwell Oliver had the task of chairing these meetings, but being at heart a conservative, he had little sympathy for radical changes in government, and simply wanted curbs on royal power and justice for the army. Nevertheless, the proposed solutions were eventually put in a document called *The Agreement of the People* demanding freedom of religion, frequent parliaments and equality before the law.

Oliver and Ireton had found themselves shuttling between Putney for the debates and Hampton Court for negotiations with the king, where he had been moved and was living in royal state, though confined to the palace and its grounds having given his parole not to escape. Oliver had appointed Colonel Edward Walley with his regiment of horse to guard the king as Walley was someone Oliver really trusted. He was the son of Oliver's aunt Frances and had joined Oliver's cavalry at the beginning and fought with him in all the major battles. Oliver, Ireton and Walley treated the king with due respect and consideration and a reasonably amicable relationship was built up between them during talks. As such, rumours began to spread amongst the Agitators that Cromwell was intending to sell them out for an earldom. This was, of course, nonsense, but shows the difficulties of Oliver and Ireton's position. These rumours became even stronger when it became known that Elizabeth Cromwell, Bridget Ireton and Walley's wife Judith had been presented to the king and entertained by him for the evening with their husbands.

It must have been a very memorable experience for Elizabeth and her shy daughter to literally be royally entertained in the grand surroundings of Hampton Court Palace by an attentive and gracious king. However, this was to be a one-off occasion as on 11 November the king escaped from Hampton Court having broken his parole in the belief that Agitators intended his assassination—or so he said in a letter he left for Walley. The king and those who helped him escape were not sure where to make for, possibly Scotland or to join the queen in France. They decided to make for the Isle of Wight because it was believed that the governor there had Royalist sympathies.

Their intelligence was wrong. The governor was Colonel Robert Hammond who was married to Oliver's cousin Mary, the daughter of John Hampden. Hammond received the king with respect but confined him to Carisbrooke Castle under Oliver's orders.

The news of the king's escape created an emergency that resulted in an end to the Putney Debates. The delegates agreed that for the sake of army unity the *Heads of Proposals* should be accepted and regiments should swear loyalty to Fairfax who had recently recovered. The oaths of obedience were to take place in three different locations starting with Ware, yet the first regimental rendezvous did not start well. Harrison's regiment turned up in an aggressive mood with soldiers wearing the Agitator's *The Agreement of the People* proposals in their hats and only came around when they were addressed by the much-respected Fairfax. Then Robert Lilburn's regiment arrived in an even more mutinous mood. Oliver drew his sword and went among them pulling *The Agreement* from hats. He then arrested four ringleaders and summarily condemned them to death for mutiny. He added some drama by having them publicly draw lots and the least successful was shot by the other three. After this, the oaths of allegiance went ahead without a hitch.

The grievances of the army remained, but discipline was restored and Cromwell returned to London to encourage parliament to reach a final settlement with the imprisoned king at Carisbrooke. Although Drury Lane was just a short trot by horse from the Commons, Oliver decided it was necessary to be within easy walking distance from parliament. He therefore moved the family to a house in King Street, almost opposite the Commons.[8] As Henry Ireton worked extremely closely with Oliver, both politically and militarily, it could be that he and Bridget also moved to the new house or at least found somewhere nearby. The Cromwell family had spent barely a year in Drury Lane and, having just begun to feel settled, was off again. With Oliver so busy, it would have fallen to Elizabeth to carry out the numerous tasks for moving a big family. Admittedly it was not far, but still entailed the disruption of a move and settling down all over again in Whitehall, although with the advantage that they were close to St James' Park. Elizabeth was used to Oliver having those who shared his political views round to the Drury Lane house for discussions where she provided them beer with bread and butter. Being so close to parliament in King Street, even more like meetings were expected, as was a greater call for more beer with bread and butter.

While Oliver and Henry were busy in the Commons, the king was busy in his own way on the Isle of Wight. Being under open arrest meant that he was still able to meet people and have private conversations, including delegates from Scotland. On 26 December the king signed a secret treaty with the Scots that they would undertake to invade England to restore him to the throne on condition that he would establish Presbyterianism. Cromwell was unaware of the actual agreement, but he and the Army Council had heard from some intercepted documents that the king was trying to come to an accommodation with the Scots. For some time, Ireton had felt that the king was too untrustworthy for any lasting agreement to be possible. Now Oliver agreed with him, as did many members of the Commons. Just three days into the new year of 1648 Oliver and Ireton managed to get parliament to agree to the *Vote of No Address* in which the question of the future government of the country was to be decided without reference to the king. The vote was carried with the biblical quotation: 'Thou shalt not suffer a hypercritic to reign', ringing in every ear. Despite the continued dominance of Presbyterians, parliament at last moved in the direction Oliver wanted.

Parliament's mounting distrust of the Scots resulted in the Committee of Both Kingdoms being dissolved and replaced by an English Committee of Safety based at Derby House. The army prepared for the increasingly likely possibility that it would have to be deployed against its former allies the Scots. These were uncertain and challenging times for Oliver who still faced plenty of political opposition. Amongst all the political intrigue, Elizabeth probably noted that over the course of the previous six months Oliver's feelings of depression had evaporated, especially once he was back amongst the army once more. Political scheming and manoeuvring had become an unfortunate part of his life, but with the army he was able to be a man of action and that action was soon to come.

Chapter 8

Cruel Necessity
1648–1650

'Tho art dearest to me than any creature; let that surfice.'
   Oliver Cromwell to his wife Elizabeth, 30 September 1650

As 1648 began it was felt that it was only a matter of time before the Scots invaded, supported by a Royalist uprising in England. Although the king had made a few unsuccessful attempts to escape, which certainly did not bode well, little happened that year and Oliver was able to spend some time on domestic matters. In February he reopened negotiations with Richard Mayor concerning the marriage between his daughter Dorothy and Richard. These negotiations dragged on with the additional involvement of third parties, such as Colonel Norton, a good friend, who was MP for Hampshire. The difficulties revolved around not only the size of the dowry, but also whether Dorothy and her family were godly people. Needless to say, Elizabeth would have not only followed the progress of the proposed marriage with considerable interest, but would have been directly involved behind the scenes.

Ever the family man, Oliver did not neglect the uncle and godfather, after whom he had been named. Sir Oliver Cromwell of Ramsey Abbey and his son Henry had been on the losing side in the Civil War and were subject to fines of £841 each. As the estate only brought in £1,200 a year and was seriously in debt, they were unable to pay. Oliver used his influence with the Sequestration Commission to ensure that the fines were set aside. Whether his uncle ever forgave him for taking his plate for parliament when he visited five years previously is not recorded.[1] Elizabeth would have known Sir Oliver and Henry and would have been pleased that they had been saved from hard times.

In the spring, troops in Wales mutinied over lack of pay and declared for the king and it was Cromwell who was dispatched to deal with them. By the time he arrived many of the rebels had been defeated by local parliamentary troops, but the remainder fled to Pembroke Castle and after a two-month siege surrendered to Oliver on 11 July. At much the same time there was a

Royalist uprising in Kent. The Second Civil War had begun. Fairfax defeated the Kentish Royalist at the Battle of Maidstone on 1 June then turned north to put down a Royalist rising under Sir Charles Lucas in Essex. He beat back Lucas who retreated to Colchester where Fairfax then began a long siege. Royalist risings also occurred in the north, the largest of which was led by Sir Marmaduke Langdale in Cumberland. Fairfax appointed John Lambert as Major General of the North; a 29-year-old who had already proved himself many times as a successful cavalry commander and had made great headway in putting down the northern Royalists when the Scots invaded England under the Duke of Hamilton's command. Hamilton's army linked up with Langdale and some troops from Ulster then marched south, with Lambert harassing them as it went. Oliver received news of the Scottish invasion and marched north with his still unpaid army, many of whom were in tattered clothes and shoeless. He managed to purchase shoes, stockings and other supplies as he went north and eventually caught up with Lambert on 14 August.

Finding that Hamilton's army of about 10,000 were strung out over a large distance, Oliver led his combined army of 8,600 to attack the Scots near Preston. The Hamilton's levies were barely trained and melted away when battle was joined, but there was stiff resistance from Langdale's horse, until it too was put to flight. Hamilton and Langdale managed to flee with 3,000 horse but were pursued by Lambert and surrendered at Uttoxeter. Two thousand of Hamilton's men had been killed and 9,000 taken prisoner, while Oliver had lost only about 100 men. Preston was a resounding parliamentary victory and marked the effectual end of the Second Civil War. Colchester surrendered to Fairfax on hearing the result of the battle and Royalist resistance in the rest of the country virtually ended. Oliver had proved a great cavalry leader at Naseby and Marston Moor, but Preston was the first battle in which he had been in full command, earning him the reputation for being a great general.

Preston had also sealed the king's fate. Royalists who had surrendered at the end of the First Civil War had given their parole not to bear arms against parliament, so those who rose up in 1648 broke their parole and could expect punishment. And punishment they got. A number of leaders were executed, eventually including the Duke of Hamilton. Those who had served voluntarily for Hamilton's army were shipped off to Virginia, Barbados and even Venice as indentured labourers. The big question was what to do with the king. It was he who had brought about this new bloodshed and was, indeed, afterwards referred to in the army as 'that man of blood'.

Back in London Elizabeth and the family would have been delighted with the news of Preston. It must have been a relief that the war appeared to be over and Oliver and the two Henrys were safe. Oliver and Elizabeth's son Henry had been in a skirmish at Appleby and then fought at Preston without injury. Henry Ireton had been with Fairfax in Kent and Essex and soon returned to them, unharmed. Oliver, on the other hand, was not lucky enough to return home so quickly, having been dispatched to Scotland to ensure all Royalist resistance was over. He arrived in Edinburgh to find a new Covenanter government in control under the Earl of Argyle. Cromwell was welcomed by Argyll and was received as a friend, albeit a rather menacing one. After supervising the disbandment of all Scottish forces and assuring himself that Scotland was safe under Argyll, Oliver left Edinburgh in October. He was not able to return home right away as Pontefract Castle was still in the hands of Royalists and he ended up carrying out a siege that lasted for eight weeks.

Meanwhile Members of Parliament in Westminster and the Army Council in Windsor were in endless discussions about what form of settlement should be imposed on the king. Ireton shuttled between Windsor and Westminster, as always, in the thick of it. Following meetings with other members of the Army Council, he had drafted a document called the *Remonstrance* calling for the king to be put on trial. By mid-November this had received general agreement by the army, although not by Fairfax. The *Remonstrance* was put to the Commons and Holles and the Presbyterian majority had the *Vote of No Address* repealed and put forth new, more lenient proposals to the king. On 1 December the *Remonstrance* was widely rejected by 125 to 58.[2] Ireton and the majority of the army, who had had enough of compromise, moved on London on 4 December and camped in Hyde Park. At virtually the same time, the king agreed parliament's proposals in a very watered-down form and these, in turn, were accepted in the Commons by 129 to 83 votes. That was too much for the army. On 6 December Colonel Thomas Pride and his regiment of foot stationed themselves outside the Commons and only allowed entry to those on his list deemed supportive of the army. This process of checking MPs went on for several days, at the end of which twenty-five were arrested, 100 or so excluded, or decided not to take their seats, and just 154 were authorised entry.

This was not in the best traditions of democracy, but the army had a compliant House of Commons and was, in effect, a military coup. This had been plotted while Oliver was in Pontefract, but he may have been made aware of the plan and even encouraged it as the principal actor in this major event was Oliver's son-in-law. Ireton almost definitely ordered Pride to purge the Commons and certainly oversaw the whole process himself. Elizabeth and the rest of the Cromwell family in King Street would have had a grand stand view of the whole proceedings. With Oliver away, there would not have been political plots or meetings taking place at the Cromwell house, unless Bridget and Henry Ireton lived with them, in which case there would have been many. If meetings did take place wherever Bridget and Henry were living, would Bridget have overheard anything? Or would Henry have discussed it with her, bearing in mind they had a close relationship, and would often pray together? We will never know, but we can assume that even if Bridget was not aware of Pride's Purge before the event, she would have given her husband full support after it had occurred.

Cromwell returned to London on the evening of 6 December, the first day of Pride's Purge. He had been away from home for seven months, but events moved too fast for him to have time to catch up with Elizabeth and the girls upon his arrival. He attended the Commons the next morning and also the Army Council but seems to have left Ireton to take the lead in the great matter of bringing the king to trial. Over the next few weeks numerous urgent meetings took place to discuss differing proposals, including meetings on Christmas day. Many hoped that the threat of a trial would bring the king to agree to their demands and induce him to abdicate in favour of his youngest son, the Duke of Gloucester. Ireton had long been convinced that the king must be executed and replaced by a republic. After much prayer, Oliver came to the same conclusion. Ireton and Cromwell having decided that it was God's will that the king should die, they had the difficult task of bringing it about. Large sections of the army would support the king's death, but not the majority of the population.

A great deal of effort would need to be expended in persuading, threatening and exercising downright deception to bring about God's will. The king had already been moved from Carisbrooke to Hurst Castle and then to Windsor. On 4 January an ordinance was passed by the eighty or so remaining members of the Commons to try the king for the treason of 'levying war against Parliament and the People of the kingdom of England'. This was rejected by the Lords, but their rejection was disregarded. A 135 strong High Court of Justice was appointed to act as both judge and jury for the king. As many, like Fairfax and St John, refused to take part, the High Court of Justice ended up with only fifty-three members, but it was enough. After a lot of hard work, all ended up in place, especially after others had refused participation, and a lesser known judge called John Bradshaw was persuaded to become President of the Court.

On 8 January the High Court of Justice assembled in the Painted Chamber[3] and the trial itself began in Westminster Hall on 20 January. It did not start well. When the names of the High Commissioner were read out and Fairfax was recorded as absent, a lady wearing a mask in the gallery shouted, 'He has more wit than to be here.' Then when the charge was read that the king was indicted for treason 'in the name of all the good people of England', there was another interruption. The same lady shouted 'It is a lie, not half, not a quarter of the people of England. Oliver Cromwell is a rogue and a traitor!' The lady was removed from the chamber; she was Lady Fairfax.[4]

Although the king refused to recognise the court, the trial continued with evidence against him being given privately in the Painted Chamber without Charles being present. Then, on 27 January in Westminster Hall, the same setting that had witnessed the overthrow of both Edward II and Richard II, Charles was pronounced guilty and sentenced to death. The desired result from Cromwell and Ireton's perspectives, but they needed sufficient signatures on the death warrant to cement the sentence. They had begun collecting signatures before the verdict and for the next couple of days persuaded and cajoled fifty-nine Commissioners to sign the warrant in the Painted Chamber. The twenty-two signatories other than Cromwell and Ireton also included some of Oliver's relations such as Walley, Walton and Ingoldsby, as well as senior officers such as Pride, Harrison, Ludlow and Geoffe. On the cold morning of 30 January, the king walked from St James' to the Banqueting House. He came through a window of the Banqueting House to a newly erected scaffold surrounded by troops to keep the crowds at a distance. In less than fifteen minutes the show was over and the king's head was held aloft by the executioner.

Oliver was at prayer with the Council of Officers when the execution took place. On receiving the news of the king's death, he declared that it was obviously not been 'the pleasure of God that he should live'.[5] Elizabeth would have been at their home not 100 yards from the Banqueting House and though she probably did not witness the execution, she would have been well aware of the soldiers, crowds and preparations. Elizabeth may have even heard the huge sigh that came from the crowd as the king's head was severed. She would very probably have received word of Lady Fairfax's outburst against her husband and of the heart-rending farewell that had taken place between the king and his two children, the 13-year-old Princess Elizabeth and the 10-year-old Duke of Gloucester. What did she think about the execution of the king who she had met personally and had treated her so graciously at Hampton Court—an execution in which her husband and son-in-law were the primary instigators?

Elizabeth's gentrified background made her, like Oliver, conservative by nature. Oliver had believed in the traditional order of government by king,

Lords and Commons. He was opposed to the king on religious and other grounds but had tried very hard to reach a settlement with him. It was only in the last month that he had come to the conclusion that the king could not be trusted to make or keep a settlement, and so would have to die. Oliver was not one to keep his emotions to himself and Elizabeth must have witnessed this change in him at close quarters. Did they talk about it together? Did Elizabeth try to dissuade him? We do not know. It is probable that she was horrified by the idea of executing the king but knowing that Oliver had firmly decided that it was God's will, found it useless trying to dissuade him from his divine mission. When Oliver returned home to Elizabeth and the family on 30 January he was most likely in the same state of euphoria that he had exhibited all day. Whatever fears and misgivings Elizabeth may have had about the monarch's execution would probably have been set aside to support the husband she loved.

Oliver would have had little time to talk at length to Elizabeth or other members of the family over the next few months about events. The king may have been dead, but the monarchy was not and there were a thousand and one things to be done to establish a new and secure method of government. Ireton had produced his revised *Agreement of the People*, which provided a blueprint for a government without king or lords and biennial parliaments elected on home owner suffrage. This was by no means supported by all, especially by the Levellers who wanted universal male suffrage.

Not only had a new constitution needed to be agreed upon but had to be implemented with all that it entailed, from new flags and coinage, to appointing reliable Republican officials to all positions of authority. Cromwell would have been well aware that although he and Ireton had been prime movers in the king's execution, they would be just two of the prominent figures in the new regime. There were other men involved like William Lenthall the Speaker of the Commons, Fairfax the Lord General, Warwick the Admiral, and forceful members of the Commons, such as Vane and Haselrig. Oliver could only use his influence and army backing to try to bring about a secure and godly nation.

Work began quickly in the Commons. On 5 February the House of Lords was abolished, as was the monarchy the next day. On 14 February a Council of State was established to oversee the running of the new republic. Cromwell was a member, but Ireton was not elected because his high handed and unbending manner had made him unpopular with his fellow MPs. Despite this, he continued to work closely with Oliver behind the scenes. There was no money for the new government and so all sorts of measures were used to bring money in, from demanding loans from the

City of London to selling cathedral lands and the Crown Jewels. Money was needed urgently, not just to pay some of the army arrears, but to prepare for more fighting.

No one had asked the Scots before executing their king and as a result Argyll changed sides and proclaimed the late king's son, King Charles II of Scotland. Charles himself was in France and had gathered a small fleet under Prince Rupert, which had just arrived at Kinsale. In Ireland the Earl of Ormonde still supported the king and made an alliance with the Irish Catholics of Kilkenny and those under Owen Roe O'Neill. With all these new problems arising, Oliver had more than enough to think about, but still made time to write to Richard Mayor about the marriage settlement. Throughout life, Cromwell always gave family matters a high priority, even at this difficult period when the very government of the country was in flux.

There were now three seats of power in the land. The Council of State, the Army Council and the House of Commons. Oliver often sat as Chairman of the Council of State and had managed to persuade Fairfax, St John and Vane to become members. Fairfax was nominally in charge of the Army Council, but his persistent suffering from a kidney stone and gout meant that in his absence proceedings were chaired by Oliver, with Ireton by his side, who also had to be in the Commons to try to sway members both inside and outside the chamber. There must have been very little time for him to relax at home with the family and any opportunities to do so were further hindered when on 15 March parliament proposed that Cromwell be the general to lead an expedition against both the Royalists and Catholics in Ireland. This certainly meant that Oliver and Ireton had to devote the majority of their time to planning the detailed arrangements for the Irish expedition.

At the same time, large sections of the army were being radicalised by the Levellers who played on the army's grievances concerning the pay issue which had yet to be resolved. Mutinies eventually broke out and Oliver and Fairfax dropped everything to deal with them, taking up most of the month of May. These mutinies were put down following a few skirmishes, which culminated in the deaths of some of the ringleaders who were shot against the walls of Burford churchyard. After this, Cromwell returned to London, via Oxford, just in time for England to be declared a Commonwealth.

This busy and momentous time had not distracted Oliver from arranging Richard's marriage, which he wanted to take place before he left for Ireland. In a letter to Mayor dated 14 March he continued to haggle over the marriage settlement offering a jointure of £300 a year if Richard died (to be provided from Elizabeth's lands when she had died). If Richard had no male heir, Mayor had wanted £3,000 to go to any daughter, but Oliver insisted on £2,000, writing: 'I have two young daughters to bestow ... according to your offer I have nothing for them ... If my son die, what consideration is there for me, and yet a jointure parted with. If she die there is little; if you have a male heir, than but £ 3,000.'[6]

There must have been a satisfactory answer because on 6 April Oliver instructed his lawyers to complete the contract. Then on 15 April there was a hitch over the settlement's estimate of revenues for lands in Glamorganshire, but after that was resolved the marriage deeds were signed on 28 April. On 1 May the marriage took place at Mayors' estate in Hursley near Winchester. Oliver attended the wedding, but there is no record of Elizabeth doing so, although she may have done. Oliver and Elizabeth must have had concerns about Richard. He had shown no interest for the law while at the Inns of Court and had been, briefly, a member of Fairfax's life guard, but gave that up. He had a mild, easy-going personality, was lacking in religious fervour and was generally very different from his father. It seemed that he would be best off as a country gentleman and that was exactly what his marriage would achieve. Oliver had met Richard Mayor once during the negotiations and found him a sound and godly man who could help steer his son Richard in the right direction when the married couple moved in with the Mayors at Hursley. He had also found Dorothy an attractive and suitably pious maiden. Fortunately, Richard had met Dorothy a few times before the wedding and had fallen in love with her. All in all, the wedding was a success and it was a relief to Oliver and Elizabeth that Richard was to settle down with a good wife on a large family estate.

After the wedding Cromwell resumed his preparations for Ireland. Parliament made Oliver not only Commander-in-Chief for Ireland, but also Lord Lieutenant, and Ireton was appointed his major general. In July the City of London wanted to honour the new Lord Lieutenant so invited Oliver and Elizabeth to a state dinner. This may have been one of the first major official functions that Elizabeth had attended and no doubt she acquitted herself well. However, the more prominent Oliver became, the more she came into the public eye and became a target for press criticism. The Royalist pamphlet *Mercurius Elencticus* said that Elizabeth had made a fool of herself at the dinner describing her as 'Pusse Rampant of Ely, cloaked all over in innocent white (her beloved's own colours) with the Clerk of the Kitchen both in the Coach'.[7]

Comments of this sort may have been hurtful, but they had become a fact of life for Elizabeth. From early 1648 Oliver had been a target of

Royalist propaganda and was usually referred to as 'Old Noll' or 'Ruby Nose'. In early 1648 Elizabeth began to be targeted in the Royalist *Mercurius Melancholicus*, which ran a series called the *Cookoo's Nest at Westminster* describing how Elizabeth and Anne Fairfax were cuckolding their husbands, misappropriating money and in rivalry with each other to be queen. This particular series had been running for two years, so Elizabeth must have become hardened to vicious propaganda against her.

Elizabeth was probably thinking about Oliver's imminent departure, which had become more urgent as the Earl of Ormonde had taken Wexford and was threatening Dublin. Despite being busy organising the expedition, Oliver still had misgivings about Richard and on 19 July wrote to Richard Major: 'I have delivered my son up to you, and I hope you will councel him; he will need it, and I believe he likes well what you say, and will be advised by you. I wish he may be serious.'[8] This letter was written when it was planned that Elizabeth would travel with Oliver to Bristol to see him off and then stay with Richard and the Mayors at Hursley. For some reason this did not happen and Oliver departed alone on 11 July in some style as Lord Lieutenant, in a fine coach drawn by six grey Friesian mares and accompanied by an honorary life guard of eighty officers. He would not return to London for over a year. He travelled first to Bristol then on to Milford Haven to embark. On board ship, Oliver still could not get his concerns for Richard out of his head, and wrote the following to his new daughter-in-law whom he had obviously become very fond of:

> 'To my beloved Daughter Dorothy Cromwell, at Hurslley, My dear daughter, your letter was very welcome to me. I like to see anything from your hand, because indeed I stick not to say I do entirely love you and therefore I hope a word of advice will not be unwelcome or unacceptable to thee. I desire that you make it above all things your business to seek the Lord; to be frequently call upon him ... I desire you provoke your husband likewise thereunto ... The Lord bless thee, my dear daughter, I rest thy loving father, Oliver Cromwell.'[9]

We will never know, but this may have been written because Oliver knew that Elizabeth would not be visiting Hursley and where she might have intended to ask Dorothy to keep an eye on Richard's spiritual well-being.

On 15 August Oliver landed in Dublin and that day Henry Ireton set sail from Milford Haven with 4,000 troops in seventy-seven vessels. Oliver and Ireton had made careful preparations for the expedition, but they were faced with major problems, not least of which was that the country was suffering a bout of Bubonic plague. The military situation in the country was highly confusing with Ormonde commanding the united Royalist / Catholic Confederation, separate Catholic troops in Ulster under Roe O'Neal and bands of Catholic brigands called 'Tories' roaming about. Oliver was fortunate that just before he arrived Ormonde's force had been defeated at Rathmines by the Dublin garrison and had retreated north. Oliver's first objective was to pursue Ormonde by first capturing Drogheda and then move south to take the other major fortified town of Wexford. His total force was 8,000 foot and 4,000 horse, which he took thirty miles north to Drogheda. The town refused to surrender and was stormed in September. Oliver's troops killed 3,500 people after its capture. The slaughter consisted of 2,700 Royalist soldiers and anyone carrying arms, and the rest were civilians, prisoners and catholic priests.

It must be remembered that Oliver hated papists, especially the Irish who he believed (wrongly) to have carried out the massacre of Protestants in 1641 and who had sent a contingent to England to fight in the Second Civil War and were still threatening the new republic. Oliver wrote to parliament of his actions:

> 'that this is a righteous judgment of God upon these barbarous wretches, who have imbrued their hands in so much innocent blood and that it will tend to prevent the effusion of blood for the future, which are satisfactory grounds for such actions, which otherwise cannot but work remorse and regret.'[10]

The merciless capture of Drogheda did not prevent the effusion of at least some blood, but it encouraged other towns to surrender when summoned. Before long, Dundalk surrendered, and Oliver sent a column to Ulster, which took the surrender of Newry and Belfast. Oliver returned to Dublin in September and Elizabeth arrived from England bringing with her various household items. This would have been quite a trip for Elizabeth, especially as it would have included her first sea journey. She would have arrived tired and already missing her family in London but would have been obviously pleased to be reunited with Oliver and see where he was living in Dublin. Ireland was by no means conquered for parliament, but at least in Dublin Oliver could live the life of His Excellency the Lord Lieutenant. It was probably both strange and enjoyable for her to be treated as a viceroy's wife. However, it would not be for long, as Oliver had to return to his military duties. All too soon after her initial arrival, Elizabeth made the return journey home, probably breaking it for a pleasant stay with Richard, Dorothy and the Mayors at Hursley.

By the time Elizabeth returned to London her son Henry would have left for Ireland having been made colonel of a new regiment and sent to reinforce his father. The King Street home she came back to was now an all-female household, consisting of Elizabeth her mother-in-law, her two daughters Mary and Frances and Oliver's sister Catherine and her daughter Lavinia. It is also likely that Bridget stayed as well while Henry was in Ireland. Bridget had at least one child and would have appreciated having her family around her. It must be remembered that poor Bridget had not only been separated from her husband while he was in Ireland, but also whilst in London when Ireton had been enormously busy with bringing about the king's execution and the establishment of the Republic. In these circumstances, she too would have relied on the company of her mother and sisters for some time.

Despite Oliver's haggling over Richard's marriage settlement, the family was more well off than they had been as a result of him receiving his general's pay and various grants of land in East Anglia, Hampshire, Gloucestershire and South Wales, bestowed by a grateful parliament. It has been estimated that his total annual income would have been in the region of £10,000.[11] That was as much as a particularly wealthy earl might have made before the Civil War. On top of this, Cromwell also received the pay of Lord Lieutenant. At last Elizabeth no longer had any financial worries and was able to spend what she liked on herself and the family. As a careful Puritan lady this would have been no more than was necessary to support a household appropriate to her husband's station. There would have been little or no extravagance, but she would have been able to enjoy the luxury of purchasing new gowns for herself and the family or good quality household items, such as hangings and furniture with no concern about the cost. As a necessity rather than an extravagance, she would probably now have a coach with Oliver's coat of arms of the lion rampant on the side and a barge and watermen for going about London on the Thames. All rather different from life in St Ives.

What did remain a concern for the family was that now three of its male members were far away at war in Ireland. There was the obvious danger of death or injury in combat, but that seemingly remote and backward land also harbored other threats, such as plague and fevers fostered by abysmal hygiene. There was also the threat of pneumonia brought on by exposure to the relentlessly bad weather, which seemed to afflict those engaged in sieges who spent month after month without proper cover. In late October Elizabeth would have heard that Oliver was so ill that Ireton had to take over as commander. This was probably the first bout of low malaria fever, which was to recur at later times in his life. It must have been extremely worrying for Elizabeth to have heard that Oliver was so ill he could not exercise command, and frustrating to have no proper idea of what type of illness it was, or how, or even if, it could be cured.

As soon as Elizabeth had left Dublin, Oliver marched out to besiege Wexford which he reached on 1 October. The garrison refused to surrender, but later the castle itself was betrayed by some of the Royalist garrison. Before arrangements could be made for surrender, Oliver's troops took over the castle, then ran amok in the town. Two thousand Irish troops and up to 1,500 civilians were killed and much of the town torched. Oliver was annoyed that the town had been destroyed but took no disciplinary action against those responsible. In theory this massacre, like that at Drogheda, was legitimate as the town had refused to surrender when summoned. Nevertheless, it is hard to reconcile Oliver's actions on these occasions with those of the same man who was so compassionate to his troops, so kind to his friends and so loving to his family. What can be said is that they worked militarily.

It was at New Ross that Oliver had been laid low with illness, but Ireton continued the campaign taking Carrick and getting Cork to surrender. By late November Oliver was sufficiently recovered to resume command and marched to take Waterford, but bad weather forced him to go into winter quarters in Youghal near Cork. On 29 January 1650 Oliver took to the field again, captured various Munster castles, then marched on Ormonde's family seat the Castle of Kilkenny, which surrendered in late March. By this time parliament had become very concerned about the situation in Scotland where Argyle and the Covenanters were firmly in control and had proclaimed Charles Stuart their king. On 9 April Oliver was ordered back by the Council of State to deal with the Scottish threat and departed for England on 26 May leaving Ireton in command.

Cromwell received a hero's return being given a triple gun salute as his ship entered Bristol and being formally welcomed by the Council of State and large crowds when he arrived at Windsor five days later. Elizabeth had been there to meet Oliver at Windsor and accompany him home, for what would turn out to be a very short stay. News had arrived from France that Charles Stewart had set sail for Scotland and taken the Covenant, and so an invasion of England was expected. The Council of State had decided on a preemptive strike and intended that this should be led by Fairfax with Oliver as his second in command. Fairfax felt it was wrong to make an unprovoked attack on a neighbour nation and resigned his commission the day parliament declared war. Cromwell suddenly became not only the commander of the

Scottish expeditionary force, but Lord General of the Army. Having been just four short weeks with the family in London, he left for Scotland on 28 June on the Great North Road. He took an army of 12,000, which would grow to 16,000 as he picked up additional contingents on the journey. The senior officers he chose were Fleetwood as his lieutenant-general, Lambert as his major-general and Walley as second in command of the horse.

Oliver's views of the Scots differed from those he had of the Papist Irish. The Scots had been allies after all and were Protestant, and although he disliked Presbyterianism, he believed in liberty of conscience. On the other hand, Argyll had broken his trust after the Battle of Preston and was now threatening the new republic. Providence had made him God's instrument with the goal of destroying their army and exacting retribution. It was in this state of enthusiasm that Oliver crossed the border into Scotland on 22 July. He had expected the Scots general, David Leslie, to intercept him, but Leslie fell back to Edinburgh and for the next few months Oliver was unable to draw him into battle, yet had his army continually harassed by raiding parties. The English army had no tents to protect them from Scottish wind and rain and by September several thousand suffered in sickness, not helped by a shortage of supplies. Oliver was in Dunbar intending to move to Musselburgh to ship the sick out and it was at this point that Leslie seized an opportunity and deployed his army to occupy the high ridge above the town, cutting off any retreat to the south.

Oliver's sick force of 11,000 was encircled by a Scottish army of 23,000. The situation remained hopeless until the Scots decided to descend from high ground on 2 September, ready for battle the following day. At 4am the next morning Cromwell drew his troops into position to attack the Scots at first light, before they were ready for battle. The English cavalry charged, followed by the infantry, and fierce fighting continued for many hours until some of the cavalry broke through the Scots line. Oliver then ordered his reserve cavalry to attack this vulnerable point and the Scots lines broke. By 6pm the Scots army was in flight and Cromwell had won a resounding victory. Leslie lost 3,000 men who were killed and 10,000 were taken prisoner. The Scottish prisoners who survived the march without food to Durham were dispatched to New England and the West Indies as indentured labourers. English prisoners were enlisted into the New Model Army. Leslie himself retreated to Stirling.

The day after the battle Oliver wrote very long detailed summaries of the battle for parliament, the Council of State and for Sir Arthur Haselrig in Newcastle and Henry Ireton in Ireland. He managed to make time to write thoughtful letters to his family as well. In a letter to Richard Mayor he included this light-hearted chiding about Dorothy and Richard:

'I pray tell Doll (Dorothy) I do not forget her nor her little brat. She writes to me very cunningly and complimentary to me; I expect a letter in plain dealing from her. She is too modest to tell me whether she breedes or no. I wish a blessing upon her and her husband. The Lord make them fruitful in all that's good. They are at leisure to write often– but indeed they are both idle and worth of blame.'[12]

Oliver also wrote the following to Elizabeth:

'My dearest, I have not had leisure to write much, but I could chide thee that in many of thy letters thou writest me, that I should not be unmindful of thee and thy little ones. Truly, if I love you not too well, I think I err not on the other hand much. Tho art dearest to me than any creature; let that surfice. The Lord hath showed us exceeding mercy; who can tell how great that is. My weak faith hath been upheld. I have been in my inward man marvellously supported; although I assure thee, I grow an old man, and feel infirmities of age marvellously stealing upon me. Would my corruptions did at last decrease. Pray on my behalf in the latter respect. The particulars of our late success Harry Vane or Gil: Pickering will impart to thee. My love to all dear friends. I rest thine, Oliver Cromwell.'[13]

This is one of the two letters from Oliver to Elizabeth that have survived. Elizabeth was obviously finding it difficult with Oliver being away in far off Scotland and so obsessed with his duty that he seemed in danger of forgetting about her and the children. In this letter Oliver tries to put her mind at rest and declares his deep love for her. Clearly, she was far more than the wife of some arranged marriage; she was his partner in life. It is unlikely that she had any influence over Oliver's major decisions, as these would have been made, rightly or wrongly, based on him acting as the agent of God's will. What we can say is that she seems to have exerted some influence over her husband, not least by being a strength and support to him throughout his life.

After the battle, Oliver took over the town of Edinburgh, although the castle still held out against him. A few days later Glasgow surrendered. The only Royalist/Covenanter army remaining was that of Leslie at Stirling in the north which was about 3,000 strong. That left Oliver with the only army in southern Scotland and able to subdue the resistance as remained. There was considerable rejoicing when the news of Dunbar reached London. Parliament decided that Oliver should be rewarded and part of that was to be granted official accommodation in the Cockpit. The Cockpit was the part of the sprawling twenty-four-acre Royal Palace of Whitehall, which had been given over to entertainment and consisted of the tennis court, bowling green and old tilt yard, as well as the cockpit itself, which Charles I had converted into a small theatre. The house called 'the Cockpit,' in this jumble of buildings, would put him in close proximity to the new government offices such as the Council Chamber and committee rooms.

In about October, Elizabeth and the family moved from King Street to the Cockpit. It was only a short move in terms of distance as the Cockpit was at the other end of King Street almost opposite the Banqueting House. Nevertheless, the move still required the whole disruption of their general routine and having all their possessions loaded on to carts, transported and unpacked in their new home.[14] Elizabeth's new home was a fine house just inside the Holbein Gate, which had been the residence of another Elizabeth, James I's daughter, the ill-fated queen of Bohemia. Ultimately, the move would have been worth the disruption as it was larger than the King Street house, faced the Privy Garden and looked out on to St James' Park at the back. Elizabeth was not particularly interested in status, but this would have been regarded as an impressive address to go with the fact that she was now being referred to as 'Lady Cromwell'. There was little chance that the honorary title would have gone to her head when she was being given less complimentary names in the Royalist press, such as *News from the Royal Exchange,* which said that she had slept with most of the officers and men of Oliver's own regiment![15]

In December Oliver sent Lambert to south-west Scotland where he crushed the remaining Covenanter resistance and on Christmas Eve Edinburgh Castle surrendered. In the same month Oliver received the only letter that survives from Elizabeth to him. She gently chides him for not writing more often and says that she sends him three letters for his one, then continues:

> 'thenk to writ sometimes to your deare frend me Lord Chef Justes (St John) of whom I have oftune put you in mind ... And truly, my deare, if you would thenk of what I put you in mind sume, it might be to ase much purpos as others, writitng sumetims a letter to the President, and sumetime to the Speikeir. Indeed, my dear, you canenot thenk the rong you doue your-self in the whant of a letter, though it were but seldume.'[16]

This letter shows Elizabeth to be in her supporting role, with a good understanding of the political situation and not afraid to offer advice–but realising that it may not be taken!

Above: Hinchingbrooke House – ancestral home of the Cromwells and later the Earls of Sandwich. Now the Sixth Form centre of Hinchingbrooke School.

Below: Cromwell's House in Ely, quite substantial but by no means a palace. Now a visitor attraction and tourist office.

Elizabeth Cromwell née Bouchier, mother of Oliver who lived with him most of her life.

Elizabeth Cromwell née Steward, wife of Oliver, who became Her Serene Highness the Lady Protectress.

Elizabeth ('Bettie') Claypole the favourite, fun loving daughter of Oliver and Elizabeth.

John Claypole, Oliver's son-in-law who he made a baron and Master of Horse.

Richard Cromwell, son of Oliver and briefly Lord Protector of England, Scotland and Ireland.

Dorothy Cromwell née Mayor, wife of Richard and Lady Protectress. This is the only known picture of Dorothy and may not be an entirely accurate likeness.

Lieutenant General Henry Cromwell, son of Oliver who made him a knight and Lord Lieutenant of Ireland.

Lieutenant General Henry Ireton, first husband of Cromwell's daughter Bridget who died while Lord Lieutenant of Ireland.

Bridget Fleetwood, devout daughter of Oliver, picture painted at time of her wedding to Ireton.

Lieutenant General Charles Fleetwood second husband of Bridget and briefly Commander-in-Chief.

Victorian painting entitled 'Cromwell's family interceding for the life of Charles the first' – a romantic idea but it never happened.

Lady Frances Russell in middle age, daughter of Oliver and thought good looking in her youth – one of his 'little wenches.'

Mary Countess of Fauconberg, spirited daughter of Oliver – one of his 'little wenches.'

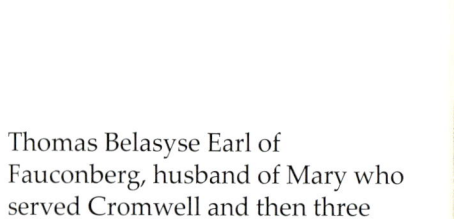

Thomas Belasyse Earl of Fauconberg, husband of Mary who served Cromwell and then three Stuart monarchs.

The year ended with Oliver and his forces in control of the whole of Scotland south of the Clyde and Forth, but with the Royalist/ Covenanter forces to the north ready to melt into the impenetrable Highlands if they were threatened. Ireton had made considerable progress in Ireland, but it would take at least two more years before the whole country was under control. Elizabeth found herself with a husband controlling much of Scotland and a son-in-law ruling much of Ireland. A unique situation, but Elizabeth was more interested in Oliver returning safely from Scotland and resuming his role as a 'family man', and the two Henry, son and son-in-law, coming back safe and sound from Ireland.

Chapter 9

Finding a Settlement
1651–1653

'Depart, I say; and let us have done with you. In the name of God, go!'

Oliver Cromwell to the Rump Parliament,
20 April 1653

In January 1651 Bridget went to Ireland to stay with her husband, taking with her their eldest child, the 4-year-old Elizabeth. Their other daughter Jane was less than a year old and was very probably left in the care of her grandmother in the Cockpit. Bridget sailed from Milford Haven as part of a three-warship troop convoy and after a mercifully calm crossing arrived at Duncannon. She and Elizabeth were met by Henry at nearby Waterford and from there, travelled to Dublin. The Ireland to which Bridget had arrived was under greater English control than the one Oliver had left. Henry had continued Oliver's work with his usual energy, taking control of the Wicklow Mountains and then besieging Waterford, which led to its surrender. He was also fortunate that the Catholic leader Roe O'Neil had died and the Royalist/Catholic confederation was falling apart. The Protestant Royalists had deserted Ormonde and the Confederates no longer trusted him, having removed him as commander in the summer of 1650. Despite their setbacks, the Catholic Confederates still held some strongholds, in particular, Limerick, which Henry had intended to besiege after Waterford, but abandoned because of bad weather and being forced to move the army into winter quarters.

Bridget, therefore, arrived in Dublin while the army was resting in winter quarters and Henry was able to be there until the start of the new campaigning season. He had been made President of Munster before Oliver left and, on Oliver's departure, became commander of the New Model Army forces and Lord Deputy. In short, Bridget was married to the military and civil ruler of the country. Although the country was not fully conquered, in Dublin Henry received all the trappings of supreme authority. These things mattered little to Henry, who in the words of Fleetwood: 'never regarded what clothes or food he used, what hour he went to rest or what horse he mounted'.[1] Henry was well used to the authority of his position, but it must have been rather special for Bridget to witness her husband's power and be treated with the appropriate deference. Puritan lady as she was, she probably rather enjoyed the vice regal position she found herself in as the Lord Deputy's Lady.

Back in Scotland the Royalist/Covenanter threat remained and was reemphasised when in January 1651 Charles Stewart was formally crowned King Charles II at Scone, with Argyll placing the crown on his head. Oliver had taken a very short winter break then headed for campaign in Linlithgow, in the snow. The weather and exertion took its toll and on 8 February he was taken ill where he remained very weak for a month and had to be fed by his French valet, Jean Duret. No sooner had Oliver recovered than the faithful Duret fell ill himself. Oliver visited him regularly and was with him at his death when he commended his mother, sister and family in France to Oliver's care.[2] Oliver immediately wrote to Elizabeth to arrange this, which she did. The Duret family were sent for and entertained by Elizabeth at her own table and became attached to her household.

Oliver's recovery was short and on 11 March he was ill once more and wrote the following letter to Elizabeth on 12 April:

> 'To my beloved Wife Elizabeth Cromwell, at the Cockpit these
>
> My dearest, I praise the Lord I am increased in strength in my outward man: but that will not satisfy me accept I get a heart to love and serve my heavenly Father better; and get more of the light of His countenance, which is better than life, and more power over my corruptions: in these hopes I wait, and am not without expectation of a gracious return. Pray for me; truly I do daily for thee, and the dear family; and God Almighty bless you all with His spiritual blessings.
>
> Mind poor Bettie of the Lord's great mercy. Oh, I desire her not only to seek the Lord in her necessity, but in deed and truth to turn to the Lord; and keep close to Him; and to take heed of a departing heart, and so being cozened with worldly vanities and worldly company, which I doubt she is too subject to. I earnestly and frequently pray for her and for him. Truly they are dear to me, very dear: and I am in fear lest Satan should deceive them—knowing how weak our hearts are, and how subtle and advisary is, and what way the deceitfulness of our hearts and the vain world make for his temptations. The Lord give them truth of heart to Him. Let them seek Him in truth, and

they shall find Him.

My love to the dear little ones; I pray for grace for them. I thank them for their letters; let me have them often.

Beware of my Lord Harbert his resort to your house. If he do so, 'it' may occasion scandal, as if I were bargaining with him. Indeed be wise, you know my meaning. Mind Sir Hen: Vane of the business of my estate. Mr Floyd knows my whole mind on this matter.

If Dick Cromwell and his wife be with you, my dear love to them; I pray for them: they shall, God willing, hear from me. I love them both dearly. Truly I am not able as yet to write much. I am wearied; and rest.

Thine,
Oliver Cromwell'[3]

The letter brings out some of the things that were on Oliver's mind that he wanted to share with Elizabeth. For once he does not show concern about Richard but is worried about Bettie. The bright, pretty and cheerful Bettie had settled down to married life with her husband John Claypole at his estate in Northborough, near Market Deeping. She had given birth to one child, who had been named 'Cromwell,' and was probably pregnant with a second. Despite, no doubt, having a respectable life as a wife and mother, Oliver was concerned about her being 'cozerned by worldly vanities and worldly company'. This was probably because John Claypole was a cheerful, outgoing cavalier in temperament and Bettie was in the same mould, rather than being a prim Puritan like her sister Bridget. Strangely, it was Bettie's *joie de vivre* that made her Oliver and Elizabeth's favourite daughter despite concerns about her spiritual welfare.

The reference to 'Lord Harbert' shows how their two 'little wenches' at home had grown into marriageable age. 'Harbert' is Henry Somerset, Lord Herbert, the eldest son of the Marquis of Worcester. The Marquis was both a Royalist and a Catholic whose estates had been confiscated and his Monmouthshire lands transferred to Oliver as a gift from parliament. His son hoped to rectify the situation by professing himself to be a Protestant and making a bid to marry Oliver and Elizabeth's daughter Mary, who was 14-years-old. It need hardly be said that the marriage did not happen.

Back in Ireland, the campaigning season started and Bridget left Dublin with little Elizabeth and returned to London. Bridget had certainly impressed at least one person as the wife of the Lord Deputy. Thomas

Patient, an Anabaptist preacher attached to Ireton's headquarters, wrote the following about her in a letter to Oliver of 15 April: 'I do by good experience find, as far as I can discern, the poer of god's grace in her soul, a woman acquainted with temtations and brething after Christ.'[4] Bridget does not seem the sort of person to be the life and soul of a party, but there again, Dublin during the winter stand-down from campaigning would hardly have been a social whirl. The mainly dour New Model Army officers were not accompanied by their wives and the atmosphere must have been set by the serious, workaholic Lord Deputy.

During the lull in the campaigning season Ireton had busied himself with removing the native Irish to remoter parts of the island and colonising strategic towns with soldiers of the Protestant faith. For example, the citizens of Waterford were ordered to leave within six months. The redistribution of Catholic lands resulted in a windfall for many members of the army including the Lord Deputy himself who accumulated 13,753 acres.[5] Henry was certainly not avaricious and before setting out for Ireland had turned down £2,000 of arrears of pay, asking that it be put towards the war effort. For a man with no inheritance this was a typically selfless gesture. He, like Oliver, saw the colonisation of Ireland by English settlers as the best way to install the Protestant religion and so help turn it into a godly nation. With spring come and Bridget gone, Henry returned to campaigning in County Clare then in June took a force of 8,000 to begin the siege of Limerick, which would last the next six months.

In Scotland Cromwell continued to fall in and out of illness, but was well enough to write the following short letter to Elizabeth on 3 May:

'My Dearest

I could not satisfy myself to omit this post, although I have not much to write; yet indeed I love to write to my dear, who is very much in my heart. It joys me to hear thy soul prospereth; the Lord increase his favours on thee and more. The great good thy soul can wish is, that the Lord lift upon thee the light of His countenance, which is better than life. The Lord bless all thy good councel and example to all those about thee, and hear all thy prayers, and accept thee always.

I am glad to hear thy son and daughter are with thee. I hope thou wilt have some good opportunity of good advice to him. Present my duty to my Mother, my love to all the family. Still pray for

Thine
O. Cromwell'[6]

This is one of three surviving letters from Oliver to Elizabeth and shows how much he loved her in his own way. It also shows that he has not forgotten his mother and was still concerned about Richard, hoping that he would, in time, respond to good advice.

Oliver's illness returned again in May and Charles Fleetwood acted as commander in Scotland, but no real progress could be made until the Commander-in-Chief was well enough to direct operations. By June Oliver was sufficiently recovered to begin to formulate a plan on how to destroy the Royalist/Covenanter army in Stirling without it retreating into the inaccessible Highlands as he advanced. Busy though he was, he made time to concern himself with family matters, in particular Richard, the regular source of worry to him and Elizabeth. On 28 June he wrote the following in a letter to Richard Mayor asking him to communicate it to Richard:

> 'I hear my Son hath exceeded his allowance, and is in debt. Truly I cannot commend him therin … i desire to be understood that I grudge him not laudable recreations, nor an honourable carriage of himself in them; nor any matter of charge, like to fall to my share, a stick with me. Truly I can find in my heart to allow him not only a sufficiency but more for his good. But if pleasure and self-satisfactions be made a man's life, so much cost laid out upon it, so much time spent in it, as rather answers appetite than the will of God … and after a long passage about the speech of Uriah to David concludes: I think it lieth upon me to give him (in love) the best council I may; and know not how better to convey it to him than by so good a hand as yours. Sir I pray you acquaint him of these thoughts of mine … And remember my love to my daughter (Richard's wife Dorothy); for whose sake I shall be enduced to do any reasonable thing. I pray her happy deliverance, frequently and earnestly.'[7]

Richard enjoyed the leisurely existence of a country gentleman and seemed to be settled down to married life with the attractive and level-headed Dorothy. They had one daughter and another was soon to be born. His father-in-law had arranged for him to become a magistrate and Richard appeared to assume a respectable position in the county. It must have been really disappointing for Elizabeth and Oliver to know that after having gone to so much trouble to marry Richard to a wealthy heiress, that he only then put himself into debt. Oliver had heard about Richard's debts from Richard Mayor and told Elizabeth about them. Richard certainly did not live up to Oliver and Elizabeth's thrifty Puritan standards.

Having done what he could about Richard, Oliver concentrated on formulating a strategy to break the stalemate that had existed in Scotland since the Dunbar victory. He dispatched Fleetwood south to prepare to defend London and mobilise the militia. John Lambert was sent to take a seaborne expedition to Fife to by-pass the enemy defences around Stirling. Lambert landed his 4,500 force, but was soon met by 4,000 from David Leslie's Stirling army and a battle took place at Inverkeithing resulting in a resounding victory for Lambert. This action had broken the stalemate, giving the English control of the Firth of Forth by out flanking Leslie. Oliver moved the rest of his army northwards and by 1 August had pushed on to Perth. In doing so Cromwell deliberately left the route to England open. Charles and Leslie decided to advance into England and make for London, anticipating that they would pick up Royalist supporters on the way. They easily moved into Oliver's trap.

On 5 August the Scottish army had arrived in Carlisle and Charles was proclaimed king of England. A pardon was offered to all who had opposed the Crown in the past, but with three exceptions: Cromwell and the judge and prosecutor at Charles I's trial. Oliver left George Monk with some troops in command of Scotland and set off in pursuit of Charles. He sent Lambert and his cavalry ahead to harass the Scots from their rear, while he led the main body at breakneck speed in pursuit. As Charles and Leslie advanced south into England they found that they only had a trickle of Royalists joining them. They decided that instead of heading for London they would go first through Lancashire and then proceed to the Welsh borders where there was traditional Royalist support. This still did not make an appreciable difference to recruiting for the Royalist army, which was viewed by most as Scots invaders. Charles and Leslie arrived at Worcester on 22 August with 22,000 rather dispirited men. Oliver had by then been joined by more cavalry under Desborough at Warwick, and at Evesham he linked up with Fleetwood who had mobilised the militia bringing the total force up to 31,000. The Royalist army was outnumbered, but, having destroyed bridges, had the advantage of the natural defensives of the Rivers Severn and Teme.

Oliver ordered the construction of pontoon bridges for both rivers and on 3 September, the anniversary of the Dunbar victory, launched the attack. The morning was spent putting the bridges in place, after which Fleetwood attacked over the River Teme in the south while Lambert attacked from the west. Oliver led his cavalry round from a position to the east of the city to cross the pontoon over the Severn and attacked with his battle cry 'The Lord of Hosts!' The Scots troops were forced back into the city and panic ensued, followed by 2,000 being cut down as they sought refuge in the narrow streets of Worcester. Charles had led a brave counter attack to no avail and was obliged to escape the city through the north gate, as did about 4,000 of the fleeing Scots army. Fleetwood led the pursuit and Charles decided to take a small group and hide from the pursuers.

This was by any standards a great victory. The Scots had lost 3,000 men and the 10,000 who were taken prisoner ended up as indentured labours in New England and the West Indies. Among those captured was their general, David Leslie, who was sent to the Tower. Charles was a fugitive and after several weeks on the run managed to travel to France on a coal barge. The last Royalist army had been destroyed and Charles' hopes of regaining his kingdoms were in ruins. For Oliver, the victory was brought about by the hand of God and was the clearest possible evidence of His support and favour.

On 12 September Oliver entered London in triumph, welcomed as the saviour of the Republic. It must have been a huge relief for Elizabeth and the family to have him home at last. Apart from the time consumed mopping up operations in Ireland, resistance in all three kingdoms was finally over. Neither he nor Elizabeth would have known it for sure, but Oliver's days of operations in the field were now at an end. He was Lord General and would remain faithful to his soldiers as, indeed, most of them would remain totally loyal to him. However, from now on it seemed Oliver no longer enjoyed the exhilaration of winning battles as God's chosen instrument. Instead, he was faced with the lesser rewarding task of trying to create a godly republic as a politician, but not before he was able to return to his family and see how they had established themselves in their new home at the Cockpit.

The family in the Cockpit still consisted of the two Elizabeths, wife and mother, as well as Mary and Frances, who were quickly becoming young ladies, being schooled in French and other social graces. Also at the Cockpit was Oliver's sister Catherine, whose husband Roger Whetstone had died, and with her was their daughter Lavinia. Since Roger Whetstone's death Oliver had given Catherine an annual annuity of £150 to supplement her widow's income and eventually invited her to live with him and Elizabeth. In addition, Bridget also stayed with them, with her three children, while Henry remained in Ireland. Bridget had intended to visit Ireland again in September to be with Henry when the campaign season had ended, but decided not to go, probably because she was pregnant. Oliver returned to the bosom of his female dominated family and came to know his grandchildren, ever increasing in number.

In October there was good news from Ireland. Henry Ireton's force had at last managed to make a breach in Limerick's town walls leading the

Royalist members of the garrison to surrender, which in turn, forced the Catholic Confederates to surrender on 27 October. The fall of Limerick had been a major success for Ireton, but had come at a price, as about 2,000 members of the besieging force had perished with disease. Any celebration of the news from Limerick back in the Cockpit would have been short lived for soon after word arrived that Henry was dead. With his usual lack of care for himself, he had driven himself too hard. He had ridden through a snow storm to visit the siege of Galway and when he returned to Limerick fell ill with a fever. The doctors bled him, which weakened him further, and within a few days he died, with his brother-in-law Henry Cromwell by his side.

The death was devastating for the pregnant Bridget and her three children. As the tall, fit Henry always had so much energy and it must have been hard to come to terms that her godly husband had died at the age of only 40. Fortunately, she could receive some comfort from Elizabeth and the rest of her family around her in the Cockpit. No doubt Oliver tried hard to help her to accept the mysterious ways of God's workings with suitable quotes from the bible. Certainly her deep religious conviction would have been a strength, together with belief that Henry, being one of God's elect, was now with the Heavenly Host.

Oliver was said to have been in deep sorrow to have lost not only a son-in-law, but someone who had soldiered with him from the very beginning and who had been his right-hand man and driving force for the creation of the republic. The Council of State also felt the loss of Ireland's Lord Deputy who had successfully subdued the country. A state funeral was ordered and Henry's embalmed body was shipped to Bristol where it was received with much ceremony, attended by 4,000 citizens on 17 December. After the body arrived in London it lay in state at Somerset House for six weeks in a room hung in black draperies, with an effigy of the late Lord Deputy set up for the public to show their respects. It was not until 6 February 1652 that Henry's body was at last interred in the Henry VIII Chapel of Westminster Abbey. The procession to the Abbey was magnificent. It was led by regiments of horse and foot with muffled drums and arms reversed. The numerous official mourners were led by Oliver, accompanied by four heralds and the sword, mace and symbols of Henry's office including his horses, which were covered in embroidered gold on crimson velvet. Lastly came the carriage carrying the body, covered in black velvet and drawn by six horses with the pall held up by mourners on foot. It was quite a send-off, and absolutely the last thing the unpretentious Henry Ireton would have wanted.[8]

The whole drawn out state funeral must have been harrowing for Bridget. At least she knew her husband had been honoured in death, even if many had disliked him in life. Parliament decided that Bridget should be cared for and granted her the £2,000 back pay that Henry had donated to the war effort. On top of this, Bridget received income from Henry's recently acquired lands in Ireland. Had it been necessary, she would have also received financial support from her father who was, by now, a rich man. In addition to his pay as Lord General and the fortune he had already accumulated, parliament had voted to give him £4,000 a year from confiscated estates as a reward for the victory at Worcester. Oliver was always concerned to ensure he had sufficient funds for the needs of himself and his large family, but was never avaricious. In fact, he decided to no longer accept his remuneration as Lord Lieutenant of Ireland, but still retained the appointment. That winter Oliver also showed his generosity and care for his family by remembering his unmarried sister Elizabeth living in Ely with the family of Dr Richard Stone. He sent her a letter with some money writing: 'I therefore send you £20 as a small token of my love.'[9]

Since returning to London, Oliver had been occupied with the death of Ireton and catching up with family matters. By the beginning of 1652 Elizabeth would have noticed a restlessness in him. His hopes of trying to establish a godly state seemed to be moving nowhere and this was because no political settlement had been found. Monarchy was over, but what should replace it? Scotland was, in effect, under the military rule of George Monk and Ireland was still in the process of being conquered by Ireton's second-in-command, Lieutenant General Edmund Ludlow, who had taken over after Henry's death. Both Monk and Ludlow were under Oliver as Lord General, but were also directed by the Council of State, which was itself answerable to the Rump Parliament. No one person dominated the Council. Cromwell was certainly very prominent, but there were others such as Sir Henry Vane, Sir Arthur Haselrig, Oliver St John, now Lord Chief Justice, and it was John Bradshaw, the president for the king's trial, who often chaired the meetings. There were also other major figures such as William Lenthall, the Speaker of the Commons, and prominent peers like the Earl of Warwick who had retired from public life after the king's execution.

Holles, who had tried so hard to reach a settlement with Charles I, had escaped to France after Prides Purge, but there were others such as the MP and lawyer, Bulstrode Whitelocke, who thought that a limited monarchy should be restored. The likely royal candidate for this was the young Duke of Gloucester who was held in Commonwealth custody. However, the restoration of the monarchy in any form was a total anathema to the army, and, thus, not an option. Month after month passed with no settlement in sight and the army became increasingly frustrated that the creation of a godly country that they had fought so hard for at Dunbar and Worcester was no nearer. Oliver saw himself as a Moses figure leading God's chosen people of England to the Promised Land of a godly country. God's providence had enabled him to cross the Red Sea of the king's execution and although the victories in Ireland, Scotland and Worcester had demonstrated that God used him as his agent on earth, he was now mired in seemingly hopeless committees and political wrangling.

To all appearances Oliver dominated the government. Envoys had been sent to the new English Commonwealth by France, Spain, Holland, Sweden, Portugal, Denmark, Tuscany, Oldenburg, Neuburg, Genoa and Venice and they were in no doubt who was in charge. As Paulucci, the secretary to the Venetian ambassador, wrote: 'General Cromwell is the one who has the first word and the last also for the necessary decisions.'[10] Despite this Oliver did not feel he had the last say. He was overruled by the Rump Parliament on a number of issues, such as his desire to offer clemency to Royalists and his scheme called the 'propagation of the gospel' for appointing of Puritan clergy to parishes. In May parliament happily launched into war with Holland over the trivial matter of Dutch captains not striking their flags to English men-of-war in the channel. Oliver was given little option but to go along with the war, yet he regarded the Dutch as fellow Protestants who should be allies rather than enemies. Frustrated though he was with parliament, Oliver used his best efforts to prevent a breach between it and the army.

What was this period like for Elizabeth? On the one hand, she had her husband back at home and much of her family with her, including grandchildren. She lived in a fine house, received the respect due to the wife of the Lord General and they were rich enough for them to live the lives of aristocrats, as far as their Puritan principles would allow. On the other hand, Oliver had lost the elation that had followed his victory at Worcester and was moving towards a 'Slough of Despond' where God's will was no longer clear and put considerable energy into trying to facilitate Providence through prayer and work. Elizabeth must have felt despite her husband living with her, he was becoming a stranger. Oliver's workload was considerable. He had responsibilities as Lord General and as chair of the Army Council, having to deal with an increasingly fractious army and operations that were still continuing in Scotland and Ireland. On top of this was the new war with Holland. He was actively involved in numerous Commons committees, attending at the Council of State, which met twice a day, and dealt with the many foreign emissaries who vyed for his attention. Other responsibilities included being Chancellor of Oxford University, which took up time, as well as managing his own complex holdings of estates scattered throughout different parts of the country and which needed to be rented out. Such was the call upon him that some of the Commons committees would start at 6am. How much time Oliver had to actually spend relaxing with Elizabeth and the family can only be imagined and when he did, it was probably apparent that he was deeply frustrated that so much work yielded so little result. However, there was another, much more immediate matter that marred the happiness of the Cromwell household in the Cockpit. Bridget was a grieving widow.

It probably mattered little to Bridget, but in Ireland the military situation had improved and by May General Ludlow took Galway, the last rebel stronghold. Although Ireland was basically conquered, there remained Catholic gangs called 'Tories' who carried out guerrilla warfare from the mountains and who continued to occupy the 34,000 strong English army, among which was Henry Cromwell. At the beginning of the year parliament had decided that Lieutenant General John Lambert would be made Lord Deputy of Ireland and replace Ireton.

Frances, Lambert's wife, had accompanied her husband on the Scottish campaign and had every intention of accompanying him to Dublin and taking up a first lady position in society. She was charming, with excellent taste and although suitably pious, enjoyed the good things of life. John and Frances liked to do things in style and spent a considerable amount of money purchasing the dinner services, furnishings and other trappings befitting the post of Lord Deputy. For Frances, she could hardly have been more different as a Lord Deputy's wife than the God-fearing Bridget had been.

It was rumoured that the two ladies had met in St James' Park and that Frances had given Bridget some offence in commenting on how she and her husband would run things in Dublin. As a cost saving measure, on 19 May parliament decided to abolish the posts of Lord Lieutenant and Lord Deputy. Lambert was offered the job of running Ireland as commander-in-chief and civil commissioner, but without the previous title and prestige. He angrily refused. What was more he felt that it was Cromwell's doing after Bridget had complained to him about Frances. Lambert was an officer Oliver valued and respected so he went to great lengths to persuade him that he had not instigated the decision to abolish the post and that had been the responsibility of parliament. Relations were eventually smoothed over when Oliver gave him £2,000 to defray the expense of his extravagant outlay in preparation for being Lord Lieutenant. Lambert was appeased and remained staunchly loyal to Oliver in the Council of State.

Something positive did come out of the incident between Bridget and Frances Lambert in St James' Park. Charles Fleetwood had been second in command at Worcester, but his joy from the victory had been short lived as his wife Frances died three months after the battle leaving him with four children. He had returned to London and had been made a member of the Council of State, as was appropriate for someone who was not only one of the country's best generals, but an able administrator. Fleetwood was someone of whom Oliver was particularly fond, who had served under him from nearly the beginning of the Civil War and shared the same type of deep religious beliefs. It is thought that Fleetwood had witnessed Bridget's upset after her conversation with Frances Lambert and had comforted her. He and Bridget would have known each other since he was stationed in Ely in 1643 and they shared the grief of both having lost their partners. In a remarkably short time their relationship blossomed into love and they were married on 8 June.

Oliver was surely delighted at the union of two such pious people. He called Bridget 'Biddy,' would later write of her 'dear Biddy who is a joy to my heart for what I hear of the Lord in her'.[11] Exactly a month after the wedding Fleetwood was nominated to take command in Ireland and in September General and Mrs Fleetwood departed for Ireland. Like Oliver, Elizabeth must have been relieved that Bridget was now happy again and once more married to a man who shared her own uncompromisingly strict religious convictions.

At the same time, in some ways a settlement of the former kingdoms was beginning to take shape. Ireland was incorporated into the new Commonwealth in August and talks were being undertaken with Argyll concerning Scotland to become part of a united Commonwealth. That was all well and good, but the army could see no progress in establishing a commonwealth ruled by the godly. For this they blamed the Rump Parliament for not wanting to relinquish power. On 3 August a newsletter described a typically long meeting attended by Oliver: 'His Excellency and the Council of Officers sat yesterday from nine in the morning till six at night, they kept all private.'[12] The discussions were not private for long as the Council had produced a declaration to dissolve parliament and various measures to replace 'profane office holders' with 'men of truth, fearing God and hating covetousness'. Although Oliver had not signed the declaration, but fully agreed with its sentiments, it was clear that the army and parliament were moving towards the conflict that Cromwell had tried so hard to avoid.

As well as the normal business of government, over the next eight months meetings took place between senior officers of the army and members of the Rump about calling a new parliament or at the very least filling the many vacant seats caused by Pride's Purge. Elizabeth must have been becoming rather tired of having so many people tramping in and out of her house, and having to direct her servants to provide refreshments, with all the meetings taking place in the Cockpit. By April 1653 Cromwell felt his position was strong enough to demand that the Rump establish a caretaker government of forty members drawn from both the army and the Rump. Parliament eventually accepted this on 19 April and on the morning of the next day Oliver chaired a meeting of the Army Council at home at the Cockpit. The meeting was disrupted by a messenger arriving to say that the Rump were in the process of debating their own bill for a new government. Parliament had gone back on its agreement and were trying to perpetuate their little oligarchy. This treachery by the Rump was too much and Oliver stormed off to the Commons.

Oliver gave himself no time to change and took his seat in the Commons still wearing his black house coat and grey worsted stockings. He then rose and gave a speech, which began calmly, but then built up into a crescendo of anger in which he stalked up and down the chamber stamping his foot on the floor and denouncing individual members as corrupt, drunkards and whoremongers. He ended his rant by saying; 'You are no parliament, I say you are no parliament, I will put an end to your sitting!' With that he gave a sign to Major General Thomas Harrison standing outside the chamber and in marched about forty musketeers. Harrison pulled speaker Lenthall from his chair by his gown and Cromwell grabbed parliament's mace with the famous word 'take away that bauble!' MPs were cleared out by the musketeers and Oliver locked the doors of the chamber and marched off with the keys in his pocket. Cromwell then returned home to tell the officers waiting in the Cockpit what had happened and afterwards, set off with Lambert to the Council of State to inform its members that the parliament was over and that they had been dismissed. The military coup was complete.

Elizabeth must have been aware that some major event was taking place and no doubt heard about it from the officers assembled in her home. It is probably when Oliver returned to the Cockpit for a brief moment of respite that he had time to at last read the order paper that parliament had been debating. It transpired that members were not trying to go against the agreement with the army and the whole thing had been a huge misunderstanding. They had simply wanted a vote for completely new elections to be held in November, to be followed by a new parliament every two years, thus trying to enact exactly what the army had wanted—they were not seeking to perpetuate their own oligarchy. Oliver must have been completely taken aback by what he had done in his rage. He was so full of emotion from the day he would have poured out his feelings to a startled Elizabeth. No doubt she offered such supportive words that she could summon; probably to little avail. However, it is also likely that although his actions had been based on a mistake, Oliver would have put it down to the guiding hand of God who was at last showing him the way.

Having dispensed with the Rump, the question was where to go from there. Lambert argued for a council of eleven. Thomas Harrison, leader of the extreme Puritan sect the Fifth Monarchists who believed the second coming of Christ was imminent, wanted a council of seventy based on the number of rabbis in the Sanhedrin courts of biblical Israel. Oliver was no Fifth Monarchist extremist, but he saw merit in a group of selected godly people replacing parliament. On 30 April it was agreed that parliament should be replaced by a Nominated Assembly, but it would be larger than the Sanhedrin with a total of 140 members, including men from Scotland and Ireland. It was then a matter of the Army Council seeking advice and coming up with suitably godly people for the task.

Naturally enough, the Army Council nominated some senior officers such as generals Lambert, Harrison and Desborough. Then there were people Oliver himself thought reliable, such as his son's father-in-law, Richard Mayor. Nevertheless, there were many others who were indeed godly, but who were extremists, such as the Fifth Monarchist, Praise-God Barbon, a leather seller nominated by the City of London. It was the presence of these extremists that quickly led to the nickname 'Barebones Parliament'.

One military nominee was Colonel Henry Cromwell who had returned to England a few months before. Elizabeth had lost Bridget and her new son-in-law to service in Ireland so it was some recompense to have another child back safely. Henry was now 25-years-old and it was high time he was married, at least that was what his spirited younger sister Mary thought as while visiting her father's friend Lord Wharton she had proposed a match between Henry and his daughter. Oliver, knowing that there was no love between the two, put an end to what he called 'Little Mall's (his name for Mary) fooling'. As it was, Henry's heart lay with Dorothy Osborne, which came to nothing as she had fallen in love with William Temple. On the rebound, Henry decided to marry Elizabeth Russell and the marriage took place on 10 May in the village of Kensington just outside London. Henry had known Elizabeth for a long time as her father, Sir Francis, and his wife Catherine were close friends of Oliver and Elizabeth. Their home was in Chippenham, but Sir Francis had been MP for Cambridgeshire and fought beside Oliver in East Anglia from the start of the Civil War and took over from Oliver as Governor of the Isle of Ely.

Henry and Elizabeth did not have a society wedding, in fact the whole thing was rather low key. This probably had to do with all the preparations taking place concerning the Nominated Assembly. It is an indication of Oliver's importance that the marriage of his younger son should be reported by the Venetian ambassador who made the point that despite Elizabeth not being an heiress, the alliance had practical advantages as she was 'the daughter of a colonel of scanty fortune but of great influence among the military'.[13] After the wedding Henry and his Elizabeth went to her parents home in Chippenham, but with the opening of the Nominated Assembly drawing near, they were given lodgings in Whitehall.

The Cromwell family continued to multiply and concentrate themselves in Whitehall residences. Elizabeth had Henry and her new daughter-in-law just down the road in Whitehall, but, of course, Bridget and Fleetwood were away in Ireland for the foreseeable future. Elizabeth would have missed having Bridget's children at the Cockpit, but at least would see her other grandchildren when Richard and Dorothy and Bettie and Claypole visited London. Oliver the family man must have relished having so many of them around him, and since his disbandment of parliament, it was generally agreed that he was in a relaxed and affable mood. It must have been a relief to Elizabeth that his previous signs of depression mixed with semi-manic behaviour had subsided now that he saw the Lord's will was about to be manifested in the creation of the rule of the godly assembly.

Oliver opened Barebones Parliament on 4 July with high hopes that it would soon produce a reform of the church and then the legal system. The church was in a chaotic state with bishops and the whole hierarchy having been expelled, along with most Anglican clergy. Parishes had a variety of preachers: some Presbyterian, some Baptist, some Congregationalist or Independent and others Fifth Monarchists, but no mechanism in place for the church to raise money to pay for the clergy or church upkeep. It soon became clear that although the Nominated Assembly was composed of godly people they had very different ideas on what form godliness should take. The principal split was between moderate Puritans and extremists, such as the Fifth Monarchists who believed in the imminent Second Coming of Christ. In all discussions, whether they be on church or legal matters, there was a strident discord and after a few months many moderate members simply gave up bothering to attend. Oliver soon realised that the constitutional experiment had been a failure and was not in receipt of God's blessing.

By December moderates in the Assembly had had enough and on 12 December presented Oliver with a petition, signed by eighty members, that it should be dissolved. In the meantime, Lambert had come up with a new constitution called *The Instrument of Government*, which was supported by the army dominated Council of State. The *Instrument* was based on Ireton's previous work and stated that the united countries of England, Scotland, Ireland would have triennial parliaments, sitting for at least five months, and have as the executive a Lord Protector elected for life. On 15 December the Council agreed the *Instrument* and elected Cromwell as Lord Protector and the remaining members of Barebones Parliament were removed from the chamber with the encouragement of musketeers. The next day, at a simple ceremony at the Chancery Court, the Lord Mayor presented Oliver with the Great Seal, Sword of State and Cap of Maintenance and he became installed as head of state. Providence had suddenly shown the way. Oliver would at last be able to create the godly Commonwealth for which he had so long yearned.

PART 3

The First Family

Chapter 10

Their Serene Highnesses
1654–1655

'A protector, what's that, 'tis a stately thing,
that confesseth itself but the ape of a king
a regal Caeser acted as a Clowne;
or a brass farthing stamp'd with a kind of crown.'

Anon 1654

Elizabeth had no doubt heard Oliver and their son Henry talking about the *Instrument of Government* and probably thought it was just another constitutional paper under discussion at the Council of State. There had been any number of draft constitutional papers over the years so the boring subject hardly affected her and was best left to the men. It must have come as a major surprise to Elizabeth when the *Instrument* was suddenly agreed and she realised that Oliver was to be head of state. There had been a brief discussion over what title he should have, whether it should be 'King' or 'Lord Governor', but 'Lord Protector' was decided upon. Whatever the title, Oliver had been converted into king in all but name. She and the family would probably have watched from the windows of the Cockpit as Oliver, dressed in black, but with a golden hat band, walked down Whitehall in a procession of dignitaries and numerous soldiers to Chancery Court for a short investiture and then a little later as Lord Protector to Banqueting House. Suddenly the boring constitutional document called the *Instrument of Government* had changed the lives of Elizabeth and her family. For one thing from about 2pm on that day Elizabeth had become 'Her Highness the Lady Protectress'.

Having made the decision to create a Lord Protector, the Council of State was eager to see Oliver properly set up in that position. That would mean such things as having the coinage changed to bear his head and him taking over Whitehall Palace, Hampton Court and all other former royal palaces such as Windsor Castle. Of course a whole lot of preparations would have to be made for that to happen and these were pursued with energy. There was a huge amount to be done. The palaces had old servants and squatters living in parts of them, roofs were leaking, most of the furnishings, paintings, tapestries and other decorations had been placed in store or sold. It is recorded that Elizabeth was not at all happy with having to move from the Cockpit, which she had made into a family home, to Whitehall Palace with its 2,000 rooms. It would take almost four months of hard work before Whitehall Palace was in a fit state for them to take up residence.

If Elizabeth was unhappy leaving the Cockpit, Oliver's mother was highly displeased. She was now 89 and was in no mood to exchange her familiar quarters for a drafty palace. On the other hand, the two 'little wenches,' Mary and Frances, were most excited by the prospect.[1] These two girls, so close in age, had received a strict Puritan upbringing, but they were also spirited and pretty teenagers. They were too young to remember the financial worries of St Ives and for their recent years had lived the equivalent lives of the daughters of a powerful peer. They embraced the latest fashions and wore rich and colourful gowns. Oliver may have disapproved of their extravagance, but could be an indulgent father.

Mary being the eldest may have been flattered that she had received the attention of Lord Herbert, but would have been even more so when later she had heard that the Duke of Buckingham had put out feelers in regard to marriage.[2] Buckingham was in exile with Charles Stuart in France, but later abandoned Charles as a lost cause and returned to England in the hope of prospering under the new regime. Like Herbert, Buckingham hoped that a marriage to one of Oliver's daughters would enable him to recover his confiscated lands. Unsurprisingly, Oliver had no intention of countenancing such a thing. Despite that, having any suitors at so young an age did marvels for the young lady's confidence, which was further bolstered by the fact that she and her sister would be living in a palace with their own personal servants and all the trappings of princesses. It was no surprise that Mary and Frances were excited about their future.

In the meantime, although still living in the Cockpit, Oliver was treated with the respect due to the head of state. The post of Master of Ceremonies, which was responsible mainly for the management of ambassadors, was already held by the old courtier Sir Oliver Fleming. The Council directed Sir Oliver to establish the Lord Protector's position with due dignity. As early as 11 January 1654 Oliver received the first ambassador to deliver a letter of appointment to the new government. This was the Spanish ambassador and the whole event was expertly choreographed by Fleming in the manner of the Stuart court. The ambassador had to ceremoniously go through four doors before he reached Oliver who was seated with three members of the Council on each side of him. Oliver raised his hat and then replaced it as was the custom of the king, while the ambassador stood bare headed.[3] The protocol for the Protectorate was just as formal as that for royalty with ambassadors being instructed to ask their monarchs to address the Lord Protector as 'brother' when writing to him. Foreign heads of state had little option but to accept these marks of respect, although Cardinal Mazarin quipped that regarding Louis XIV, he did not think Oliver had a French father.

In February the Venetian ambassador described Oliver's attendance at a sumptuous banquet given by the Lord Mayor.[4] A costly coach of six collected him from the Cockpit, accompanied by Lambert and Monck and followed by members of the Council in other coaches. They made their way to the Guildhall where Cromwell was received by the Lord Mayor and Aldermen in gowns, together with trumpeters and heralds and the Tower of London firing a salute. Oliver's son Henry had been a member of the Council during the Barebones Parliament, but had not been selected for the Protectoral Council as Oliver wished to avoid nepotism; he was, nevertheless, invited to the banquet because he was the son of the Lord Protector. We must assume that, Richard, although the eldest son, was not invited because he was just living quietly in the country with no involvement in public affairs. As for Elizabeth, although Lady Protectress, she too was not invited because, as with so many events during the new regime, these were all male affairs. How different from Charles I's time when Queen Henrietta Maria accompanied him on nearly all occasions.

Whether they liked it or not, Oliver's family took on the role of first family. Henry was called 'Lord Henry,' and his elder brother 'Lord Richard'. Their sisters all became 'Lady', no doubt to the particular delight of Mary and Frances. Bettie and Richard were still living out of London so their father's elevation did not immediately affect them other than Richard being given various appointments in the county. Bridget was already in an exalted position as the wife of Fleetwood who was soon to be given the restored appointment of Lord Deputy. Pious Puritans though Bridget and Fleetwood were, they had to keep up appearances and they and their large combined family lived very comfortably in Cork House in Dublin during the winter and Phoenix House in the summer, while hosting large formal events in the state rooms of Dublin Castle.

Feverish preparations were carried out at Whitehall Palace. The Council had appointed Colonel Philip Jones, who had served with Oliver in Wales, as Comptroller of the Protectoral Household, where he recruited servants, many of whom were experienced having previously worked for the late king. Two sets of plate were ordered at a cost of £6,000, as were silk curtains and red velvet upholstered furniture. There was also the matter of retrieving old royal furnishings and decorations, some of which had been sold by Parliament in 1649. Tapestries had to be taken out of store and royal collection paintings assembled. For example Raphael's cartoons of the Seven Deadly sins needed to be removed from the Tower to Whitehall Palace.

Clement Kinnersley, Charles I's former Chief Officer of the Wardrobe, was reappointed and instructed to follow Her Highness Lady Elizabeth's instructions on furnishing the Protectoral apartments in Whitehall Palace. This was a major task for Elizabeth and by no means an easy one. There would have been numerous interior design issues to decide on, and the matter of making their more private quarters reasonably homely while at the same time ensuring the grandeur becoming a head of state. Whatever she decided she could expect that her taste would receive the criticism from those who envied her position.

The large sum of money set aside for the refurbishment of Whitehall Palace together with assembly of former royal furnishings and artwork came to the value of £35,497 16s 6d.[5] Both Oliver and Elizabeth understood that they were not seeking to establish an extravagant lifestyle for themselves and their family, but provide surroundings to signify the dignity and authority of the Commonwealth's Lord Protector. Oliver and Elizabeth were each assigned their own butlers and there were two stewards for below stairs to manage the small army of servants to run the Palace, for which a grant was made of £16,000 per quarter. As Lord General, Oliver was used to having his own Life Guard to accompany him while on the move, but this was enhanced and he was provided with a household regiment of foot guards based at St James' to provide protection for him in the palaces and other static locations. The soldiers were given the same uniforms as the more senior household servants, footmen and pages; that is grey coats with velvet collars, with silver and black welted lace.

Although not included on the Council, Oliver gave Henry an important mission to sound out the situation in Ireland or as Ludlow described it: 'To feel the pulse of the officers there touching his (Oliver) coming to command that nation.'[6] Henry arrived in Dublin in early March and no doubt Bridget was delighted to see her brother and catch up on family gossip. Fleetwood, although always pleasant and polite, may have been less happy about Henry's visit knowing Oliver would use his son to report to him on Ireland, rather than himself as the Lord Deputy. Henry only stayed for three weeks and in that time saw that Major General Ludlow, Fleetwood's deputy, was a staunch Republican who did not wish to accept Oliver as Lord Protector.

On returning to London Henry reported to the Secretary of the Council, John Thurloe, and explained that apart from Ludlow, offices in Ireland supported Oliver in his position as Protector. Thurloe was not only the Secretary of Council, but also head of intelligence and, as such, took a considerable interest in those suspected of disloyalty. As Secretary of State, Thurloe was in effect head of the civil service and became Oliver's right-hand man in the running of the country. Thurloe was intelligent, incredibly hard working and built up a formidable intelligence network for the Protectorate. Oliver was right to put great trust in Thurloe, not least for the fact that he became utterly devoted to the service of Protector and his family. Thurloe telling Oliver about Ludlow's disloyalty would have meant the latter's days were numbered, and it would also have cast doubts about Fleetwood who had not taken steps to dismiss him.

Henry had gone off to join his wife Elizabeth at Chippenham just before Oliver and the family spent their first night in the newly redecorated and refitted Whitehall Palace on 14 April. About a week later Elizabeth found herself carrying out her first official engagement as Lady Protectress. This was a simple enough affair as the Portuguese had sent Conde de Cantenerio as a special emissary to deliver a letter to Oliver. He then proceeded to Elizabeth's apartments in the palace to pay his respects to her. This audience would have been a short one, mainly consisting of bowing and perhaps the presentation of a gift, but Elizabeth must have been apprehensive about finding herself in a queenly role. Royalists would poke endless fun at Elizabeth as a gauche country woman unable to behave in high society, but the fact was that she took on her new position with dignity and humility.

Three days later the more formal event of hosting the Dutch ambassadors took place. The Dutch party arrived at Whitehall to sign the peace treaty, having been brought by state coaches with footmen running alongside in the Protector's grey livery. They were received with a fanfare of trumpets and then taken through to dine. Dining at Whitehall was very different from what it had been in the Cockpit and far less intimate. There was 'a Table for His Highness, a Table for the Protectress, a Table for Chaplains and Strangers, a Table for the Steward and Gentlemen, a Table for Gentlewomen, a Table for Coachmen, Grooms and other domestic servants and a Table for Inferiors or Sub-Servants'.[7] On this highly important occasion, Oliver and the three ambassadors sat on one table and members of the Council of State on another. On a third table Elizabeth and her daughter Mary, together with Frances Lambert, hosted two of the ambassadors' wives. Music was played throughout the meal after which there was the singing of a psalm.[8] One hopes that the Dutch ladies could speak English, or there were some interpreters present, otherwise it could have been a rather trying meal for all concerned.

That evening, probably, fully brought it home to Elizabeth how much her life had changed. She was now the consort of the head of state with public duties to perform and responsibilities for overseeing the running of palaces. She would probably have been consulted about the food and arrangements for entertaining the Dutch ambassadors that evening. Elizabeth was living in the full glare of the Protectoral court with privacy a thing of the past and her behaviour under constant scrutiny. Perhaps most of all, there were now moral dilemmas of how to reconcile the trappings of semi-royalty with the humility of a devout Puritan. Apart from her own strength of character, what must have helped her cope with her new unwanted position would have been that she and Oliver were sharing this strange and difficult new way of life together, and they would have both accepted it as God's will.

Elizabeth would have many more official engagements before her, but these did not include the opening of Oliver's first parliament in September. It was a glittering occasion. The Venetian ambassador described Oliver as being in 'a very gorgeous coach accompanied by 100 gentlemen, bareheaded and by his guard of horse and foot'.[9] The procession included the Master of Horse walking immediately behind the Protector's coach, leading the horse of state 'with a rich saddle embroidered in gold and pearl'. Henry was back in London having been elected MP for his father's old seat of Cambridge and had travelled to parliament in the same coach as his father. Richard on the other hand had been allowed by Oliver to continue enjoying the life of a country gentleman, rather than be dragged into the great events in the capital. Still, with Henry returned, the majority of Cromwells were coming to live in London.

By September the family had become settled in Whitehall Palace and even Oliver's mother had grudgingly moved in and made herself comfortable. Oliver had chosen his daughter Bettie's husband, John Claypole, who had been elected MP of Carmarthenshire, to have the important appointment of Master of Horse and gave the couple apartments in Whitehall Palace. Elizabeth and Oliver would have been delighted to have Bettie back with them together with her two children. As a bonus, they also gained an additional grandchild when Henry's wife, Elizabeth, gave birth to a daughter who was given the rather unoriginal name of Elizabeth. In their new home, the family would retire to their private apartments in what had been Queen Henrietta Maria's part of the palace, where they were able to relax to some extent, although still surrounded by servants. The Cromwell family now lived very publicly with Elizabeth having her ladies in waiting and Oliver his gentlemen of the bedchamber. (Fortunately the latter achieved some progress in improving Oliver's appearance when they assisted him in his dressing and ablutions. He even took to wearing a rich scarlet cloak to brighten up his otherwise dark clothes.) Nevertheless, in the privacy of their own quarters Oliver could sit down with a glass of sherry or sack (fortified Spanish wine), both of which he was partial to, along with an occasional pipe of tobacco, while his musicians played chamber music or small groups of singers performed for him. Different though it was from their former life, Oliver and Elizabeth quickly adapted to their duties; and Mary and Frances to the delight at being young 'princesses'.

All in all Oliver and the family quickly accustomed to their new situation. Oliver's aged mother was less adaptable and in continual fear that her son as Lord Protector would be a target for assassination. Oliver was also secretly concerned about such a threat as was shown in an incident when he and Thurloe were riding by carriage through Hyde Park. For a bit of fun Oliver tried his hand as coachman. He was an excellent equestrian and all went well until the horses were spooked for some unknown reason and bolted, catapulting him from his seat on to the pole, then with his legs entangled with the harness, he fell under the carriage at which point a pistol he was carrying in his pocket for self-protection went off, scaring the horses even more. He was then dragged by the foot for some distance until he lost his shoe and he fell free. Oliver fractured his ankle and was severely bruised, but also very badly shaken and had to take to his bed for a few weeks.

Oliver was naturally despondent after hurting himself in the accident, but he was also frustrated over government matters. Fortunately the war against the Dutch was over after English naval victories had resulted in the Treaty of Westminster, but his hopes of turning them in to an ally for the Protestant cause went nowhere. In addition to this was the wider problem of deciding on which of the two great rival powers in Europe to support, because most countries had to come down on the side of one or the other. The Council was divided on whether to support Spain or France. Spain was the home of the Inquisition and would never be forgiven for the Armada, but was a good customer for English wool, whereas France had supported the Royalists, but appeared to be prepared to abandon Charles Stuart for good relations with England. Another frustration for Oliver was that he wanted to heal the wounds of the Civil Wars by allowing Royalists to rent back confiscated lands and, more importantly, ensure that the government accepted, to a degree, freedom of worship, but both policies were blocked by parliament.

It was at this time when Oliver was low from his injuries and frustrated by lack of progress, that a personal disaster struck. On 18 November his mother Elizabeth died. It was a major loss. They had lived together for the fifty-five years of his life and he had always held her in very high regard. In his letter of 6 December the Venetian ambassador provides the following assessment of Elizabeth and her relationship with Oliver:

> 'A woman of ripe wisdom and great prudence. Never a week passed but he (Cromwell) went to see her, treating her with filial affection and great respect. It was said on good authority that towards the end of her life she had pointed out to her son the dangers of having risen so high. She begged him to reflect seriously upon his state, and she did admonish him that, if his intentions were good, God would protect him, but otherwise he would be punished and abandoned. Cromwell answered her with tears in his eyes, his strong spirit overcome by his sorrow at his mother's last wishes. And so he left her full of sorrow, and the same night she died. The Protector feels the loss keenly and shows it outwardly.'[10]

Thurloe left this record of Elizabeth's final prayer to her son: 'The Lord cause His face to shine upon you and comfort you in all your adversities, and enable you to do great things for the glory of your most high God, and be a relief unto his people; my dear son , I leave my heart with thee; a good night.'[11] This loving dying prayer from the mother with whom he had spent most of his life must have been both a comfort for Oliver and strength in his determination to do great things for the glory of God.

As so few records have remained about Elizabeth it is impossible to be sure what influence she had on her son. What could be said was that they were very close and Oliver had considerable respect for his mother who was generally regarded as being a level headed, sensible woman with a strong Puritan faith. It is unlikely that she swayed him in making any of his major life decisions because Oliver's actions were based upon what he considered were God's requirements of him. What his mother did do, however, was to have brought him up in the Puritan faith and was able to communicate with him as one Puritan to another. Elizabeth must have had some share in creating Oliver's unshakeable faith and determination to be an instrument of God's providence, which were the hallmark of his actions. Also, given Oliver's periodic emotional mood swings, she would have provided a rock of stability as someone in whom he could confide and draw strength from. If Elizabeth had died young or been a different personality, would it have made Oliver a different person? We will never know, but what we do know is that she meant a great deal to him and he was heartbroken by her loss. The rest of the family would also have been stricken by grief for the loss of such a strong character who had always been a presence in the home. Oliver's wife Elizabeth must have particularly felt the loss having spent virtually her whole married life living under the same roofs as her mother-in-law.

Elizabeth's funeral took place on the following Sunday evening and was befitting the mother of the head of state. Among the funeral cortege were 100 gentlemen carrying lighted torches accompanying the hearse as it made solemn progress to Westminster Abbey where Elizabeth was interred in Henry VIII's chapel, among the former kings and queens of England. His mother's death, coming on top of his accident, sent Oliver into one of his depressions. Elizabeth would have been grateful that it was not the type of deep depression he had experienced in St Ives, but it was a depression nonetheless, and one that brought government business to a near halt for the next two months.

One decision that was made at this time was that the Council recommended that Henry Cromwell should be made Major General for the troops in Ireland and Oliver agreed. It was a difficult decision as Oliver was very fond of Fleetwood and did not want to undermine his authority. On the other hand, Fleetwood seemed to have done nothing about dealing with the disloyal Ludlow, and Henry, whose presence Oliver valued in London, would provide a safer pair of hands in Ireland as Fleetwood's replacement. It was all rather difficult and because of this, Henry's departure for Ireland did not take place for almost a year. One decision that Oliver did make and see through during his melancholy, however, was to dissolve parliament on 22 January 1655. It had resisted his attempts to establish freedom of worship and made no progress towards creating a godly society. The last straw occurred when Levellers and others who did not fully support the *Instrument of Government* debated putting the militia under the control of parliament rather than the Protector. Thus, with the obstacle of parliament removed, Oliver was able to rule with the advice of his Council until a more satisfactory and pliant form of government had been devised.

Having taken the step to dismiss parliament, Oliver's depression seemed to lift and he, once again, seemed to enjoy life. A major part of his enjoyment was time spent at Hampton Court. Oliver had turned down Windsor Castle as a secondary residence and decided upon Hampton Court for the good reason that the estate was an excellent choice for his two great passions of falconry and hunting with buck hounds. It soon became his custom to leave Whitehall on a Friday for Hampton Court and return on Monday morning;

as a result, he is credited with inventing the weekend. Elizabeth and the family often accompanied him to Hampton Court, travelling either by coach or in the Protector's state barge with its grey liveried watermen whose uniforms were richly embroidered front and back with his personal coat of arms.

Cromwell's coat of arms was the Commonwealth shield with the crosses of St George and St Andrew and the harp of Ireland, but superimposed in the centre of which was the Cromwell family's silver lion rampant. The shield was surmounted by a royal six-barred helmet with crown, crested with a lion rampant and supported by a lion and a dragon; the dragon to commemorate the family's Welsh origins. On either side of the supporters was the monogram 'O' and a 'P' standing for 'Oliver Protector'. Beneath was Oliver's motto as Protector: *Pax Quacritier Bello* (Peace sought after war).[12] The coat of arms had been devised by the College of Heralds and, although elaborate, was very appropriate to a member of the Cromwell family who had become head of state. Having been created, it began to be placed on numerous items relating to Oliver as Lord Protector, including coinage, and so visually reinforcing his right to rule.

Oliver's choice to occupy Hampton Court Palace required that Elizabeth supervise the furnishings and decoration, once she had completed the main work for Whitehall. Hampton Court Palace had been repaired and redecorated to the same standards as at Whitehall and had been adorned with fine furniture, tapestries and much of Charles I's great art collection. For example, the fabulous *Abraham* tapestries bought by Henry VIII were hung in the Great Hall and Mantegna's *Triumph of Caesar* panels adorned the Long Gallery. As in Whitehall Palace, the bedchambers of both Protector and Protectress had expensive furniture, rich window curtains and even carpets on the floor, a luxury few people experienced in those days. Oliver's own bedchamber did not have religious paintings, but five fine tapestries illustrating the stories of the gods, Vulcan, Mars and Venus. It had a dressing room and a private kitchen attached. The details of Elizabeth's personal bedchamber are not known, but would have been suitably opulent and comfortable. As time went on Oliver made significant improvements to the already very grand palace, for example having the impressive Diana fountain removed from Somerset House and installed in the Privy Garden and a number of semi-nude classical statues erected, to the horror of some prudish visitors.[13] Elizabeth quite probably also made her mark on palace improvements, but whether she supported the erection of the semi-nude statues is not recorded.

Stag hunting and falconry were Oliver's main recreations, together with the occasional game of bowls, but music was his favourite form of relaxation.

He appointed John Hingston, an organist and viola player, as his Master of Music and had seven full-time musicians. Various singers and additional musicians were also engaged by Hingston depending on the musical entertainment required. Oliver liked organ music as long as it was not in a church, in which case was regarded as sacrilegious. An organ was installed at Whitehall Palace and the particularly valuable organ from Magdalen College Chapel in Oxford was removed to Hampton Court's Great Hall, on which Hingston taught both Mary and Frances how to play.[14] It should not be thought that Hampton Court was a quiet rural retreat for the Cromwell family because they were far from alone. As well as the resident Hampton Court staff, the Protector travelled with his guards, personal servants, chaplains and gentlemen of the bedchamber and Elizabeth with her own personal servants and ladies in waiting. It was also necessary to have some members of the government service present together with messengers. Oliver sometimes spent longer periods than weekends at Hampton Court, particularly if he was unwell. In those circumstances, members of the Privy Council would take up residence to attend meetings, as would John Thurloe and the secretariat. For all that, Hampton Court was a more relaxed atmosphere than Whitehall and Thurloe's Latin Secretary, the great poet John Milton, who was a talented organist, probably played for Oliver in the Great Hall.

On 21 February Oliver hosted the wedding of his favourite niece, Robina Sewster, at Hampton Court Palace. It must have been a happy family affair. Robina had become close to the Cromwells ever since Oliver's sister Anna had died and Oliver fully approved of the bridegroom Sir John Lockhart. On the face of it, the match was rather strange. William Lockhart, a Scotsman, was the eldest son of Sir James Lockhart of Lee and had joined the Dutch army at the tender age of 13, then later enlisted in the French army and became a captain of horse. When the Civil War broke out he returned to Scotland to fight as a Royalist, rose to lieutenant colonel and was knighted by the king. He was captured after the Battle of Preston, but a year later paid a fine to be released. He returned to Scotland, but fell out with Argyll then changed sides in 1652 and travelled to London where he visited Oliver.

Oliver was so impressed by Lockhart that he made him one of the commissioners for justice in Scotland and then a member of the Scottish Privy Council. Oliver would not normally warm to someone who was either Scottish or a former Royalist, but recognised Lockhart as a man of talent. The marriage also indicated Oliver's current policy of reconciliation with both the Scots and former Royalists. To reflect this the wedding was celebrated with a poem, an extract of which is: 'Tell our friends on both side Tweed, | That the nations are agreed Sewster, Lockhart tie the knott, | 'Twixt the English and the Scott.' (The poem was written by an 'AP'; it might have been a better idea to have had Milton or Andrew Marvell write it.)

Robina was much the same age as Mary and Elizabeth and her marriage probably put them in mind of romance. They had certainly become highly eligible young ladies. Mary was by now 19 and had already attracted the interest of Lord Herbert and the Duke of Buckingham. She would have many more hopeful, but unsuccessful suitors, including the son of the Prince de Condé of France, and nearer home, Anthony Ashley Cooper who was a member of the Council and later to become Lord Shaftesbury, the leader of the Whigs. Although Frances was only 16 she too attracted potential suiters. The most interesting of which, according to reports by both Pepys and Lord Broghill, was the possibility of marriage to Charles Stewart, being explored by Charles himself.[15] Lord Broghill had become a close friend of Oliver's and described how Oliver had dismissed the idea out of hand saying that: 'the young gentleman (Charles Stewart) cannot and will not forgive the death of his father'.[16]

Oliver was, in effect, ruling alone, under consultation of friends such as Broghill and St John, as well as the Council of State. He missed Fleetwood over in Ireland, but John Lambert had successfully filled his place. Lambert had travelled in Oliver's coach on the way to the opening of parliament and had carried the Sword of State at the ceremony. Cromwell eventually began to refer to Lambert as 'Dear Jonnie' and was quite smitten with his charming and intelligent wife Frances who shared his own religious views. Despite this, he had gone against Lambert's advice to ally with Spain and accepted the decision of the majority of the Council to oppose Spain, and by implication try to ally with France. It was decided that rather than oppose Spain directly in Europe, it would be better to carry out attacks on her Caribbean empire. An expedition of ships carrying 8,000 soldiers was launched and sent to Barbados as a mounting base. Unfortunately, it was poorly supplied, had a divided command and was unable to obtain the provisions and men it had expected in Barbados. In mid-April it landed in the Spanish colony of Hispaniola (the island which today consists of Haiti and the Dominican Republic) and within a few days the English force was decisively repulsed and fled back to the ships to sail away having lost 1,000 men.

It was not until the end of June that news reached England of the defeat. The reaction was one of shock to a population that had been used to a long series of victories, including the recent war with the Dutch. Oliver was furious with the two leaders of the expedition, but more importantly was severely shaken as this was his first military defeat and a clear sign that God no longer supported his actions. There was much soul searching regarding how he might have offended God and his whole role as an instrument of the Divine was severely shaken. We can only sympathise with Elizabeth who had to contend with her husband's torments at close quarters. She may also have shared Oliver's anguish that the defeat was a sign of God's disfavour and if so, what could be done to redeem the situation.

Fortunately, a month later news arrived that the expedition had sailed 100 miles west of Hispaniola and had successfully taken the surrender of the lightly held Spanish garrison in Jamaica. This was not an unqualified success as the lack of rations, failure to issue water bottles and disease resulted in about half the 7,000 English force dying before the end of the year. Nevertheless, it was probably viewed by Oliver as his return of God's favour, as the guiding hand of Providence. In fact, Oliver had had every reason to feel that the Almighty blessed his policies on foreign affairs as the Commonwealth had become a major power in Europe. He had improved relations with France, sufficiently enough for a commercial treaty to be signed with Cardinal Mazarin in October, which included in its provisions that neither country would support the other's rebels. The Commonwealth would, therefore, not support Condé's Fronde rebellion against Louis XIV, but, more importantly, France was to no longer support Charles Stuart's claim to the throne and promised to expel him from France.

Oliver was also seen as a champion of the Protestant faith and it was largely through his influence with France that the Duke of Savoy ended his persecution of the Protestant Vaudois sect in the Piedmont. Admiral Robert Blake had won a reputation for the Commonwealth navy in his victories during the Dutch War and also sailed to the Mediterranean to successfully deal with the Barberry corsairs and establish British naval dominance of the seas while his fleet was present. The leaders of Europe wanted Cromwell as an ally, with his renowned Ironsides and powerful navy. By September 1655, in that year alone there had been thirty-two foreign missions in London. The large number of ambassadors and emissaries had to compete for Oliver's attention and used gifts to do so, such as the presentation of a lion and leopard by the Sultan of Morocco.[17]

The various emissaries also paid their respects to Elizabeth, who, in turn, also entertained their wives when necessary. She too would have received gifts, although not as exotic as a lion and leopard, which were safely placed in the Tower of London menagerie. Elizabeth collected portraits of foreign heads of state and their wives and made it known through Sir Oliver Fleming that such gifts were very acceptable. Some of the ambassadors were more favoured by Oliver than others, such as the Dutch and Swedish ambassadors who, unlike other envoys, were invited to Hampton Court. When the Swedish ambassador, Count Christer Blonde, was invited, he was entertained in some style. Blonde had been received by Oliver and with a small party, including Fleetwood and Claypole, dined on oysters, then retreated to the gallery to listen to music, after which was followed both a hunt through the park to kill a stag and a game of bowls. Blonde was then taken to the Lady Protectress' apartments where he kissed her hand and paid respects to Mary and Frances. Finally, after a few glasses of Spanish wine, Blonde made his farewells and returned to London.[18]

Of more interest to Elizabeth than foreign affairs would have been family matters, particularly in Ireland. In June Richard and Dorothy presented her with a new grandchild called Oliver and in the same month Henry and Elizabeth produced another grandson, also called Oliver. The timing of the arrival of Elizabeth's baby Oliver was not ideal as it coincided with the decision that Henry would at last take up his duties as Major General in Ireland. Elizabeth with her little girl and new baby accompanied Henry via Chester and Holyhead and arrived in Dublin on 9 July. Bridget was only able to enjoy her brother Henry's company for two months before she and Fleetwood returned to London.

The whole changeover had been difficult and Cromwell had been at pains to explain to Fleetwood that he needed him as an adviser in London. To make the point, Fleetwood kept the post and pay of Lord Deputy. Henry was left to run Ireland with his six-man council on a day to day basis, while Fleetwood controlled appointments and still required major decisions to be referred to him in London. This undercut Henry's authority and was not a recipe for good government especially as he was a conscientious, decent and honest man, who was loyal. Henry had done his best in a difficult situation as he had replaced Ludlow as Major General who returned to England in October and was arrested for refusing to take the oath of allegiance to the Protector. Nevertheless, Cromwell had no wish to punish one of his best generals and, after interviewing him, allowed Ludlow to retire to his home in Essex.

Henry would have been relieved that the departure of Ludlow had at least removed one of his problems. His wife Elizabeth would have been well aware of Henry's continuing frustrations with incomplete authority, but very probably enjoyed her new public and political station. Her life had been transformed from that of a wife to a simple army colonel to one of 'Lord Henry', the son of the Lord Protector. Another transformation was also obvious. She may not have been the wife of a Lord Deputy, but she was certainly the wife of a commander of 23,000 troops and the most powerful person in Ireland.[19] Suddenly she had the respect and trappings of the first lady, with the servants and residences of both Cork and Phoenix House, which went with them.

Oliver and Elizabeth would have been sorry to see Henry and his family leave for Ireland, but were no doubt consoled by the return of Bridget and her four children. Oliver also had Fleetwood, a man who shared so much of his own views, once again at his side. The Council gave Fleetwood Wallingford House in Whitehall as a residence. It was a fine house, but rather a come down for him and Bridget after their residences in Dublin. On the plus side, it did mean that he was within walking distance from both the Council Chamber and Whitehall Palace, Oliver's seat of power.[21] In fact, Fleetwood had returned at an important time because Cromwell, with Lambert's encouragement, had decided upon a new experiment to create a godly government.

As both an ordinary parliament and a nominated parliament had failed, Oliver introduced governmental management through Major-Generals. There had been a brief Royalist rising earlier in the year, and the division of the country under the jurisdiction of generals worked to enhance security. Of more importance, perhaps, was that Oliver's generals, moreover, would be pious men who could be relied upon to enforce the standards needed to achieve a godly society. This meant the imposition of strict Puritan standards. Christmas and saints' days had been abolished some years before, as had pastimes such as Maypole dancing, and traditional sports such as bear baiting and cock fighting, together with restrictions on ale houses and the closure of theatres. Major-Generals would have control over a local militia to enforce these rules and others in the future.

In a type of pilot scheme, Oliver's brother-in-law, John Desborough, was made the first Major-General with responsibility for Devon, Cornwall and the south-west of England. On 9 August other Major-Generals were appointed to cover all regions of England and Wales. For example, Edmund Walley was given the Midlands, Lambert the North of England, and Fleetwood East Anglia and Oxfordshire, although the latter two both delegated the responsibility to their officers and so remained available to attend the Council of State. Thurloe also made use of the Major-Generals to introduce draconian security measures such as preventing Royalists travelling more than a short distance from their homes without a licence from their Major-General and introducing the decimation tax on Royalists to pay for the Major-Generals' staff and administration. The severity of the rule of the Major-Generals differed between areas, but race meetings and gambling were outlawed and in some areas, people were imprisoned for riding their horse on the Sabbath or women placed in the stocks for swearing. It need hardly be said that this experiment was intensely unpopular and would be abandoned within a year and a half.

By the time that the country was experiencing the trauma of godly military control, the Protectorate court was well settled into its routine. Elizabeth and the family would have become used to the forty-strong Yeoman of the Guard halberdiers in the Guard Chamber, the prestigious guard of Gentlemen Pensioners in the Presence Chamber, the black and grey liveried pages and footmen; indeed, the whole grandeur, protocol and routine of court. That routine included Oliver dining weekly with his senior officers to keep in touch with the army and having Thursdays set aside for an audience with emissaries. Court entertainment became better organised so that as well as John Hingston's musical performances, there were events organised by William Davenant, the semi-official Master of Revels. Davenant was said, especially by himself, to be the illegitimate son of William Shakespeare, but the plays and operas that he wrote for the Protectorate court do not indicate that he had inherited the appropriate genes.

A Lord Chamberlain was not appointed until a little later, but by the end of 1655 Elizabeth would have become very adept at organising the stewards, keepers of the wardrobe and other senior staff at each palace. The fabric of the two palaces was maintained and the Council ordered that £1,000 be spent on their repair and maintenance. It was a matter of pride to the Council and parliament that their head of state lived in surroundings of appropriate splendour. Elizabeth would have become accustomed to some of the Protectorial luxury that was specifically for her. For example, the cost of materials for upholstering her private coach was £38 for velvet, £15 for damask and £10 3s for a fringe.[21]

As the year 1655 came to an end Elizabeth's mind would not be on the trappings of power, but on the health of her family. Oliver once more fell ill. They called it the ague, but it was probably a gall stone. Unfortunately, Oliver taking to his bed became a regular occurrence. Of greater concern, however, was the health of Bettie who had become seriously ill. Bettie too was to begin a pattern of becoming ill, then recovering, then being ill again; each time becoming weaker and her good looks wasting away. Oliver and Elizabeth became very concerned at her decline and unknown to the physicians, cancer was claiming her. In a letter to Henry Cromwell in Ireland dated that December, one of Bettie's physicians wrote: 'I never saw two parents so affected (or more) than my Lord Protector and her Highness.'[22]

Elizabeth and Oliver had a close relationship that was not altered by the potential barriers created by the duties and ceremonial of being head of state. During the various bouts of Bettie's illness they were drawn even closer together and the health of their daughter would take clear precedence over affairs of government. Bettie's illness also brought their children closer together. It is touching to read the many letters between Bettie's brothers and sisters about her health. There can be no doubt that the power and luxury that came with their semi-royal status did not change the Cromwells from being a loving and caring family. It was, of course, also a family in which all its members shared a deep religious faith. The strong family bonds and acceptance of God's providence would help to sustain them in future years when the Heavens ceased to smile on them.

Chapter 11

A Future Queen?
1656–1657

'For to be Cromwell was a greater thing
Than ought below, or yet above a king.'

Andrew Marvell

By early February 1656 Oliver was sufficiently recovered to attend the wedding of Lavinia Whetstone, the daughter of his favourite sister Catherine. Catherine and Lavinia had lived with the Cromwells since Catherine's husband had died back in 1646 and so Lavinia was like a daughter to Oliver and Elizabeth. The groom was Richard Becke, a wealthy landowner with estates in Yorkshire and Buckinghamshire. The marriage took place at Whitehall Palace, but we know nothing of the details other than it was in 'great magnificence'. Beck was eventually placed in command of Oliver's Life Guard. Not long after this wedding there was another in which Lavinia's mother Catherine married Colonel John Jones, a friend of Cromwell's who had fought for parliament in Wales and then served in Ireland under Ludlow. He had also been one of the judges at the king's trial and had signed the death warrant. In fact, he was so dedicated a Republican, he had not supported the creation of the Protectorate. Despite this, Oliver stood by him as an old friend and new brother-in-law, making him Governor of the Island of Anglesey and continuing to pay his sister Catherine the annual annuity of £150 that he had paid her since her first husband's death.

The year 1656 was a romantic one for Oliver's sisters. His youngest sister Robina had been married to Rev Peter French, a canon of Christ Church, who had died the previous year. Oliver was Chancellor of Oxford University and had appointed French and Dr John Wilkins, the Warden of Wadham, as part of the small committee to deputise for him as Chancellor. On French's death, Wilkins probably saw an opportunity for advancement and decided to court Robina. As Robina had been left a clergyman's widow with two daughters to support, marriage was an attractive proposition. Just a year after Peter French's death she followed her sister Catherine's example and married Wilkins. As with so many members of the family, they were given apartments in Whitehall Palace. Although the Palace was huge, it must have been pleasant for Oliver to have so many of his family near him and able to dine with him and Elizabeth.

Elizabeth was used to doing her duty as Protectress, receiving ambassadors and the like and ensuring she played her part in the management of the two palaces. In fact, that man of great taste, the diarist John Evelyn, visited Whitehall Palace in February 1656 and, ardent Royalist though he was, recorded: 'I ventured to go to Whitehall, where of many years I had not been, and found it very glorious and well furnished, as far as I could safely go.'[1] Elizabeth had been active in deciding the furnishing of Whitehall and so deserves some recognition for her good taste. Naturally, Royalist propaganda made great fun of Elizabeth as a jumped-up farmer's wife pretending to be queen, and making a complete hash of it. They liked to call her 'Joan', which was a name usually associated with the lower orders, and made much mirth over stories of her endless streams of supposed *faux pas* and bad behaviour. It was particularly popular, to liken her to a parsimonious, kitchen maid and say she sat around with her drunken lady friends making lewd toasts.

The reality was very different; she remained in the background, but carried out her role with quiet dignity and efficiency. There was a comptroller and two stewards for Whitehall Palace, as well as several other senior officials to advise and assist Elizabeth in the major operation of running the Protectorate Household. There was also the matter of running the huge palace of Hampton Court. It is hard for us today to take in the enormity of the task of housing, feeding and generally looking after those working or visiting the Protectoral Court, but a small indication can be given from the annual purchase of 7,560 gallons of Spanish wine and 5,040 of French wine for Whitehall Palace alone.[2] The Protectoral Court ran very effectively thanks to the professionalism of the senior members of the Household, but Elizabeth's general oversight made a contribution to its success.

Elizabeth did not just slavishly follow the precedents of former royal households, but added a few touches of her own. For example, she arranged that leftover food from Household dining was sent to the churches of St Margaret and St Martin-in-the-Field to be distributed to the poor. Elizabeth had employed six daughters of impoverished Puritan ministers to work in her own apartments to produce needlework. She created a new dairy for Whitehall Palace in which butter milk was a speciality, and had an area of St James' Park fenced off for the cows.[3] The menus selected for the household and guests were of high quality produce, but seldom fanciful and she and Oliver ate simple food when dining privately by themselves or with the family. Oliver was usually busy, but Elizabeth had time to enjoy the presence of her family.

As Bettie's husband was Master of Horse, the couple were also entitled to accommodation at both palaces. Bettie and John Claypole's lodgings in Hampton Court had been formally occupied by the Duke of Hamilton, the Master of Horse for Charles I. It consisted of a bedroom, with dressing room, a withdrawing room with furniture upholstered in yellow cloth and cased in red baize, next to which was a small closet hung with liver-coloured serge, giving access to their family dining room. Next to this was an impressive formal dining room with six tapestry hangings. There were three other working rooms for servants and cooks. Claypole's manservant had his own room in another part of the palace, as did Bettie's gentlewoman, who was placed in a partitioned off area of the Guard Chamber. The rest of the huge Guard Chamber with its fifteen priceless tapestries and furniture covered in sky blue taffeta, embroidered with silver and gold, was rather unwisely given over to a playroom for Bettie's children.[4] Altogether Hampton Court provided a pretty congenial weekend retreat for the Claypoles.

Elizabeth would have been delighted to be seeing so much of Bettie's children: Cromwell, Henry and Martha, and also receiving frequent visits from Bridget with her seven children, and probably those of Fleetwood from his first marriage. As if that was not enough grandchildren, Richard and Dorothy would regularly visit from Hursley with their four children and had also been given an apartment in Whitehall. As well as her daughters and grandchildren, Elizabeth also had Oliver's sister Robina living with her new husband as a chaplain at Whitehall Palace together with Oliver's niece Lavinia and her husband Richard Beck. The Becks had apartments at Whitehall and Hampton Court because of his post as commander of the Life Guard. Elizabeth was not short of company just with her relations, but no doubt also entertained her own friends perhaps visiting from Ely or members of her Bourchier family based in Felsted or London.

As well as her private family and social life and time spent with senior members of the Protectoral Household, Elizabeth would have also had close contact with Oliver's personal staff and officials. There were three principal chaplains, the most important of which was Hugh Peters, who had been given Archbishop Laud's old apartments in Whitehall Palace. Peters was very close to Oliver and would have had a strong religious influence on Elizabeth. Then there were five physicians, of which Dr Bates was the most eminent.[5] Their position in Elizabeth's life became increasingly prominent as Oliver's health began to fail and Bettie had her recurring bouts of illness. There was Oliver's private secretary William Malyn who tended to look after his personal correspondence and no doubt would have done the same for Elizabeth. Lastly there were Oliver's principal government officials of which John Thurloe was by far the most important. Stuart kings had had two Secretaries of State, but Oliver had only one; the highly capable Thurloe.

Thurloe was a workaholic who combined being Secretary of the Council with Secretary of State. He was also in charge of the government service, was government Leader of the Commons, Postmaster General and head of intelligence. Although always a subordinate, he was treated by Oliver as a friend and was indeed a true friend to the Cromwell family. As part of his duties he needed to be in regular correspondence with Henry over in Ireland, but his letters, although respectful, are more like those of a family friend. Thurloe was intimately connected with the Cromwell family in many ways, such as being one of the executers to the administration of the property given to Bridget by parliament after Henry Ireton's death. No doubt Elizabeth saw quite a bit of Thurloe and also a certain amount of people like John Milton and Andrew Marvell who worked for him. Finally, Elizabeth would have had the company of her five ladies-in-waiting. With regard to them, she had not forgotten the French family of Oliver's old valet Duret. Madame Duret was appointed a maid of honour and her son a page. Such personal attendants were rather different from the aristocracy who had filled such posts in royal times.

There are very few records of Elizabeth's life as Lady Protectress, but we can assume that it was a busy and pleasant one that combined family and friendships with official and household duties. Although to some extent cocooned from the real world in the magnificence of a palace, she was a down to earth, intelligent woman who would have kept herself aware of life outside her sumptuous environment. She would have known that Oliver's great experiment of creating a godly government through the rule of the Major Generals was badly received. One of the most extreme Major Generals was William Boteler who was responsible for Huntingdonshire, Northamptonshire, Bedfordshire and Rutland, an area Elizabeth knew well and one in which many of her friends still lived. Boteler was severely anti-Royalist and illegally imprisoned the Earl of Northampton for the non-payment of a fine. He had an equal dislike of Quakers and wanted to have the Quaker leader James Nayler stoned to death for blasphemy. Fortunately, Nayler's sentence was reduced to just having a 'B' branded on his head and two years hard labour in prison.

However, it was the disruptions to the lives of ordinary people which caused most resentment. Elizabeth would have been particularly aware of the repression that was going on in London. Philip Skippon, the commander of the London Trainband militia, was nominally Major General responsible for Middlesex, Westminster and London, but as he was old, had delegated it to Colonel John Barkstead, the Lieutenant of the Tower of London. Barkstead provided excellent service for Thurloe's intelligence department by being the Protectorate's principal interrogator, indeed, Oliver had knighted him in January 1656. He had equal enthusiasm in stamping out ungodly acts in London. Elizabeth, as a staunch Puritan lady, probably supported the shooting of all bears and breaking the necks of all cocks in London to prevent bear baiting and cock fighting and applauded the punishments imposed for swearing, gambling and drunkenness. Even she, however, may have thought it a bit much when a maidservant could be put in the stocks for being caught mending her dress on a Sunday.

Whatever Elizabeth's own views, she would have been well aware that the banning of football and other sports on Sundays and outlawing all celebration of Christmas, including the eating of mince pies in December, was highly unpopular. In London Barkstead's zealous enforcement of strict Puritan standards drained most of the traditional pleasures that relieved the hard grind of daily life endured by the majority of citizens. Added to this was high taxation. In May Oliver summoned all his Major Generals to discuss progress in the creation of a godly nation. The discussions soon moved from the success or otherwise in imposing godly standards, to the more mundane matter of funding. There was insufficient funds to support the militia used by the Major Generals to police and enforce the strict Puritan standards. Worse still was that the naval war with Spain and the maintenance of a 55,000 strong army had contributed to the Commonwealth running an annual deficit of £700,000. The government was out of money and needed the funds necessary to clear the deficit and maintain the strength of the navy, army and militia. The Major Generals all agreed that the only way to raise the money was to call a new parliament to vote the necessary taxation.

Oliver was less than enthusiastic about the value of parliaments. His first two had been fractious and uncooperative and he initially opposed the idea of calling another one. Eventually he was persuaded that this was the only way to avoid what was turning into a financial crisis. Most of the Major Generals were also of the opinion that they had sufficient influence in their respective areas to ensure only government supporting MPs would be returned. Oliver reluctantly authorised the writ to call parliament and elections were held in September. Under the *Instrument of Government*, which had now become England's first constitution, Roman Catholics and known Royalists were not only debarred from standing for election as an MP, but were also denied a vote. On the face of it, this and the influence of the Major Generals should have produced a strong government victory at the election. That was not the case. What had not been taken into account was how much the rule of the Major Generals was detested and, by association, the government of the Protector. Of the 400 or so MPs elected, ninety-three were potentially anti-government because they were either Republicans or Royalist sympathisers. Fortunately the *Instrument of Government* had a remedy for this irritation. The Council was able to exclude 'ungodly' MPs and so excluded all ninety-three, who they pronounced as being 'Not of known integrity, fearing God'.

On 17 September Oliver opened his new rather depleted parliament with due pomp and ceremony. In a long address to members, he emphasised the need for money to pay for the war against Spain, particularly since Charles Stuart, styling himself 'King Charles II,' had formed an alliance with Spain and there was a chance that Spanish troops might support him to invade the country. Having made his patriotic appeal, Oliver left the Commons in high hopes that having removed potential opposition, MPs would swiftly vote the taxation needed. This was not to be the case. The Commons began debating the legitimacy of debarring the ninety-three elected MPs. On 22 September a vote was taken on the matter and was won by the government supporters. Less promising was that a further fifty MPs resigned in protest thus reducing parliament to about 250 MPs and seriously undermining its legitimacy. In October the reduced number of MPs voted to extend the naval operations against Spain to all-out war. Despite this, they still did not vote to raise the taxation necessary to prosecute the war.

MPs may have thought that the war would be self-financing for news had arrived that Captain Stayner had successfully attacked the Spanish treasure fleet of four capital ships the previous month. One Spanish ship had escaped, then hit a rock and sunk and two others caught fire and also sank, but the third was captured with its cargo of plate valued at £600,000. This victory demonstrated the power of the British navy to the rulers of Europe and further increased Oliver's prestige abroad. On 8 October Thanksgiving Services were held in London and Westminster, but the bottom line was that parliament had not carried out the principal purpose for which it was called—to vote for taxation. Frustrating though this was for Cromwell, the matter was suddenly overshadowed by a family bereavement. Oliver's sister Jane, who was married to John Desborough, died after a short illness.

There are few records to indicate how close Oliver was to Jane, who was seven years his junior, but Oliver had a strong sense of family and would have been naturally protective of his younger sister. Their lives had been closely entwined. The Desboroughs lived in Eltisley in Cambridgeshire, within easy reach of Oliver and Elizabeth when they lived in Huntingdon,

St Ives and Ely, and we may assume they met regularly. John Desborough, like Oliver, had served as an MP and had joined Cromwell's cavalry troop at the very start of the Civil War. They had often fought side by side together and Desborough had risen in rank with Oliver to become a Major General and then a member of the Protectorate Privy Council.

The two families must have been close and so the sudden death of Jane would have been a blow to both Oliver and Elizabeth. Oliver acknowledged his love for Jane in death by giving her a funeral appropriate for the sister of a head of state. In the words of the Venetian ambassador: 'On Monday at two o'clock at night, she (Jane Desborough) was carried with great pomp to Westminster and buried in one of the tombs which, in other days, were reserved for royal bodies only.'[6]

The gruff, plain speaking Desborough was a Republican at heart and probably did not appreciate his wife being interred with royal grandeur. Whatever his views, and although still grieving for his wife, he threw himself back into his work as an MP. He decided to take action to solve the financial impasse in parliament that held up the funding of the Major Generals. Christmas day had, of course, been made a normal working day with shops open and work as usual. Although the Commons sat, attendance was understandably lower than normal and Desborough chose this opportunity to bring a motion that the Decimation Tax on known Royalists should be made permanent. This ploy did not work because the vote was not taken till 28 January of the new year 1657, when the Commons was back to its normal level of attendance. There were many army officers sitting as MPs, but they were easily outnumbered by the remainder who were sick and tired of the interference of the Major Generals in their daily lives. Desborough's bill was defeated by 124 to 88. This meant that there would be no funding to support the Major Generals and their militia and so the rule of the Major Generals would have to end.

Oliver must have felt that his instinct not to call a parliament had been right as it had not only failed to provide the vital government funding, but had put an end to his dream of the creation of a godly nation through imposition of Puritan moral standards by the Major Generals. Unknown to Oliver, this parliament might have been even more damaging for him because there had been an assassination plot to be carried out at the opening, back on 17 September. Oliver's mother had often worried about her son being assassinated. In fact, Edmund Ludlow rather joked about it in his memoirs saying if she even heard a musket fired she would think it was being aimed at Oliver.[7] As it happened, the sensible old lady had been right all along. The particular threat came from a few remaining Levellers led by Colonel Edward Sexby, a former New Model Army officer who, being a Leveller, believed in the complete equality of men, and so found the concept of a Lord Protector anathema.

Sexby regarded Cromwell as a traitor to republicanism and decided to ally with the Royalist exiles and the Spanish to achieve his overthrow. Thurloe's intelligence department was well aware of Sexby's activities, but did not know that he had recruited another Leveller and former officer, Miles Sindercombe, to assassinate Cromwell. Sindercombe and two other conspirators hired a house in King Street and, hiding a blunderbuss in a viola case, took it to an upstairs window with the intention of shooting Oliver as he left Westminster Abbey on his way to open parliament. The conspirators had not taken into account the large crowds coming to see the spectacle who masked the line of sight to their target, resulting in the operation being abandoned.

Sindercombe was not a man to be easily deflected from his task and next hired an upstairs room in a house in Hammersmith which Oliver would pass in his coach on his Friday visit to Hampton Court. In this case Sindercombe took no chances and set up a battery of six blunderbusses that could be fired simultaneously. This well laid plan also came to nothing as Oliver had decided to travel to Hampton Court by river in his state barge. Undeterred, Sindercombe's next plan was to shoot Oliver as he rode in Hyde Park, but this scheme also had to be abandoned when the getaway horse went lame just before the planned assassination. The inventive Sindercombe then came up with a very ambitious plan to start the new year of 1667 by setting fire to Whitehall Palace and shooting Oliver as he escaped. Incendiary material was placed in the Chapel of the Palace of Whitehall, together with a slow fuse. This operation had required careful planning and obtaining the cooperation of some of the palace staff to gain access. Fortunately, one of those who learnt of the plan was an informant for Thurloe, which enabled Sindercombe and an accomplice called John Cecil to be arrested on 8 January. On interrogation in the Tower by Thurloe and Sir John Barkstead, Sindercombe remained silent, but Cecil admitted the various assassination attempts. Both were sentenced to death, but Sindercombe had a final plot up his sleeve and had his daughter bring a fatal quantity of arsenic to him in paper on her farewell visit the day before his execution.[8]

The revelations from the Sindercombe Plot must have been very worrying to Elizabeth and the rest of Oliver's family. They also knew that the death of Sindercombe and Cecil had not brought the threat of assassination to an end. Sexby was still active on the Continent and was about to publish a pamphlet with the self-explanatory title, *Killing No Murder*, for distribution in England. Equally worrying was that some of the Protector's household had assisted in the plot to set fire to Whitehall Palace. Additional security measures were put in place and the Life Guard was increased from 45 to 160, organised under ten officers into eight squadrons.[9] At least one member of the Life Guard was complicit in the Sindercombe Plot and so those who Thurloe's intelligence staff had doubts about were removed and Thurloe ensured that he had informants in the larger regiment. Oliver, having made Richard Becke, the husband of his niece Lavinia, Commander of his Life Guards, looks less like nepotism than having trusted family members about him. It was about this time that he made Sir Gilbert Pickering Lord Chamberlain. Pickering was a relation and friend, who was MP for Northamptonshire, and who had been one of the judges in the king's trial; just the sort of person to be trusted in keeping an eye on members of the household.

Parliament's rejection of the Major Generals was not a rejection of Oliver, and when the Sindercombe Plot became known there was general rejoicing at the Protector's deliverance. In fact, support for Cromwell resulted in parliament actually voting £400,000 for the Spanish war. This was a very pleasant surprise for Oliver, but a greater surprise was to come on 23 February when Sir Christopher Packe, a former Lord Mayor of London, stood up in the Commons and asked Cromwell's permission to read a paper to him. The paper was entitled *The Humble Address and Remonstrance*, which proposed a new constitution re-establishing the House of Lords and making Oliver king. Although this document was presented by Packe, the authors had included Oliver St John and Lord Broghill who believed that it was time that the country was brought back to traditional government. They felt that the recent threat on Oliver's life demonstrated how fragile was the Protectorate, resting as it did on the life of one man. The proposal was greeted with uproar, with staunch Republicans and the majority of the army members calling Packe a traitor. Others could see the logic of Packe's words, and discussion of the matter was to dominate parliament for nearly three months.

On 27 February 100 officers led by Fleetwood, Lambert and Desborough came to Whitehall to see Oliver to protest against Packe's proposal. Oliver told them that he 'liked not the title (of King), a feather in a hat, as little as they did'.[10] However, he made the point that it had been the Major Generals who had given him assurance of a compliant parliament and left them with the impression that having unsuccessfully tried different forms of government, kingship could not be ruled out. The officers left dismayed, but hoped that Oliver would be persuaded to completely reject the notion of becoming king. Over the next few weeks parliament continued to consider Packe's document. On 11 March a bill was passed to create an Upper House of seventy members chosen by the Lord Protector, but writs would not be issued until the great issue of kingship had been resolved. *The Humble Address* was gradually amended to include making parliament responsible for taxation and reducing the size of the army and the final document was transformed into *The Humble Petition and Advice of the Parliament England, Scotland and Ireland*. On 25 March parliament passed *The Humble Petition* by a vote of 123 to 62 and on 31 March the Speaker formally asked Oliver to accept the new constitution and with it the Crown. This was a huge decision for Oliver and one in which he needed time to agonise over. But there were other things that demanded his attention, not least for him and Elizabeth to console Bettie who had just lost her youngest child.

The country was also at war with Spain and it had become important to ensure that England had a close relationship with France. The year before Oliver had decided to select a talented person who was related to him by marriage for the task. He selected Sir William Lockhart, the husband of his niece Robina, for the post of ambassador to France. Without the influence of her uncle, Robina might have expected to have been married off to a member of the lower gentry, but now she was Lady Lockhart of Lee and wife of the ambassador in Paris. She had left for Paris in some style having been given a number of items from the former royal collection by Clement Kinnersley, the Keeper of the Wardrobe, to assist her while she entertained at the embassy residence. These included twelve large pieces of tapestry and silver tableware amongst which were sixteen dishes, thirty-six trenchers and six salt cellars.[11]

In fact, life was not as glamorous as it might have seemed as the English were very unpopular in France, mainly because they were viewed as extreme heretic Protestants who had executed their king. At first Robina and her little boy, Cromwell, were largely confined to the embassy, but Sir William gradually gained acceptance as ambassador. Although Louis XIV was 18-years-old and of age, Cardinal Mazarin effectively ruled the country on his behalf. Sir William's charm enabled him to establish a firm friendship with Mazarin and when Robina gave birth to a second child in Paris, the baby boy was christened Jules in honour of Mazarin. In March 1657 the relationship with Mazarin was so strong that the Protectorate was able to form a treaty with France to attack the Spanish Netherlands. The agreement was that France would contribute 20,000 men, England 6,000 and her fleet, with the objective of capturing Gravelines for France and Mardyck and Dunkirk for England.[12]

On 20 April Admiral Blake won a major victory against Spain, further increasing the prestige of both the British navy and the Protectorate. Rear Admiral Richard Stayner had led the assault on the silver fleet as it was in the harbour of Santa Cruz in Tenerife. All seventeen ships of the Spanish fleet were captured or destroyed with the loss of no British ships. Blake's fleet then returned home a few months later, but sadly Blake died of old wounds in sight of Plymouth. He was given a state funeral and Stayner received a knighthood from Oliver. Although the reputation of the Protectorate flourished abroad, it had a much more difficult time back in Britain.

There were many important matters of government to consider since the end of March, but the one issue which dominated Cromwell's mind was whether or not to accept the Crown. Although parliament had voted with a very strong majority in favour of his acceptance and the return to traditional stable government, the army was strongly against. The decision for Oliver was truly agonising and he became withdrawn and started smoking very heavily. The matter was finely balanced. As a conservative country squire Oliver had by nature accepted the custom and legality of kingship. It was only when there was, in his view, an unjust king that he had rebelled. If he accepted the Crown he could ensure that the rule was a just one. Kingship also had the legal advantage that made any plot or rebellion against the monarch treasonous. This meant that his supporters would be safe from any reversal of order having acted on behalf of the legal anointed king. On the other hand, being king meant sticking to the established limitations of kingship. A king could not get away with a measure such as the rule of the Major Generals as a Protector had. Importantly, if the monarchy was constitutionally restored, there was a young gentleman overseas ready and willing to come and claim it with the help of Spanish troops. A restoration of monarchy might well encourage a Royalist uprising to restore Charles Stewart.

In addition, there was the matter of the views stemming from the army. Apart from a few officers who were closely tied to Oliver, such as Colonel Sir Richard Ingolsby who was married to Oliver's cousin Elizabeth, and Colonel Charles Howard who had commanded his life guard, the great majority of the army were implacably opposed to the idea of monarchy. What was more, Ludlow, so popular within the army, used all his influence to whip up opposition to kingship. To many in the army he appeared to be a strong candidate to take over from Oliver on his death, but if Oliver became king his heir could be the virtually unknown civilian, Richard Cromwell. The army was Oliver's power base, there were 3,000 troops in London alone, so could he defy its clear wishes? Oliver probably felt that his prestige in the army was so high that despite murmurings they would accept him as king, but that could not be guaranteed. The decision was one of the utmost importance and so like all important decisions for Oliver was left to the guiding hand of Providence.

While Oliver waited for a sign from God on what decision he should take, his 'two little wenches,' Mary and Frances were more concerned with romantic matters. They very probably rather liked the notion of becoming princesses. Indeed, they were already referred to as princesses by foreign ambassadors. They were also celebrities in their own rights and when they went to take the air by coach in Hyde Park, they were pursued by crowds hoping to grab a sight of them. Frances had many suiters and, to complicate matters, had been semi-promised to William Dutton. When William's wealthy uncle John had died, he left in his will the request that Oliver be responsible for William's education and mentioned that it had been agreed that William would later marry Frances. Oliver did indeed look after the boy's education and employed Andrew Marvell to be his tutor in 1653. As time went by, Marvell moved to work for Milton in the Secretariat and the Dutton match seems to have been quietly forgotten.

By 1657 Frances had fallen in love with Robert Rich, the son of Lord Rich and the grandson and heir of the Earl of Warwick. On the face of it this would be a perfect match. Warwick was an old friend of Oliver's and had commanded the Parliamentary navy, but, as with Richard, Oliver wanted to ensure he had the right match for his offspring. Two issues arose. The first was whether Robert Rich was of a suitable moral standard and the second was the familiar thorny matter of agreeing the marriage settlement. Back in June 1656 Mary wrote about Frances to her brother Henry in Ireland:

> 'truly I can say it, for these three months I think our family, and myself in particular, have been in the greatest confusion and trouble as ever poor family can be in ... I suppose you heard of the breaking off of the business ... After a quarter of a year's admittance, my father and my Lord Warwick began to treat about the Estate; and it seems my Lord did not offer that that my Father expected ... but if I may say the truth, I think it was not so much the estate as from private reasons that my father discovered to my sister Frances and his own family, which was a dislike to the young person. Which he has reports of his being a vicious man given to play and other such things.'[13]

In the same month Fleetwood wrote to Henry saying that the sticking point was Oliver's demand for a £15,000 portion: 'As for my Lady Frances, that buysnes is concluded twit themselves. My lord Warwick not answering his

Highness' demands upon his giving £15,000 portion prevents at present the consumation, but I do not see how it can breake off, both parties being engaged.'[14] In fact, it looked as though the negotiations would break down completely as Warwick wrote to his grandson: 'If my lord Protector insists upon these high demands, your business will soon be at an end, and I assur you nothing could have made me come to half that i have offeered but seeing your great affection for my Lady Frances and her good respect of you.'[15] By April 1657 the marriage negotiations had gone nowhere for over a year and poor Frances became very frustrated. Nevertheless, Oliver would have to be completely satisfied over Robert Rich's moral standing, as well as the size of the marriage portion before agreeing to the union. Frances would have known that with her father preoccupied with anguishing over the offer of kingship, he would have no inclination to resume negotiations on the portion.

Frances must have been particularly irritated that unlike herself, marriage plans seemed to progress for her older sister Mary. Mary had been pursued by a number of hopeful suiters, such as Edward Hungerford, heir to the Farleigh Hungerford estate, and Sir Edward Mansfield, who had considerable property in Wales. Oliver disregarded them as he had a suiter of his own in mind and this was the surprising choice of the 29-year-old Thomas Belasyse, Viscount Fauconberg of Newburgh Priory near York. Fauconberg had supported parliament and was Protestant, but came from a Catholic family and both his father and grandfather had been Royalists. He was a charming and intelligent man whose wife had died the previous year and who had sought permission to visit France. On Oliver's instructions, Thurloe wrote to Lockhart in Paris asking him to look out for Fauconberg 'an able gentleman from York who the Protector much respected and desired him to notice'.[16]

Lockhart made it his business to come to know Fauconberg, and was able to report that he was 'a person of extraordinary parts' and was not a Catholic. He did, however, ask that further checks were carried out upon Lockhart in England to confirm his wealth and clarify whether there was a truth in a rumour that he was already promised to Lady Katherine Howard. Thurloe's efficient intelligence organisation was well placed to carry out the necessary checks and was soon able to report that the rumour about Lady Howard was false and the Fauconbergs had an annual income of £5,000 a year. In March Fauconberg called on Locklart and gave him a letter for Cromwell containing a profession of loyalty. Fauconberg asked Locklart if he could have a clear invitation from the Protector to make his address to Mary, but Lockhart replied that modesty would prevent that happening.

After all the encouragement he had been given, Fauconberg was not sure whether he should proceed and, indeed, whether Mary would be happy with her father's match for her. Mary had probably come across the attractive Fauconberg in London, and Elizabeth and Oliver would have talked to her about the proposed marriage. No doubt she was excited about the prospect, but also rather anxious about an arranged marriage to someone she hardly knew. However, as with so much, talks would not progress until her father had finally wrestled over the decision on kingship.

Frances and Mary were not the only members of the Cromwell family who suffered from Oliver's indecision about the offer of kingship. Richard Cromwell wrote to his brother Henry in Dublin: 'I can say that you are somewat more happy than others (of) your relations for that you are oute of the slattering dirte which is thrown aboute here.'[17] More importantly, Oliver's protracted decision making also brought political instability. Some, like the Fifth Monarchists, actively opposed the notion of kingship with their slogan 'there should be no king but Christ'. Major General Thomas Harrison and some of the other Fifth Monarchist leaders were arrested. Oliver's cousin Edward Whalley describes how worrying the situation had become in this extract from a letter to Richard Cromwell:

> 'I beleve yf the parliament continue to adhere to theyr former vote of kingshipp, his Highness will rather accept of that title then ether revert to the instrument of government, which is now become very odious, or leave us in confusion, which inevitably we shall runne into yf he refuses. There is onely this bad expedient left for us, to disolve into a commonwaelth, which many ayme at, but I hope they expectation wilbe frustrated. My lord the times are dangerous.'[18]

Elizabeth would have been very concerned at the effect the difficult decision to be made had on Oliver. She knew that her husband saw himself as being guided by Providence, like Moses leading his people to the Promised Land of a godly Britain. He was wracked with the difficult question of whether he would be better able to lead his nation to the Promised Land if he were king. There can be little doubt that as Elizabeth and Oliver were such a close couple they talked about whether or not he should accept the Crown. We can only surmise what her thoughts and advice might have been, but it is likely that Elizabeth would have thought the prospect of her husband becoming king, and therefore herself becoming queen, was quite absurd. She was prepared to do her duty having had the position of Lady Protectress thrust upon her, but to wear a crown was a step too far.

Elizabeth had spent the great majority of her life as a member of the lower gentry and had no ambitions other than to have a reasonable level of financial security for herself, Oliver and their family. She and Oliver fulfilled the functions expected of them in the Protectoral Court with confidence and dignity, but for two Puritans to assume the status of royalty would be entirely unnatural. What was more, if Oliver became king it would affect the lives of their children. The girls would become princesses, Henry would be Duke of York and Richard, Prince of Wales. Poor, pleasant, easy going Richard, who was happy with Dorothy and the children living the pleasant life of a wealthy squire, would become heir to the throne. On Oliver's death he would have the burden of kingship placed upon his shoulders and had neither the capacity nor the desire to bear such weight. We may assume that Elizabeth had strong reservations against Oliver accepting the Crown and would have made her views known to him.

On 6 May Oliver went for a walk in St James' Park and was joined by Fleetwood, Lambert and Desborough, who had been waiting for him. They told him plainly that if he accepted the Crown they would not oppose him, but they would resign their commissions. Oliver remained uncommitted and resumed his walk. Two days later, the Council and parliament attended upon him in the Banqueting House to hear the decision that had been two and a half months in the making. After a speech apologising for taking so long to consider the matter, he ended by saying 'I cannot undertake this government with that title of King. And that is my answer to this great and weighty matter.'[9] Oliver's soul searching and the country's uncertainty were over at last.

Chapter 12

Uncertain and Giddy Times
1657–1658

'The Lord giveth and the Lord taketh away.'

Book of Common Prayer

Many have speculated about what made Oliver reject the Crown. The usual explanation is that the threats of resignation by his three closest military leaders gave him God's long-awaited sign. This may well have been the case, but it is not impossible that Elizabeth's lack of desire to be queen might have had at least some subconscious influence on his decision. Oliver's rejection of the Crown was a surprise to many and left parliament with the urgent priority of creating a new constitution. The Commons hurriedly amended the *Humble Petition* to make Cromwell Lord Protector for life and authorised to nominate his successor and members of a second chamber.

The next step to Oliver's slightly enhanced status having been agreed to, was to re-install him as Lord Protector with increased powers. The ceremony was far more elaborate than his first installation. On 26 June Oliver arrived at Westminster in his state barge and was met with great ceremony and conducted to the Painted Chamber where he agreed to uphold the new constitution in front of his Council, judges and officers of state. There was then a procession to Westminster Hall led by his gentlemen-in-waiting and other notables, followed by the heralds, with Warwick carrying the Sword of State and the Lord Mayor carrying the Sword of the City Westminster and finally Oliver. On entering Westminster Hall he went to the coronation chair which been brought from the abbey and placed under a rich cloth of state on a dais draped with pink velvet with gold fringes. In front of the throne was a table on which was a bible bound in gilt, a gold sceptre, a sword of state and a cap of state.

With everyone in position, and in front of the invited guests of ambassadors and other dignitaries, the Speaker carried out the investiture. Oliver was dressed in a long purple robe lined with ermine, had the sword fastened about him and was handed the sceptre and purple and ermine cap of state. Cromwell took the oath of office after which there was a fanfare of trumpets and the cry 'God Save the Lord Protector'. The installation ceremony over, Oliver left Westminster Hall with three pages carrying his train and proceeded to Palace Yard where he alighted into the state coach and returned to Whitehall Palace in a large procession, which included his Life Guards, and the richly adorned horse of state led by John Claypole.

The next day Oliver went by coach to Temple Bar, attended by twelve footmen and two pages in another procession of Life Guards, heralds and members of the Council. There he was met by the Lord Mayor and aldermen on horseback, dressed in their civic finery. Oliver, who was wearing a musk coloured suit and a coat richly embroidered in gold, got out of his coach and mounted a horse to join the Mayor in a joint procession to a reception at the Guildhall. After this, the procession reassembled and travelled to three locations in the City at each of which Oliver was proclaimed Lord Protector with fanfares of trumpets.[1] The pageantry and ceremony of Oliver's inauguration only lacked the presence of a crown to differentiate it from a royal coronation.

Elizabeth would have been pleased that the whole matter of kingship was over and allowed life to resume much as it had been before. A particular relief was that Oliver's anguish over the situation had come to an end and had been replaced with relaxed good humour. Another matter that revived his spirits was not only that Bettie's health improved, but she had given birth to a baby boy, who she named 'Oliver'. A further relief was that the rift about the kingship between Oliver and his son-in-law Fleetwood and brother-in-law Desborough also ended and they loyally returned to his side. Bridget must have found it very upsetting to have had her husband in potential conflict with the father she so loved and respected. It would be a relief for Elizabeth to no longer feel that she should act as family peace maker on the difficult matter. Fortunately, Oliver's refusal of the Crown had brought an end to bad feelings amongst all his senior generals, except for one.

Immediately after Cromwell had been installed, he prorogued parliament for six months and ruled as Protector with his Council. John Lambert, Oliver's close friend and probably best general, refused to take the Council's oath of loyalty to the Protector. This may have been because he was sulking over Oliver's new authority, which included giving him the right to nominate his successor. Lambert may have hoped that his popularity with the army would ensure his position as successor, but this was thrown into doubt as Oliver would be likely to nominate one of his own sons. Lambert's changed attitude towards the Protector was a blow to both Oliver and Elizabeth.

Oliver had called Lambert 'my dear Johnnie' and referred to his wife Frances as 'my jewel'; they were almost part of the family. Eventually, Lambert had an interview with Oliver and agreed to lay down his commission and retire. As this would have meant a loss of pay of £6,000 a year Oliver generously agreed to give John £2,000 a year from his own earnings.

Lambert retired to his property in Wimbledon with Frances and their ten children and devoted his time to the simple pleasures of gardening and painting. Charles and Bridget Fleetwood would have been sad that two people who they had been so close to had taken themselves from the Protectoral Court. Fleetwood may also have been secretly pleased that his main military competitor had been removed, clearly making him the most senior officer in the army, which meant that there was a good chance that Oliver would nominate him as his successor, bearing in mind that the army was the principal power in the land. He had been one of the four standing closest to Oliver in the dais during the investiture. Nothing could be certain, but a betting man would have put money on Fleetwood being nominated Oliver's heir now that Lambert had quit public life. The last thing that Bridget Fleetwood would have wanted to contemplate was the death of her dear father. For all that, it must have crossed her mind that in that sad event her husband was likely to become Lord Protector and she would succeed her mother as Her Highness the Lady Protectress. It was of course only a possibility, but the prospect of holding such a position with its duties and regal splendour would have been both alarming and exciting. If indeed, she did ever consider the prospect, she probably quickly put it out of her head for her own peace of mind.

In September Fleetwood's commission as Lord Deputy expired and Oliver conferred it upon his son Henry, ending the division of command that had caused some friction between them. Elizabeth would have been relieved that her son and son-in-law no longer had grounds for disagreement. She would have missed Henry with his open, reliable disposition and his charming wife. Although Elizabeth had numerous grandchildren around her in Whitehall, she obviously would have wanted to see Henry's children who were growing up fast in faraway Ireland. In fact, she had not even met their son Oliver who had been born in Dublin in April the previous year. At least Elizabeth was able to console herself that Henry and his wife Elizabeth were happily married, which was confirmed by Elizabeth's parents, the Russells. There is a correspondence from Sir Francis Russell to Henry mentioning a letter from Elizabeth to her mother that referred to 'such tales of love and kindness to her [Elizabeth by Henry] my wife cried for joy while I laughed'.[2] One of the few existing letters from Elizabeth to her husband Henry ends as follows: 'My deare, the messenger is in such hast to be gon that I have not time to say that as I would, but the substance of all that I am able to say is that you shall ever find me a loveing, constant wife. My dear, believe this that comes from thy affictiton wife, E Cromwell.'[3] Henry's mother must have felt satisfied that she and Oliver had done a good job in helping to arrange this marriage.

It is hard for us today to understand just how prominent a position Henry held as viceroy of the whole of Ireland. Henry and his wife Elizabeth lived a life not far removed from the semi-royal existence of his father. As ruler of the country, he had his own court and the appropriate entourage, such as his Life Guard. Henry had been made a knight by Oliver and was entitled to confer knighthoods himself; indeed, he created fourteen knights as Lord Deputy. Henry was a diligent and hard-working ruler and, like his wife, a devout Protestant, but this does not mean that they shunned the good things of life. Henry was rather disparagingly described by Lucy Hutchinson in her writings about the life of her Roundhead Colonel husband, as 'a cavalier' and so we may assume that the Lord Deputy's court flourished in some style. Henry's mother, Elizabeth, would have been aware of the privileged life being led by him and his family and no doubt rather proud that her son successfully managed the responsibilities of his high office. She knew Henry was a devout Christian and would have understood that he had to accept some trappings of grandeur in his position as Lord Deputy, just as she and Oliver had been obliged to in their positions.

Oliver had been at Hampton Court most of August suffering from catarrh, but had improved by the end of the month. With Bettie essentially recovered, and with the problem of kingship out of the way, the Lord Protector turned to settling the future of his 'two little wenches'. Negotiations were reinstigated with the Earl of Warwick about the marriage between Frances and Warwick's grandson, Robert. It was eventually agreed that the earl's estate should be settled on his grandson and if Frances outlived her husband she would receive an income of £2,000 a year. Oliver agreed to pay a dowry of £15,000.[4] This was a huge sum and shows the dramatic changes made to the Cromwell family's finances since the hard times twenty-six years earlier in St Ives. Plans could begin for a wedding.

There was also the question of Mary's marriage. By this time Oliver had received a lot of positive information about Thomas Belasyse, Viscount Fauconberg, including that he had an annual income of £5,000. In fact, he was already so taken with Fauconberg that he had given him command of Lambert's regiment of horse.[5] With Fauconberg back in London, he and Mary were at last able to come to know each other. Mary was a spirited, good-looking girl with an attractive personality and she found Thomas charming, intelligent and handsome. He was by this time 30, ten years older than her, but the age difference was quite normal and just made him more distinguished. In short, Mary fully approved her father's choice of suitor. It is also quite possible that she was secretly rather pleased at the prospect of her and Frances marrying into the nobility, unlike their elder sisters Bridget and Bettie. Before long Mary and Fauconberg were betrothed and Oliver had agreed another colossal dowry of £15,000.

Romance may have been in the air, but a wedding took place on 15 September that Oliver thoroughly disapproved of. This was the marriage of Lady Mary Fairfax, the only daughter of Oliver's old friend Thomas (now Lord) Fairfax, and George Villiers, Duke of Buckingham. After the first Duke of Buckingham had been assassinated, King Charles had brought up his son George like his own. The young Buckingham had been the future Charles II's closest companion, had fought with him at Worcester and joined him in exile. Buckingham was amusing, talented and charming; he was also entirely unscrupulous. By 1657 he was clear that there was no prospect of his close friend Charles ever regaining the throne and decided to return to England. Having been rebuffed in his scheme to marry Mary Cromwell, he looked elsewhere to regain possession of his inheritance.

At the beginning of 1657 Fairfax had been given much of the Villiers confiscated estate in lieu of arrears of pay. This part of Buckingham's former estate was considerable, including York House in London and lands producing a total income of £5,000 a year.[6] Buckingham approached Fairfax to ask permission to address his daughter, which was rather surprisingly agreed to. Fairfax's daughter Mary fell madly in love with the charming Buckingham and it seems that Thomas and Anne Fairfax also succumbed to his charm and status as a duke. So it was that this surprising marriage took place.

When Oliver heard that the Royalist leader, Buckingham, was in England and had married the daughter of his friend, he was furious and ordered Buckingham's arrest. Buckingham went into hiding and his new wife and parents-in-law were naturally very distressed at this turn of events. Anne Fairfax travelled down from Yorkshire to London to see Elizabeth and ask her to intervene with Oliver on her daughter's behalf. It must have been a strange meeting for both ladies. Anne had been the aristocratic wife of Oliver's superior officer, a person of whom Elizabeth would have previously held in some awe. Now Anne arrived as a supplicant to Her Highness the Lady Protectress. The conversation was not recorded, but we may assume Elizabeth showed at least some sympathy and agreed to speak to Oliver, but offered no strong hopes of a happy outcome. We do not know for sure whether Elizabeth's intervention with her husband on behalf of the Fairfaxs did any good, but when Buckingham was finally arrested he was given favourable treatment. Instead of being incarcerated in the Tower he was allowed to live in luxury in York House with his wife Mary.

The incident of Anne Fairfax seeking Elizabeth's help is one of the few recorded cases of someone coming to Elizabeth as a supplicant. In fact, Elizabeth must have received numerous requests for assistance in her capacity as Lady Protectress. These requests would have been for the benefit of the person making the request or for one of their relations. They covered all manner of things, from pardons of justice, to employment in the Protectoral Household or government office, such as a commission in the army or navy. Some requests were in person, but many were by letter and were probably replied to by William Malyn, who as Oliver's secretary, also looked after Elizabeth's correspondence. How much Elizabeth would have supported this special pleading would have depended on circumstances. It is likely that she would not have put a case to Oliver unless she was already confident that he would agree to it. Oliver did give positions to close friends and members of his family, but because he knew and trusted them, not through nepotism. That none of those granted posts by Oliver were members of Elizabeth's family indicates that she did not ask him to grant any of the many requests for advancement she must have received from them.

Although lack of parliament meant that the dire state of public finances continued, Oliver was in a generally good mood. Not only were the marriages of Mary and Frances sorted, but the French alliance was bearing fruit. Lockhart had moved from Paris to Flanders to keep himself on top of the war against Spain. The 6,000 English red coats of the New Model Army under Sir John Reynolds had joined Marshall Turenne's French contingent in Flanders. Reynolds was Henry Cromwell's brother-in-law and had been knighted by Oliver for his military service in Ireland. Reynolds had captured Fort Mardyck from the Spanish in September and it had become an English garrison. The naval side of the alliance was equally effective with Edward Montague, who had replaced Blake as admiral, having deployed a fleet of eighteen ships to control the Channel.

In September Richard's wife Dorothy gave birth to another child at Hursley. Oliver doted on his grandchildren and was particularly fond of Dorothy who he called 'Doll,' which must have, briefly, helped him to take his mind off Bettie's poor health which was once more in decline. Oliver's own health had improved, but he was 58 and the rigors of past hard military campaigning were catching up with him—added to which he had increasingly suffered frequent bouts of illness from gout, a troubling gallstone and attacks of what is thought to have been malaria. Oliver was slowing down, but he retained sparks of his old energy and, indeed, merriment. The autumn of the year 1657 brought him the pleasure of the weddings of his 'two little wenches'.

Frances' wedding to Robert Rich was the first and took place in great splendour at Whitehall Palace on 17 November. As the 1653 Marriage Act only authorised civil weddings, the ceremony was conducted by a justice of the peace, followed by some prayers by one of Oliver's chaplains. That over, the party began. Music was provided by an orchestra, which included forty-eight violins and fifty trumpets. Among the guests were many members of the aristocracy with connections to the jovial Earl of Warwick, including some who had supported the king in the Civil War. There was, of course, a fine wedding feast and even mixed dancing, an activity which until only a few months previously some Major Generals had used a spell in the stocks as punishment. Elizabeth, the Lady Protectress, actually enjoyed a dance with the Royalist Earl of Newport. Oliver joined in the gaiety of the occasion and wore a doublet and breeches of 'uncut grey velvet in the Spanish fashion', silk stockings with gold laced garters and gold buttons on his shoes; all rather different from his rustic and unkempt appearance of the past. He was said to have become so carried away that he engaged in boisterous horse play including spraying wine on lady guests and putting sweetmeats on their seats.

The reception continued 'with much mirth and frolics' until five o'clock the next morning.[7] That was not the end of the celebrations, however, as they moved on from Whitehall to Warwick House in Holborn and lasted for several more days with the Earl of Warwick acting as a generous host.[8] The wedding presents matched the magnificence of the occasion and ranged from £2,000 of gold plate from Robert Rich's grandmother, the Countess of Devonshire, to a couple of sconces costing £100 each from Bettie and John Claypole. The whole glittering marriage celebration was fit for a princess, which was, to all intense and purposes, Frances' position. As *Mercurius Politicus*, the main news sheet of the time, announced the event: 'This day the most illustrious lady the Lady Frances Cromwell, the youngest daughter of His Highness the Lord Protector, was married to ... Mr Robert Rich.'[9]

Oliver had intended Mary's wedding to Fauconberg to be equally magnificent, but Fauconberg had asked for it to be a small private ceremony and the money saved given to the married couple. Oliver approved his future son-in-law's disdain for worldly extravagance. Hampton Court was decided upon for this less extravagant wedding, but although there were fewer guests and lasted just a single day, it was still a splendid occasion in a stunning palace venue. The marriage took place on 19 November, immediately after that of Frances, and was also a civil ceremony. However, Fauconberg had obtained Oliver's agreement for a discreet service to be conducted using the Book of Common Prayer by Rev John Hewett, a well-known Anglican priest. The wedding feast was splendid, as was the entertainment. John Milton's assistant as Latin Secretary, Andrew Marvell, had been commissioned to write two pastoral masques.

James I and Charles I had both enjoyed masques and these were major productions with singing, dialogue, dancing and elaborate costumes and scenery. It was customary for members of the royal family and senior courtiers to take small parts themselves, representing virtues such as justice and clemency. These expensive productions had been much frowned upon by Puritans and had not been seen in England since the times of Charles I. The two masques for the wedding were not such elaborate affairs, but more a matter of simple amusement. That Oliver should have agreed to this entertainment can be explained by his love of music and possibly his daughters' influence, who as a younger generation believed that godliness should not exclude a measure of harmless fun. A feel for the masques can be taken from this brief extract from Marvell's second work which refers to Fauconberg's northern estates and Oliver as Virgil's shepherd Menalcus: 'Never such a merry day, | For the northern shepherd's son | Has Menalcus' daughter won.'[10] Though not to modern tastes, masques were much appreciated in the seventeenth century and we can be sure that Oliver enjoyed this one and quite probably took the part of Menalcus.

The married Falconburgs were given apartments in Hampton Court and Whitehall Palaces. Mary was a very happy bride and immediately after the wedding wrote to her brother Henry in Ireland: 'I was maryed on Thursday next com fortneight, and truly, dear brother, to a person that hath a greater kindness than ever I coul have expected. The Lord contenue it.'[11] Oliver and Elizabeth certainly felt that they had done their duty as loving parents as all their children were now happily married.

After the weddings, Oliver turned his attention to implementing the amended constitution, which required the creation of a second chamber of parliament, the members of which would be nominated by him. It was agreed not to call the chamber 'the House of Lords', but simply 'the Other House'. Deciding who he should nominate for the Other House was not easy. Apart from former parliamentary supporters, such as the earls of Warwick and Manchester and Lord Saye and Sele, most former members of the Lords were Royalist and therefore unsuitable for nomination. Oliver had made a couple of peers himself, such as Charles Howard, his former Captain of the

Life Guards who had been made Viscount Howard of Morpeth, and his cousin Edmund Dunch and, as such, they were selected. Otherwise, it was a matter of selecting members from relations, friends and senior members of the army. These included Fleetwood, Claypole and Whalley, Oliver St John and Henry's father-in-law, Sir Francis Russell. In total, eighteen of those nominated were Oliver's relations including, of course, his sons Henry and Richard.

Oliver had been in the continual process of raising Richard's profile. He had occupied appointments relating to his rural interests such as being Keeper and Warden of the New Forest, which were ideal for Richard who enjoyed hunting and who was more than happy to be left living the life of a squire with Dorothy and the children. His rustic idyll had been disrupted first when he was made a member of the Committee of Trade, and further when Oliver resigned as Chancellor of Oxford University in September that year and handed the job over to Richard. Now Richard was to be a member of the Other House. Lucy Hutchinson was to describe Richard as 'pleasant in his nature, yet gentle and virtuous, but became not greatness'.[12] This seems to have been a pretty accurate summary and although much preferring life at Hursley, he was always ready to fulfil his duty and took up his new responsibilities conscientiously. Richard's increased appointments meant more time in London and with the happy result that he, Dorothy and the children spent more time at Whitehall, no doubt to the pleasure of Elizabeth and Oliver. Nevertheless, what had been a happy year for the Cromwell family overall, came to a sad end with the death of Richard and Dorothy's three-month-old baby.

Oliver opened the new parliament, which included the Other House, on 20 January 1658. The opening was suitably impressive with Oliver arriving on the magnificent Protectoral barge and conducting the proceedings on a throne under a canopy of state. For all the pomp, he must have had misgivings from the start, as of the sixty-three nominated for the Other House only forty-three accepted, and of the forty-three who had accepted, only thirty-seven turned up on the day. This was disappointing, but what was of more concern was that by putting those he could trust in the Other House, Oliver had denuded the Commons of his supporters. The election of MPs had resulted in the return of some closet Royalists and a significant number of Republicans, such as Sir Arthur Haselrig and Thomas Scot. Oliver could only hope that after appealing to his parliament to grant taxation and work in harmony, its members would take his speech to heart.

Sadly that was not to be the case, as the Commons almost immediately began to challenge the legitimacy of the Other House. On 25 January Oliver called both chambers to the Banqueting House and demanded that they end their squabbling and concentrate on the business at hand. This obviously fell on deaf ears. Haselrig persuaded the Commons to begin a petition to abolish the Other House and asked soldiers to sign it. This was in clear defiance of the Protectoral constitution. News of the stratagem reached Whitehall Palace on the night of 3 February after Oliver had retired to bed, but he was woken up and informed. He acted swiftly by immediately calling his duty officers Whalley and Desborough and ordering the change of guards at Whitehall and Westminster. That done he went back to bed.

The next morning he tried to take his barge to parliament, but it was one of the worst winters in memory and the Thames was frozen. Oliver grabbed the first carriage from the palace mews and set off at speed to Westminster. He arrived at the Other House and informed them of his intention to dismiss parliament. Fleetwood was taken aback and advised his father-in-law against the dissolution, to which Oliver replied; 'You are a milksop, by the living God I will dissolve this house.'[13] And so he did, in an angry speech rebuking the Commons for not supporting the other House, which they themselves had asked to be created and filled by men of their 'own rank and quality', railing that they were 'men that I approved my heart to God in choosing ... loving the same things you love, whilst you love England and whilst you love religion'.[14]

The year 1658 had not started well. The government debt was out of hand and there was insufficient money to pay the army and navy. The various experiments with government had failed to provide a parliament that would tackle the two tasks of authorising taxation and helping to create a united and godly nation. However, soon personal events were to distract from affairs of state and bring Oliver greater cause for sorrow. One after another there were sudden deaths. Oliver's niece Lavinia, who had married Richard Becke, suddenly died. Lavinia had lived with Elizabeth and Oliver like a daughter before her marriage, and as her husband Richard was Commander of the Life Guards, she had remained part of the Protectoral Court. Within a month Elizabeth and Oliver were to lose another grandchild. Bridget Fleetwood's daughter Anne died and, because of the family's status, was buried in Westminster Abbey. Oliver and Elizabeth adored their grandchildren and Oliver would have them on his knee and play with them in a relaxed way that was fairly unusual for the time. Bridget had had a total of eight children with her two husbands and in an age of high infant mortality the loss of poor Anne was tragic, but not unique, for her and her parents. However, this was followed by another death of greater impact as disaster struck for a second daughter.

Robert Rich died of 'consumption' (now called tuberculosis) leaving Frances a widow at just 19. In March Rich's funeral took place at Whitehall after which the body was taken to Warwick House, following the progress taken by the wedding party just four months earlier. Frances was distraught and wrote to her brother Henry in Ireland:

> 'Dear brother, I culd fill this paper with giving you an account of the afflictions I have met with, but I shall not give you that trouble now. Only to tell you I have lost my husband; the Lord help me to mack a sanctyfied use of it and all His dispansations to me. Tis true I have grat marcys left me in my relations, that many of God's prescious ons want, though I think nothing in the world can repair my loss.'[15]

The death of young Robert Rich was not only a tragedy for the Cromwells, but also for his grandfather the Earl of Warwick. For Oliver's old friend and companion in resistance to Charles I, the death of his heir was too much to bear and he died the next month.[16] Oliver lost a contemporary, so much different from him in class and temperament, but one to whom he was very close.

These losses did nothing to help Oliver's health. He became listless and, according to the Venetian ambassador, began taking opium to help him to sleep, but soon stopped because of its side effects. He did not attend all the Council Meetings and as John Thurloe was ill at the time, the management of the three nations began to drift. Attention was obviously directed towards Oliver's reaction to the bereavements and poor health, but thought should be given to Elizabeth as well. She too was grief stricken and would have been the principal person to try to console her two daughters, particularly Frances. She must have thought that her almost fairy-tale life had ended and found it impossible to think she had any chance of future happiness. In addition, Elizabeth was still concerned about Bettie's health and her husband's deep dejection. We can probably assume that Elizabeth provided a major strength and support to her family at this time, and was an emotionally draining one for her.

In April Oliver's spirit began to return and his mind moved towards government business. There was still no taxation to pay government debts, but at least the French covered the cost for the 6,000 Ironsides in Flanders. That alliance remained particularly important since the 2,000 strong Royalist force was in Flanders alongside the Spanish. If the Spanish should beat the French in Flanders, they might then provide Charles Stuart with an army to invade England. Oliver decided to send a goodwill mission to France to strengthen the relationship. Of course, he already had his niece Robina's husband Sir William Lockhart as ambassador, but he had been given an additional role as commander of the English expeditionary force following the sudden death of Sir John Reynolds. Oliver felt he needed an ambassador extraordinary to pay respects to Cardinal Mazarin and the 19-year-old King Louis XIV.

Fortunately, he had the ideal person to hand in his most recent son-in-law. Fauconberg was intelligent, charming and most importantly, fluent in French. Mary must have felt a little pride that not only had her marriage turned her into a viscountess, but that her husband was selected for this highly important mission. Fauconberg set off, accompanied by a retinue of 100 carriages. His natural diplomatic skills made his meetings with Louis and Mazarin a resounding success and further strengthened the alliance. In fact, so successful was the visit that it was decided to have a reciprocal one in June, where the principal French ambassadors would be Monsieur Mancini, the nephew of Cardinal Mazarin, and the Duc de Crequi, King Louis' Chief Gentleman of the Bedchamber.

Fauconberg had departed England on 26 May, the day after the High Court of Justice had been re-established to try cases of treason unearthed by Thurloe's intelligence organisation. The Marquis of Ormonde had been sent to England by Charles Stewart in disguise to sound out known Royalists about the possibility of an uprising. Ormonde discovered that the Royalists were too badly organised for an uprising, but his movements had been under the surveillance of Thurloe's agents and so revealed his Royalist contacts. There began a general round up of those Ormonde had contacted or were thought to have been contacted by Royalist activists in order for them to appear before the High Court of Justice. One of those considered a suspect and the first to appear before the High Court was Sir Henry Slingsby who had been in prison for several years as a Royalist activist, but who had never been charged. As Slingsby was the husband of Fauconberg's aunt, this was potentially embarrassing and it was no bad thing that Fauconberg was out of the country during the trial, which resulted in his uncle being sentenced to being hanged, drawn and quartered.

Another of those to appear before the High Court was the clergyman Dr Hewett, who was accused of raising money for Charles Stewart and using his services in London as a cover for Royalists to meet to plot against the Protectorate. He too was sentenced to be hanged, drawn and quartered, as were various others who had been arrested. Hewett had been the Anglican clergyman who had privately married Mary and Fauconberg and it is believed that both Mary and Frances, and possibly Bettie, had secretly been to hear him preach at St Gregory's church near St Pauls. The evidence against both Slingsby and Hewett was flimsy, but they had stood no chance before the High Court composed of ardent Commonwealth men who acted as judge and jury. From the start of the proceedings against them, Mary, Frances and Bettie had all pleaded with their father to grant mercy.[17] This had only been partially successful as Slingsby and Hewett were merely granted the privilege of the sentence being reduced to beheading.

Oliver may have regretted not having intervened to grant Bettie her request because in June her 1-year-old child Oliver died; a blow for Oliver and Elizabeth to have lost a third grandchild within a year. Oliver doted on his grandchildren, particularly Bettie's children, Cromwell, Henry and Martha and the deceased baby Oliver. His affection is described by Andrew Marvell in the lines: 'Or with a Grandsire's joy her Children sees | Hanging about his neck or at his knees'.[18] Bettie took the loss very severely and her delicate health crumbled as a result.

Despite private sorrows, the work of state had to continue. The important return visit of the French ambassadors Mancini and de Crequi was about to take place. This high-level French emissary could not have come at a more opportune time. Marshal Turenne, supported by the English force under Lockhart, had won a major victory against the Spanish and their Royalist allies at the Battle of the Dunes on 4 June. A few days later Dunkirk surrendered to Lockhart and became an English possession. Dunkirk had been the principal base for French pirates attacking English shipping in the Channel and becoming an English garrison put that to an end. However, more than this, it restored an English possession on the Continent, which had ceased 100 years earlier when Mary Tudor lost Calais. The capture of Dunkirk was the cause of even greater national pride than the acquisition of Jamaica and could be said to be the high point of the Commonwealth and Cromwell's achievement as Protector.

Mancini and de Crequi arrived at Greenwich on 15 June for their six-day visit accompanied, according to *Mercurius Politicus* 'by divers nobility of France and many gentlemen of quality'. They were met by Fauconberg and Sir Gilbert Pickering and taken by the Protector's splendid state barge to the Tower of London. They then transferred to a fleet of coaches with Mancini and de Crequi riding in the Protectoral coach and made their way to stay at Brooke House, the government mansion in Holborn. With Fauconberg in constant attendance to ensure all the ambassadors' needs were met, the next day they visited Whitehall Palace and were received with ceremony by Oliver under a canopy of state. The following day they travelled to Hampton Court where they were entertained more informally by Oliver with some hunting in the deer park and the day after entertained by Fauconberg at a country residence at his own expense. The next day, they returned to Hampton Court and in the afternoon formalities of the visit ended with a final audience with Oliver at the end of which he did them the honour of walking with them to the entrance of his Guard Chamber. Having made their farewells to the Protector, they then went to pay their respects to Elizabeth, Mary and Frances, but not Bettie, who was grieving for her lost child. Elizabeth and the two girls were used to being treated as semi-royalty, but it must have felt rather special to be the recipients of full blown Gallic charm and courtesy from senior representatives of the king of France.

For Mary's husband, Fauconberg, the departure of the ambassadors and their retinue was a relief. The whole visit had been a great success, but he was quite exhausted after being their constant amusing host, attending to their slightest needs amid the busy programme of banquets and entertainments. An idea of the effort put into the French mission is that the additional costs came to £6,098.[19] As soon as Mancini and de Crequi had left, Falconbridge decided to have some time off and take Mary up to his estate in Yorkshire, an exciting prospect for Mary because she was to see her new home for the first time. It was even more exciting that their journey there was essentially a royal progress. As Viscount and Viscountess Fauconberg neared York they were greeted by 'above 1,000 horse of the gentry and others, besides the mayor and aldermen of the place'. When they entered the city they were formally received by the mayor and aldermen then taken to a reception where they were given a pair of silver flagons and £60 in gold. It was then off to Coxwold in the North Riding to stay at Newburgh Priory.

Mary had become used to living in Whitehall and Hampton Court Palaces, but she must have been a little thrilled to see her husband's large stately home of which she would be the mistress. Her parents had left their modest farmhouse in St Ives before she was born, but Mary would have remembered living in their rather ordinary town house in Ely. What a contrast to Newburgh Priory with state rooms, fine gardens leading to parkland and the large estate beyond, all in a beautiful setting with superb views across to what is now Kilburn White Horse.[20] This must have been a particularly happy time for Mary and an enjoyable one for her husband as he took her on tours of his estate and introduced her to his neighbours. Unfortunately, the visit was all too short, because news arrived that Bettie was seriously ill and so they began the long journey back to London.

At much the same time as Mary's visit to the north, her brother Richard was sent west. In January 1658, to raise Richard's profile further, Oliver had given him command of a regiment, although there is no record of him spending any time with it, and in May he attended the launch of a new warship at Woolwich, which was named *Richard* in his honour. In June Oliver decided that Richard and Dorothy should make a formal visit to the West Country.

This visit was also not unlike a royal progress. Three miles outside Bristol they were met by the sheriffs and 200 citizens on horseback, together with a train of 400 mounted local gentry. Cannons fired as they entered the city and there was a 'noble dinner' and then a banquet hosted by the mayor in the evening. Richard and Dorothy proved popular because of their unpretentious and gracious manner and the content and delivery of Richard's formal speeches.[21] In some ways this was to be the high point of their lives; receiving popular acclaim and respect without the cares of responsibility. This pleasant interlude in which both Dorothy and Richard must have surprised themselves of their aptitude for public duties also came to an end with the news of Bettie's deteriorating health. On 17 July they arrived at Hampton Court Palace where Bettie had been taken and the family assembled around her.

As Oliver and Elizabeth were almost constantly at Bettie's bedside, the Council moved all meetings to Hampton Court, but most public business ground to a halt. Bettie is thought to have had cancer of either the bowel or womb and tossed and turned in pain, not helped by the fact that it was an exceptionally hot and humid July. To the great relief of her husband John Claypole, Oliver, Elizabeth and the rest of the family, she seemed to rally slightly at the end of the month. This lasted only a few days and then her pains became increasingly excruciating. Marvell movingly describes how Bettie and Oliver tried to comfort each other: 'she lest He grieve hides what She can her pains, | and he to lessen Hers his sorrow feigns'.[22]

Although Marvell describes Oliver, we may be sure that Elizabeth was with him at Bettie's bedside giving what comfort she could. In the early hours of the 6 August Bettie's misery ended and she died. Her parents virtually collapsed with grief and exhaustion. Bettie had been liked by all and as *Mercurius Politicus* described her: 'A lady of any excellent spirit and judgement, and of a most noble disposition, eminent in all princely qualities … procured her an honourable mention in the mouths both of friends and enemies.' Indeed, so great was her reputation for goodness that she became regarded as an almost saintly figure in Royalist folklore. Stories circulated of her pleading with her father for clemency for Royalists and on her deathbed reproaching him about executing the king. The coffin of this kind young lady was taken at twilight down the Thames in a silent procession of barges to Westminster where it was briefly laid in the painted Chamber before being interred at midnight in Henry VII's Chapel in the abbey. Bettie's coffin had been accompanied by her husband John, brother Richard, Fauconberg and Fleetwood. Oliver was suffering from gout and far too distressed to attend and Elizabeth and their daughters remained at Hampton Court to comfort him and each other. Oliver was a broken man.

Chapter 13

A New Protector
1658–1659

'I would not take away the life of the least person in the nation to preserve my greatness, which is a burden to me.'

Richard Cromwell, 1 April 1659

His deep sorrow over the death of Bettie, and Oliver's own failing health, brought his life to an end in the autumn of 1658. The malaria fits became stronger and he had pains in the bowels, possibly because his kidney stone had turned septic. The waters brought from the spa of Tunbridge Wells that he began taking appeared to bring an improvement, and by 17 August he was able to go riding at Hampton Court. However, George Fox, the Quaker leader, met him on that day and wrote in his journal: 'I saw and felt a wafte of death goe forth against him, that he lookt like a dead man... .'[1] The next day Oliver took to his bed and on his doctors' advice, was moved by litter to Whitehall, accompanied by the family. He rallied slightly and was even able to see Fairfax who had come to protest that his son-in-law, Buckingham, had been put in the Tower for breaking his parole as he was caught leaving York House. Oliver was strong enough to turn down the request for Buckingham's release and Fairfax marched off in anger. Oliver returned to his bed falling in and out of consciousness while his physicians rushed about trying every remedy they could think of to cure what they had diagnosed as 'common tertian ague' (malaria).

We can imagine the anguish of the family seeing Oliver so stricken. Nevertheless, he had been seriously ill before and recovered, so there was always hope. Oliver himself was hopeful and said to Elizabeth, as she held his hand 'I tell you, I shall not die this hour, I'm sure on't.'[2] Thurloe and members of the Council had not been so optimistic and had begun worrying who might succeed this giant of a man who had kept the power of the three kingdoms clenched in his own hands. Thurloe thought that Oliver had named his successor in a sealed envelope, but despite urgent hunting for the envelope in his study and elsewhere, it could not be found. On Monday, 30 August Oliver was asked to name his successor and seems to have whispered 'Richard'. He was asked again on 2 September, and once more is thought to have said 'Richard'. The next day was the anniversary of his historic victories of Dunbar and Worcester and amid the greatest storm in living memory, at 3pm he died.

The reaction to the death was one of shock. It was hard to believe that such a dominant figure was no more. Oliver's family and his immediate staff were poleaxed with grief. Included among the grieving was the faithful John Thurloe who, nevertheless, immediately summoned the Council and, from there, things moved quickly. The Council accepted Thurloe's word that Oliver had named Richard as his heir and after a short meeting visited Richard's apartments in Whitehall to tell him that he was now Lord Protector.

Fleetwood, the Lord General, called the Council of the Army to inform them and ordered troops to be deployed in case of trouble. The Lord Mayor was also informed and the next day the Norray King of Arms, accompanied by heralds, trumpeters and foot soldiers, read a proclamation at Temple Bar and then at points throughout the City ending with: 'God save His Highness Richard Lord Protector!' Later that day the Lord Mayor and the Council attended Richard and he was sworn in as Lord Protector. As soon as the news of Oliver's death reached Scotland and Ireland, General Monck and Henry Cromwell immediately proclaimed Richard as Lord Protector. The transfer of power could hardly have gone more smoothly and Thurloe was able to write to Henry:

> 'It hath pleased God hitherto to give his highnes your brother a very easie and peaceable entrance upon his government. There is not a dogge that waggs his tongue, soe great a calme are wee in.' However, did add rather ominously: 'But I must needs acquaint your excellencye, that there are some secret murmurings in the army, as if his highnes were not generall of the army, as his father was; and would looke upon him and the army as divided, and as if the conduct of the army should be elsewhere, and in other hands.'[3]

Richard had become Lord Protector and Oliver's favorite daughter-in-law, Dorothy, was now Her Highness the Lady Protectress. Richard and his brother Henry had little time to mourn their father, but the women of their family were overcome with grief. For Frances the death of her beloved father came on top of that of her husband and sister. Bridget and Mary were also highly distraught and Fauconberg wrote to Henry: 'my poor wife, i know not what on eath to do with her. When seemingly quieted, she bursts out again into pasion that tears her very heart in pieces; nor can i balme her, considering what she has lost'.[4] The greatest blow must have fallen on Elizabeth. Within about two months she had lost a grandchild, her beloved daughter and the husband to whom she had been so close and whose amazing life she had shared for the past thirty-eight years. It was hard to adjust to the fact that death had suddenly snatched such a towering personality. For days, Oliver's women folk gathered about a round table with the household chaplains trying to find religious comfort to sustain them at this terrible time. We may expect that Elizabeth was doing all she could to console and support her daughters, while at the same time trying to care for Bettie's bereaved children. She also had to start considering how to hand over her position as Lady Protectress. She would have wanted to do all that she could to help Dorothy learn the etiquette and responsibilities, but for the moment all was dominated by the grieving process.

The machinery of succession moved forward with due protocol. The Protectoral Court went into mourning, as indeed did the French Court. Days of fasting and humiliation were set. The French, Portuguese and other ambassadors were swift to present their formal condolences to Richard as he stood under a cloth of state in the Whitehall Palace Presence Chamber. The accession of Richard was celebrated in many parts of the country, bells rang out and cannons were fired in York, Shrewsbury held a banquet and in Southampton the corporation set up a conduit of claret wine for all to drink. Other towns including Bristol and Exeter celebrated by bell ringing, bonfires and trumpeters, with the civic authorities in their scarlet gowns shouting 'Amen, Amen, God Preserve Lord Richard, Lord Protector.'[5]

Oliver's body was embalmed and the council decided that his funeral should be based on all the royal pomp accorded to King James I. A life size effigy of Oliver, made of wood and wax, was created and taken with due solemnity to Somerset House on 18 October where four rooms were set aside, draped in black and hung with the Protector's coat of arms. The standing effigy was dressed in a purple velvet robe with gold lace and ermine, holding a sceptre in one hand and an orb in the other and wearing a purple cap of state lined with ermine. Behind the effigy on an ornate chair, an imperial crown rested on a cushion. There the effigy stood in public view until the magnificent state funeral with its great procession to Westminster Abbey on 23 November. Oliver's actual body was quietly interred in the abbey some days before, 'without ceremony,' in accordance with the 1645 Public Worship Act. It was as well that the interment of Cromwell's actual body had waited for the public funeral as it was already badly decomposed through a botched embalming process. The total funeral arrangements for the empty coffin came to the colossal sum of £60,000.[6]

It may have been comfort to the Cromwell family that Oliver was given the recognition of so grand a funeral, but it meant that they had to wait nearly three months before his body was finally put to rest and they could start trying to move on with their lives. In the meantime, the Council had made arrangements for the new order. Elizabeth would have the title 'The Dowager Lady Protectress' and it was decided that she should move to St James (then called 'James House') with her daughter Frances, and be given £20,000 and an annual pension of another £20,000. This was a generous settlement, as was the generosity of the funeral. The only problem was that there was no money in the Treasury. Richard had inherited his father's major difficulty of shortage of funds, so issued writs for a new parliament to sit in January 1669 in the hope that it would vote for taxes. Revenue was desperately needed, not least to pay the arrears owed to the real power in the land, an increasingly discontented army.

Fleetwood, the Lord General, had been almost as grief stricken as his wife Bridget over the loss of his father-in-law, who he tearfully described as 'a dear and tender father'. He soon discovered that the senior officers of the General Council who had been ready to support their wartime leader Oliver, had reservations about Richard. Desborough, although Richard's uncle, had no respect for him because of his lack of military experience and was thought that the Protector's powers should be curtailed and possibly be even replaced by a Republic. Others were beginning to share Desborough's views. With feelings running high about arrears of pay, the Council of Officers decided that Fleetwood should take over the post of Commander-in-Chief, which was Richard's by right of being Lord Protector.

Fleetwood presented a petition to Richard requesting that he should be made Commander-in-Chief with the ability to grant commissions, including reinstating as generals Thomas Harrison and John Lambert who had been sacked by Oliver. Richard refused and on 18 November called the Council of Officers to Whitehall. He addressed them with great diplomacy and asked for their help, accepting his lack of combat experience, but saying that he would be guided by them. Richard said he would make Fleetwood commander of the army for the three nations, but the post of commander-in-chief would remain with him. The majority of the officers seemed to accept Richard's gracious speech and the issue appeared to be over, but not for long.

Fleetwood still wanted to be Commander-in-Chief and had gatherings of senior officers at his home at Wallingford House under the guise of prayer meetings. The dismissed, but still popular John Lambert, a staunch Republican, began attending the meetings and swayed officers to his views.

Opposition to Richard also began to appear in the Council where both Fleetwood and Desborough were members. Large groupings of up to 300 officers began to meet at St James and many of the more junior openly said that Richard had 'never drawn sword for the Commonwealth' and began supporting Lambert's plan for a republic. Fleetwood led the army's pressure on Richard, but was beginning to lose the initiative. It must have been of some anguish to Bridget Fleetwood that her husband was now moving into opposition to her brother Richard and being aided and abetted by their uncle Desborough. On top of this, much of the plotting was going on in her own house. Fleetwood remained outwardly respectful to Richard, but their relationship became icy with Fleetwood's mounting resentment that Richard was confiding in Thurloe and Fauconberg, rather than himself.

The Cromwell clan began to split apart and Elizabeth must have been increasingly anxious at witnessing the strains in the family. She would have been well aware of the group of disaffected junior officers who met at St James', close to her own apartments. Elizabeth pressed Richard for Henry's return from Ireland to provide support for him and moral support for herself. This went nowhere as Desborough flatly refused to agree it in Council.

Meanwhile, Richard tried his best to manage the business of government, assisted by the dependable Thurloe. Richard worked with quiet dignity, no doubt supported by Dorothy, and proved himself to be a potentially just and diligent ruler. He had confirmed all existing appointments and promoted Henry to become Lord Lieutenant of Ireland. He also conferred a few knighthoods, including Colonel Richard Beck, the husband of his cousin Lavinia Whetstone, but otherwise showed no favouritism. While he was engaged in the new and challenging experience of government, he and his wife were hit with a personal tragedy. As the news sheet *Mercurius Politicus* reported: 'On 14 November came sad news of the death of an illustrious Infant Lady, the Lady Dorothy, second daughter of His Highness who died at Hurley … the loss is entertained by their Highnesses with much sorrow of mind.' Little Dorothy was 15-months-old and was buried at Hursley on 13 November.[7]

Private feelings apart, the most important issue on Richard's mind was the forthcoming parliament. Thurloe used all his efforts to ensure that suitable supportive MPs were elected, but his gerrymandering had only partial success. The new parliament assembled and was opened on 27 January 1659 by Richard with due splendour and pageantry. He had arrived in the brand-new Protectoral barge, with its liveried watermen, and proceeded to the Lords' Chamber in a grand procession, with Claypole carrying the sword of state. In his speech Richard emphasised the need for continued war against Spain and the urgent requirement to vote for taxation. The speech was well received, but it soon became clear that Richard would have the same problems with this parliament as his father had in the past. The Commons pressed for the abolition of the Other House and although this was defeated, there were vocal members, such as Sir Arthur Haselrig and Thomas Scot, who were Republicans. There was also a large number who wanted to bring the army under control and were not prepared to vote for taxation until they had done so. For all that, about two thirds of the Commons supported Richard's rule.

The army had no great liking of parliaments and lost patience with this one. As there had been no progress in resolving the arrears of pay, on 2 April Fleetwood delivered to Richard a petition demanding payment of what was owed. The army made it clear that they were the power in the land and were to be obeyed. Parliament and the City became extremely agitated about what the army would do next. By the second week of April a rumour was circulating that senior officers had planned to seize Richard and hold him in custody. This led some of Richard's closest advisers to urge him to arrest Fleetwood and Desborough. Charles Howard, the Captain of the Protectoral Life Guard, said he was more than willing to carry this out. Richard is believed to have made his famous reply:

> 'I will have no blood spilt for me. Everyone shall see I will do no one any harm. I never have and never will do. I shall be very much troubled if anyone is injured on my accord. I shall not take away the life of the least person in the nation to preserve my greatness which is a burden to me.'[8]

Richard was not going to risk civil war and decided to put his trust in parliament and in hopes of negotiating a settlement between them and the army.

On 18 April the Commons response to the increasingly aggressive army was to lock their chamber doors for safety and vote that there should be no army meetings without the Protector's consent. Richard summoned the General Council of Officers and declared their meetings dissolved. This resulted in an angry protest from Desborough. The meetings continued in defiance of Richard, and Fleetwood and Desborough called for the dissolution of parliament. On 21 April the Commons at last began to debate funding of the army, but also its reorganising under parliament's control. This was too much for the army.

The General Council of Officers ordered all regiments of foot and horse in the London area to rendezvous at St James' Fields. Richard issued a separate instruction ordering all troops to assemble at Whitehall to support the Protector. Only a few companies came. Even the regiments under his close supporters, Whalley, Ingoldsby and Goffe, defected to Fleetwood. That evening Fleetwood and Desborough visited Richard to demand that he dismiss parliament. Richard held out against this until late at night, but on the advice of Thurloe reluctantly agreed and signed the dissolution at 5am. Richard had the support of Montague's navy, Monck's army in Scotland and Henry's army in Ireland, but there were several thousand troops massing close to Whitehall Palace, so what could he do? As Desborough told him, he could either dissolve parliament or the army would dissolve it for him. The next day both houses were informed that they were dissolved and the chambers were cleared by soldiers. Another military coup had taken place.

Fleetwood and Desborough had succeeded in grabbing power, but soon found that they had miscalculated their influence over the army in London, which had swung to Republicanism. As early as 2 May, John Barwick, a Royalist spy in London, wrote to Edward Hyde:

> 'Both Desborough and Fleetwood are now as low in the esteem of the officers as before they were high, being looked upon as self-seekers in that they are for a Protector now they have got a protector of wax whom they can mould as they please and lay aside when they can agree upon a successor whereas the common volge (voice?) of the army is for a Commonwealth and the Long Parliament revived.'[9]

On 5 May the Council of Officers decided to recall the Rump of the Long Parliament, which had been dismissed by Oliver back in 1653. Two days later Speaker Lenthall and forty-two MPs took their seats in the Commons protected by Lambert's soldiers. The parliament immediately declared that government should be carried out without a Protector or Upper House, and on 14 May Richard's great seal was formally broken. Richard and Dorothy were once again Mr and Mrs Cromwell. On 25 May Richard officially resigned and asked only for indemnity and that his and his father's debts were paid. The three nations were now a republic governed by the Rump Parliament in the Commons, with the Other House having been abolished and a Committee of Safety acting as Council. Of course the real power rested with the army, and Fleetwood was declared Commander-in-Chief. Fleetwood and senior officers dominated the Committee of Safety and, wanting to treat Richard fairly, requested that the Commons discharge him of his Protectorial debts of £29,000 and grant him an income of £20,000 and £10,000 for his posterity for ever. Elizabeth was now officially named 'Her Highness Dowager' and it was decided she should receive £8,000 and a suitable residence, such as Somerset House.[10] The Commons agreed the settlement and included other items such as £2,000 removal expenses for Richard.

Richard may have received a generous settlement (which was never paid), but this could not hide the fact that he had been unceremoniously kicked out of office. He summed up the situation when he wrote to Henry in Ireland:

> 'As for my selfe, those that were my father's friends, pretended ones only, were myne. It required time to acquit myself with tem, for though they were my relatins they forsooke me. i knowe Fleetwood and Desborough regaurds not ruen soe that they may have there ends, they are pitiful creatures.'[11]

Despite his dire situation as a semi-prisoner of the army, Richard still had the potential support of the armies of Monck in Scotland, his brother in Ireland, Lockhart in Flanders and Montague's Fleet. He could have called upon them to save the Protectorate and parliament, but chose not to do so. To have summoned them to his support would have almost certainly led to civil war. A braver man might have risked all and had a reasonable chance of winning and thus possibly establishing a Cromwell dynasty that might yet be ruling the British Isles to this day. Richard had neither the appetite for power, nor the wish to cause bloodshed. It is not clear whether Dorothy was with him at this time or in Hursley with the children. Richard and Dorothy were very close and he may well have sought her views and she may have had some influence on him, but we shall never know. It is likely that Dorothy would have been very happy for Richard to relinquish the burden of Protectorship and return to the quiet life of a country gentleman with her and the children.

Richard soon made it clear to Monck, Henry and other potential supporters that he would not seek their help and 'He was resolved to sit still and look on'.[12] Monck reluctantly accepted the rule of Fleetwood and the Rump. Henry was dismissed as Lord Lieutenant by the Rump and the Republican, Edmund Ludlow, was put in command of the army in Ireland. Henry left Ireland with Elizabeth and the children on 27 June and on 2 July he was back in London to formally report to the General Council of Officers. Henry's career was over at the age of 31. While in London Henry would have almost definitely visited his mother. It must have been a great comfort for Elizabeth to see him after so long and following the shocks of her multiple bereavements and Richard's overthrow. It is not known whether she would have also been visited by her grandchildren. If so, she would have seen little Oliver for the first time and witnessed how much the other children had grown in the four years they had been away. Whether or not she saw them, it would have been a relief for her that Henry and the family were at last back in England, even if they only had a brief time in London before moving to stay with Elizabeth's parents, the Russells, in Chippenham.

The new regime purged those who had supported Richard. Naturally Bettie's husband John Claypole was out of a job as Master of Horse and so went off with his children to the family estate in Narborough, Northamptonshire.[13] Fauconberg was dismissed as a colonel, his regiment given to Lambert. Mary and he moved to their estates in Yorkshire. Other supporters of Richard, such as Howard and Ingoldsby, were dismissed from command and their regiments given to Republicans like Haselrig. The whole structure of the Protectorate was rapidly dismantled. In this bewildering time Elizabeth and her daughter Frances remained in St James Palace not knowing where they would eventually be accommodated. Richard clung on in Whitehall Palace, for a time rather dazed by the turn of events. He was also waiting for the promised payment of his removal expenses. Thurloe had been dismissed as Secretary of State and replaced by the Republican Thomas Scot. Elizabeth's world was falling apart, largely because of Fleetwood's disloyalty to Richard. The once close friendship between her and the rest of the family with Fleetwood turned to hatred and some of this must have rubbed off on his loyal wife Bridget. We may expect that Bridget avoided her mother as much as she could to prevent the likely arguments and recriminations.

It is probable that Fleetwood had wanted to retain Richard as a puppet Protector, but the Republican pressures unleashed by Desborough and Lambert made that impossible. Although Fleetwood had once hoped that he would be nominated as Oliver's successor, it did not happen, but he had become Commander-in-Chief of the all-powerful army. Bridget found herself married to the most important man in the Republic, but at the price of a gigantic rift with the family she loved. Powerful though Fleetwood was, his position was by no means invincible. The Committee of Safety was replaced by a twenty-one strong Council of State, which had included MPs such as Haselrig, and was far from easy to control. There was also the matter of the Rump Parliament, which proved just as fractious as its predecessors. The army, although obedient to its Commander-in-Chief, increasingly fell under the influence of the popular and charismatic John Lambert. Fleetwood would have noted that when the Rump had been recalled it was Lambert who received the credit and obtained an ovation from the troops in Westminster Hall.

Bridget must have found that her husband was under increased pressure and spending more and more time seeking help and guidance in prayer. The response he received from the heavens was silence; as a result of which his anxiety increased. Charles Stuart had watched the Protectorate fall apart and, hearing of the divisions in the new Republic, he decided that the time was ripe for a Royalist uprising and the date of 1 August was set. Charles positioned himself in Boulogne to be ready to land in England supported by two troop landings totalling 1,000 soldiers, including Conde's battle-hardened veterans. The position looked serious for the new Republic, but the Sealed Knot, the Royalist resistance movement, was disorganised and as the timing clashed with the vital period of harvest, few wanted to take up arms. On top of this, Charles discovered that the Commonwealth intelligence service had obtained their whole uprising plan, and so ordered it to be abandoned.

Word that the uprising was cancelled did not reach everywhere in time and Sir George Booth went ahead, raised 4,000 men and captured Chester. Fleetwood needed to dispatch a force to put down Booth and decided that it should be led by Lambert rather than himself. He probably did not trust Lambert to be left with the rest of the army in London. On 19 August Lambert's force defeated the dispirited Royalists at Winnington Bridge. Booth was captured and sent to the Tower. The Council of State ordered the rounding up of other suspect Royalists amongst whom was Fauconberg. After all she had suffered, Mary now had the anguish of her husband being sent to the Tower. Fortunately there was no evidence against Fauconberg and he was released after a short time having provided bail of £10,000 and was able to return to Mary in Yorkshire. This must have been a relief to the whole Cromwell family in such dangerous and uncertain times.

Parliament were so grateful to Lambert for the victory that they voted him £1,000 to buy a jewel to commemorate his success. This could have helped cement relations between the army and parliament, but Lambert distributed the money among his troops. Haselrig and other Republicans were furious and saw this as Lambert trying to ingratiate himself with the army with a view to becoming Protector or even king. Haselrig could well have been right in his assessment and Fleetwood may have secretly agreed with him. Some of Lambert's returning army wrote a petition while in Derby requesting that Fleetwood be appointed permanent Commander-in-Chief and Lambert made his Lieutenant General. Haselrig called for Lambert's arrest, but Fleetwood stood by him, saying the petition had been issued without his knowledge. This failed to prevent an escalation in hostility between the army and parliament.

The General Council of Officers passed a resolution that anyone casting scandalous aspersion on the army should be punished. On 11 October Parliament responded with a vote that raising tax without parliamentary consent was high treason. The next day parliament cashiered Lambert, Desborough and six other officers, abolished the post of Commander-in-Chief and put the army under a committee of which Fleetwood was to be chairman. Lambert was enraged and marched on Westminster with 3,000 men. He was met by two regiments of infantry and four troops of horse, which parliament had deployed as its guard force. These troops went over to Lambert and when the Rump MPs arrived at the Commons they were refused entry. Parliament was thus forcibly dissolved. Another army coup had taken place and Fleetwood had been a helpless bystander.

The army set up a new Committee of Safety of which Fleetwood and Lambert were the most prominent members, but it was clear to all that the ambitious Lambert had the upper hand. Lambert's coup had removed parliament, but did not mean the Committee of Safety was now the unchallenged ruler of the three nations. There were rumours that both Montague, who commanded the Fleet, and Monck, the commander in Scotland, wanted a return of parliament and were in contact with Charles Stuart. A small group of officers felt the best way forward might be to restore Richard as Protector. Richard and his family had by this time settled to live at his father-in-law's estate at Hursley.

Richard and Dorothy were exceedingly surprised when three troops of horse arrived at Hursley to escort him back to Whitehall as Lord Protector. Richard had no appetite for power, but felt it his duty to go with them. The group had hardly gone a few miles before word arrived that the Committee of Safety had narrowly voted against restoring Richard. As there was still a chance that Richard might be restored, he was taken to Hampton Court to await events. One can only imagine the shock this must have been to Richard and Dorothy who had just been adjusting to reverting to life as country gentry when unwanted greatness was suddenly being thrust upon them and then equally suddenly snatched away.

Hursley was a pleasant place for the family to live, but their previous happy country existence could never be recaptured. To have been ousted as His Highness the Lord Protector had made Richard an object of ridicule to many who, until recently, had done all they could to ingratiate themselves with him. More important than that, Richard was pursued by debtors wanting payment for the expenses of running the two palaces and the costs of his father's funeral. The total amount creditors were claiming was nearly £30,000. Richard had been forced to lock himself in his rooms in Whitehall Palace to escape the creditors and then secretly move to the Cockpit before making a getaway to Hursley.[14] Most of the creditors had been temporarily kept at bay because it was known that the Rump Parliament had granted him a substantial settlement. Unfortunately, none of that had been paid and the Rump Parliament was no more. Richard's financial position was as unstable as the political situation.

For Fleetwood and the Committee of Safety there had been confidence that the troops in Ireland under Ludlow would remain loyal to them once Ludlow arrived to take command. In his *Memoirs* Ludlow records visiting Fleetwood at Wallingford House in December prior to departing for Ireland and hoping to persuade him to restore parliament. Ludlow writes:

> 'His lady (Bridget) over-hearing these last words from her chamber and being informed that I was alone with the Lieutenant-General, she came into the room where we were, and with tears began to lament the present condition of her husband, who, she said, had always been unwilling to do anything in opposition to Parliament, assuring me that he was utterly ignorant of the contrivances of the officers at Darby (Derby) to petition to Parliament in so insolent a manner, and had not been any part of their proceedings upon it afterwards. That as to herself she had always solicited him to comply in all things with the orders of Parliament; and that fearing the consequences of the petition from Darby, she had taken the original, and locked it up in her cabinet, where it still was. She desired me to defer my journey to Ireland till differences should be composed between the Parliament and the Army.'

Ludlow had replied that he would leave as planned because he could not bring the sides together. He ends this passage by writing: 'I confess i was moved buy the discourse of the lady.'[15] This is one of the few records we have of Bridget. It shows her to be strongly supportive of her husband and a lady of character who was not afraid to give forthright advice. It also shows that Fleetwood had not wanted Lambert's coup against parliament and was desperately trying to hold the army and government together as events slipped out of control.

Fleetwood became worried about the reaction of Monk to the dismissal of parliament and was concerned to keep him on side. He sent Monck several letters of assurance, but received noncommittal replies. Monck kept his cards close to his chest, but had ominously moved his headquarters to Coldstream near the English border. A deputation was sent to treat with Monck and at the same time Lambert was dispatched with 7,000 men to try to win him round or, failing that, block any advance into England. Problems also occurred at the other end of the country. Haselrig had gone to Portsmouth where the Republican governor declared for parliament. Fleetwood dispatched two regiments of horse and one of foot to deal with this, but on arrival they went over to Haselrig. On 5 December Haselrig's success encouraged apprentices and others to rise up in London and demand the restoration of parliament. Fleetwood ordered a regiment to put down this disturbance, but although some apprentices were killed, it merely inflamed citizens even more against the army.

To cap it all off, on 13 December the navy announced its support for parliament and a few days later Vice-Admiral Lawson appeared in the Thames with twenty-two ships from the Downs Fleet threatening to blockade London if parliament was not restored. On hearing this, Haselrig led the Portsmouth garrison to London. At their approach, the troops in Westminster mutinied against the Committee and joined Haselrig declaring that they would live or die with the parliament. They then marched into Lincoln's Inn Fields and on to Chancery Lane where they halted before Speaker Lenthall's house, fired three volleys of musketry then pronounced him not only Speaker, but Lord General. Lambert sent back some of his troops to deal with this, but on their arrival at St Albans they heard the news from London and immediately joined the demand for parliament.

Bridget Fleetwood watched in anguish as her husband was paralysed by indecision. He was still Commander-in-Chief, but instead of deciding on a firm plan, kept sinking to his knees in loud prayer and bursting into tears. This did not help to inspire confidence in the rest of the Committee of Officers. Fleetwood was still popular with the army and could have attempted to rally them to him, but he had something of a nervous breakdown. However, things are never so bad that they cannot become a lot worse. On Christmas day Lenthall and his army and naval supporters took over the Tower and then went to the Lord Mayor and aldermen to tell them that parliament was reassembling. Fleetwood's power had evaporated and he could only conclude that he had carried out some transgression to make God abandon him. In his own words, 'God hath spat in my face and forsaken me.'[16]

On 26 December Fleetwood submitted himself to the wishes of the reassembled Rump and handed over the keys of the Commons to Lenthall. The Rump's first action was to dismiss Lambert, Desborough and their followers and to instruct the soldiers serving under Lambert to quit their commander. Lambert's force were still unpaid and, having no desire to fight Monck's army, melted away. Lambert was left with just fifty troopers, so he disbanded them and returned home where he was later arrested and taken to the Tower. The road was now open for Monck to march on London if he chose.

A New Protector

Although the soldiers had said Lenthall was their Lord General, Fleetwood had not been officially removed from office by the Rump and it might have still been possible for him to show himself in support of parliament and resume his position of authority. Bridget must have prayed for him to pull himself together and take action. Whitelock advised him on an alternative way out, which was to accept that the Commonwealth was lost and seek accommodation with Charles Stuart. Fleetwood agreed to this and that Whitelock should visit Charles as his intermediary, but just as he made the decision, Desborough and Vane entered and persuaded him against it. By this time poor Bridget must have been in despair knowing that her husband's lack of any action would end in their ruin. With Fleetwood remaining paralysed by indecision, the initiative moved to Monck.

Fairfax had been observing events and decided to raise the Yorkshire gentry in support of parliament. He and his followers were welcomed into York and Monck and his army marched through the snow from Coldstream to join him. Among those who joined Monck in York was Fauconberg who was made a colonel by Monck and given Haselrig's regiment. On 1 January 1660 Monck took 5,000 of his troops on the march south supposedly to support parliament, but as parliament was already restored no one knew what his real intentions were. Was he really going to support parliament? Or was he hoping to make himself Protector by military coup? Or did he want to restore Charles Stuart to the throne? Monck was in close touch with Charles, but it is not certain that he had yet finally decided his intentions. Fauconberg on the other hand had definitely decided to support Charles, and secretly sent his secretary to the king in Brussels with a gift of £1,000. Meanwhile, Monck had asked the Rump to order all troops out of the city to which it reluctantly agreed. On 3 February Monck marched his men in to the City and received a hero's welcome.

By deft political manoeuvring, Monck managed to alienate the City from the Rump and procured popular agreement for the recall of the full Long Parliament. Hazelrig and Scot made an effort to thwart Monck by trying to have Fleetwood reappointed Commander-in-Chief, but this went nowhere. They saw their cause was completely lost and returned to their homes. The remaining members of the Long Parliament met on 20 April and made Monck Commander-in-Chief. Five days later the House of Lords reassembled. For months Monck had been in contact with Charles Stewart and by managing to have the Long Parliament returned, he had created a House of Commons dominated by Presbyterians who wanted a return to the stable government of monarchy.

On 1 May parliament received a document from Charles written in Breda promising his support for parliament's privileges, a free pardon to his opponents and religious freedom of conscience. Eight days later parliament proclaimed Charles king and began arranging for his return. On 24 May Charles embarked at Schevelling to sail for Dover and claim his crown. The ship he sailed on rapidly received new paintwork, renaming it the 'Royal Charles,' as it had been called 'The Naseby' after Oliver's great victory in 1645. The achievements of Oliver and the Protectorate were going to be similarly obliterated by the new regime. Might obliteration extend to the Protector's family? The Cromwells must have been living in fear of what Royalist vengeance was about to be unleashed against them.

Chapter 14

Survival
1660–1720

'The arch traitor Cromwell and his choicest instruments, Bradshaw and Ireton, finished the tragedy of their lives in a comic scene at Tyburn, a wonderful example of justice.'

                               Diary of John Evelyn, 30 January 1661

But what of Elizabeth during the fast-moving events that had resulted in Charles Stewart returning as King Charles II? Since Richard's fall from power Elizabeth had continued living in St James' Palace with her daughter Frances. She was Her Highness the Protectress Dowager and had ordered a refurbishment of her new apartments. Unfortunately, the funding that had been voted for her by parliament never materialised to pay for this or the upkeep of the palace and her household. Across the Park in Whitehall, Richard had been plagued by creditors until he had made a run for the relative safety of Hursley in June. No doubt creditors had also attempted to present Elizabeth with bills, and this pressure would have increased after Richard's departure. Fortunately Elizabeth was still being treated with respect and protected by her household staff. Her son might no longer be Lord Protector, but her son-in-law, Fleetwood, was Commander-in Chief and probably the most powerful man in the country. Fleetwood would have been well aware of Elizabeth's anger with him about Richard's overthrow, but he would not have wanted to do anything to harm her. In fact, quite the reverse. He had known her for so long he would have looked upon her almost as a mother and in any case, Bridget would have insisted that she was properly cared for.

    Although Elizabeth remained in comfort after Richard's deposition, she would have felt isolated, and anxious about the future. If she visited Whitehall Palace it would have seemed eerily quiet. It had been her home and the Protector's seat of government, bustling with members of the Council, clerks, courtiers, supplicants, and guards, as well as the household staff and servants. Now virtually all had left. With them had gone old familiar figures such as Thurloe, Howard, Ingoldsby, Pickering, Goffe, and Whalley, not to mention gentlemen of the bedchamber and chaplains, many of whom had become trusted friends. To make matters worse, her family was now dispersed. Henry was back in England, but living in Chippenham, Richard had gone to Hursley, Mary was in Yorkshire and Claypole had taken the grandchildren off to Northamptonshire.

It must have been some consolation at least to have Frances living with her at St James', although the young grieving widow would not have been the most cheerful company. Bridget and her numerous children presumably visited, but we may assume that the relationship had become strained after Fleetwood's coup against Richard had left her torn between her mother and family and her husband and her own family. Elizabeth would have relied more and more on her personal staff for company, but their loyalty would become increasingly tested as there would have been little or no money for their pay. It was probably in this manner that Elizabeth spent her life: neglected and forgotten during the major events of a Royalist rising, power struggles between the Commons and the Other House and both against the army leadership, which had its own power struggles.

Elizabeth's world was further destabilised in October with Lambert's dismissal of the Rump and the creation of the Committee of Safety. She would have known that Richard had gone to Hampton Court and would have no doubt fervently prayed that Fleetwood and Lambert would restore him and parliament. By early December, however, it was clear that was not going to happen and Richard had returned to Hursley.

Elizabeth did not just sit passively in St James watching Fleetwood allow the government to fall apart. The following report shows she was prepared to press him for the reinstatement of Richard:

> 'The Lady Dowerger sent one of her gentlemen to my Lord Fleetwood yesterday before he was up, and tould him he had come from her Highness who wish't him to call to minde the saying of her husband to him before his death that he would never leave his whimsies till he had put the nation in blood and wish't him seriously to consider what wrong he had done her sonne R (Richard) whether as affairs stood they had any better way to pleasure themselves and the nation than to restore him. He lay in bed the whole time and said not a word.'[1]

Fleetwood's lack of response to her message would hardly have come as a surprise to Elizabeth. She would have come to realise that events had gone beyond her son-in-law's control. Elizabeth would have heard about the London apprentices rioting to demand the recall of parliament and parts of the army defecting from the Committee of Safety to join Haselrig. She would have seen that Fleetwood was being deserted by his troops and had to ignominiously submit to the established Rump. On the one hand, she may have felt this was poetic justice for Fleetwood's bid for power at the expense of Richard. On the other hand, the change in Fleetwood's status obviously had an adverse effect on the situation of her daughter Bridget and Elizabeth herself. She would have had no wish to find her Bridget married to a man who felt genuinely God forsaken with his dreams shattered and in deep depression. She could remember her own difficult life when Oliver went through his depressions and would not have wished that on anyone, least of all one of her daughters.

With Fleetwood effectively ceasing to be Commander-in-Chief, Elizabeth no longer had a powerful protector in these uncertain times. The new regime dominated by Hazelrig and Vane was Republican and had always been totally against creating a Protector, so would have had little interest in caring for the Protectress Dowager. Elizabeth found herself deserted. Bridget and her children left Wallingford House with Fleetwood as he abandoned public life and moved away from Westminster, probably to the manor he had inherited from his first wife in the village of Stoke Newington to the north of London. Her vulnerability became clear to what remained of her household and servants began secretly stealing what they could from St James and Whitehall Palaces.

On 3 February as Monck arrived in London and took absolute control of events, Elizabeth's situation suddenly brightened. She knew that Monck had held Oliver in deep respect and would wish no harm to come to his family. What she probably did not know was just how much Monck wanted to look after the Cromwell family interests. This is clear from an extract from a letter Monck wrote to Fleetwood and the Committee of Safety the previous year, immediately after Richard had been overthrown:

> 'That you will use your endevours with all affectionate care and industry that himself (that is Richard Cromwell) and family together with Her Highness Dowager may have such honourable provision settled upon them and such other dignities as are suitable to the former great services of that family to the nation.'[2]

Elizabeth had every reason to hope that Monck, the new Commander-in-Chief, would ensure she received the safety and respect due to the widow of the Lord Protector.

Elizabeth may have even secretly hoped that Monck might restore Richard. One very good sign was that on 27 February Monck had brought back that very loyal servant of the Cromwell family, John Thurloe, as

Secretary of State. Also Montague, who had supported Richard when he was Protector, had been reinstated as General at Sea, commanding the fleet. In reality no one knew what Monck intended to do with his new power. Monck's intentions became clearer as he encouraged the excluded Presbyterian members of the Long Parliament to take their seats. It was then a short step to dissolving themselves on 16 March and enabling the election of a new Royalist dominated parliament, which would restore the monarchy. Any hopes Elizabeth had were dashed as she could see the inevitability of a Royalist triumph. Too much was going on for anyone to bother very much, but in early April it was noted that Her Highness Dowager was no longer living in Whitehall. Indeed, it was not known where she was. It eventually transpired that she and Frances had secretly moved to the Charterhouse. Colonel Philip Jones, who had been the Controller of the Protector's Household, was Governor of Charterhouse and offered them a place of refuge.

Quite what then became of Elizabeth and Frances is not clear. It is unlikely that they would have remained in London to hear the bells ringing in celebration at Charles II's arrival to the city on 29 May. They were probably far away when figures of Oliver were burnt in the streets and the highly expensive effigy created for the Protector's funeral was hung by the neck from the window bars of the Jewel House, opposite parliament. They may have slipped away to France, but it is more likely that Jones took them to his home in Wales. This would probably have been either Cardiff Castle of which Jones was still nominally governor or, more likely, his home in Cardiff. What is clear is that later in the year Elizabeth and Frances went to join her son-in-law Claypole at his home in Narborough, in the county of Northamptonshire.[3] In some ways it might seem surprising that she and Frances did not move to be with one of her sons. She was friendly with both the Mayors at Hursley and the Russells at Chippenham, but probably felt that she could do more good living with Claypole and helping to look after Bettie's children. Whatever the reason, it was at Narborough that Elizabeth based herself for the rest of her life.

Another reason why Elizabeth may have decided not to even visit Richard at Hursley was that she would have heard that his position was intolerable. The creditors had arrived in force and became menacing in their demands for payment. Virtually all the money supposedly owed by Richard was in fact the legitimate expenses of the Protectorate. Apart from the cost for Oliver's funeral, typical items from Richard's schedule of debts were £3,700 for soldiers' winter uniforms and £6,090 for supplies to the Dunkirk Garrison.[4] The debts were government debts, but the Protectoral government was no more, so tradesmen felt the only way of obtaining their money was to extract it from poor Richard. On 18 April Richard had written to Monck to say his pursuit by creditors was going to make him go in to hiding. He then tried to put his affairs in order as best he could, resigning his last public office as Chancellor of Oxford University on 8 May.

In early July Richard secretly travelled to Lewes in Sussex where the captain of a small boat agreed to take him across the Channel to Dieppe, from where he went to live under an assumed name in Paris. Richard left behind his children, the 10-year-old Elizabeth, 4-year-old Oliver and Anne who was just 15 months old. It must have been a painful farewell. Dorothy's father, Richard Mayor, had died just three months before in April and so Dorothy would now have the responsibility of running the Hursley estate by herself. On top of that, she, was eight months pregnant and had no idea when she would see her husband again. It is perhaps as well that she did not know that Richard would not return to England for twenty years, by which time she would be dead.[5]

From the moment that Monck had set the wheels in motion for the restoration of the monarchy, Elizabeth must have been in continual fear about Royalist vengeance against her family. The exiled Charles Stuart had issued his terms for his return as king in the Declaration of Breda on 4 April 1660. This had included a general pardon to all who would recognise Charles as lawful king, but then added 'excepting only such persons as shall thereafter be excepted by Parliament'. It was this sting in the tail that would have been a worry for Elizabeth, particularly in respect of her sons Richard and Henry and her sons-in-law Fleetwood and possibly Claypole.

On 14 May, even before Charles returned, parliament had given an indication of those they would exempt from the pardon by ordering the arrest of all regicides. Although a few of Elizabeth's friends, such as Edward Walley and Hugh Peters, had signed the king's death warrant, the only close members of the family to do so had been Oliver himself and their son-in-law Henry Ireton. Death was no excuse in the eyes of parliament as the next day they passed a retrospective act of attainder against Oliver, Ireton and the President of the Court for King Charles' trial, John Bradshaw. When Charles was restored to the throne later in May, parliament began considering exactly who should be punished while debating the many other immediate pieces of business that required their urgent attention.

Elizabeth and her family had to wait until 29 August for the Act of *Free and General Pardon Indemnity and Oblivion* to be passed in order to discover what penalties they might face. During that time as the bill was passed between Commons committees and then between the Commons and

Lords, where names for exemption were added and removed. There were some grounds for hope when John Thurloe was released from the Tower on 27 June.[6] He had been arrested for High Treason back in May, but although thoroughly disliked by Royalists no evidence would stand up against him. While Elizabeth would have found this encouraging, Thurloe's knowledge of intelligence made him a special case who might be of possible use to the new regime. She had to wait another two months to discover whether this indicated general leniency.

To the great relief of Elizabeth and the family, the final Act reserved the death penalty exclusively for those who had signed Charles I's death warrant or had been directly involved in his trial and execution. The only close family member who this effected was Oliver's favorite sister Catherine. After the death of her husband, Roger Whetstone, Catherine had lived with Oliver and Elizabeth in the Cockpit before marrying Colonel John Jones. As Jones had been one of Charles I's judges, the Act resulted in him being held in the Tower and then executed in October. Elizabeth would have been very sad for Catherine to lose her husband, but less sad for John Jones himself, who as an ardent Republican had opposed Richard as Protector. Although much of Jones' estate was forfeited, fortunately Catherine and her children were allowed to keep his manor in Merionethshire. The Cromwell family were largely off the hook, but some of those close to them, such as Oliver's cousins Valentine Walton and Edward Walley, and Walley's son-in-law, Major-General William Goffe, were also regicides and so subject to the death penalty. Fortunately for these three, escape had been possible. They had been all been in hiding and by the time the Act was passed Walley and Goffe were far away in Boston, New England and Walton was in Hanau, Germany before fleeing again to live in Flanders disguised as a gardener.

The Act also added three people who were exempt from pardon and would be tried for treason rather than automatically being executed. These were Haselrig, Lambert and Vane, all of whom had been in custody for some time. Finally, the Act named twenty people who were also exempt a pardon but would be merely barred from all public offices and positions of trust. Oliver St John was one of this number as was Charles Fleetwood. As Fleetwood had no intention of returning to public life this mild penalty must have been a great relief to him and Bridget. They could continue to live quietly on his estate in reasonable comfort.

Elizabeth would have had a huge burden of worry removed when she heard about the contents of the Act. Although they had done no real wrong, Richard had been Lord Protector and Henry the Lord Lieutenant of Ireland. It could so easily have been that a vengeful parliament would have demanded their heads. What must have helped to dampen any over enthusiasm for revenge was the attitude of Charles II. He was not by nature a vengeful man and was more interested in healing the wounds of a bitterly divided nation and catching up on the pleasures and extravagances that he had missed in exile. Although Elizabeth's overriding fears had not materialised, she was by no means free from worry. Creditors had made their way to Narborough and hounded both John Claypole and herself for money. What was worse, some people took advantage of Elizabeth's vulnerability, burst into her properties and ransacked them looking for jewels and other valuables that were owned by the Protectorate, but which now belonged to the king. One such case was a fruiter's warehouse in Thames Street where she had stored some of her belongings.

In November Elizabeth wrote a petition to the king, which the new Secretary of State, Sir Edward Nicholas, endorsed: 'Old Mrs Cromwell, Noll's wife petition' and recorded:

> 'She was deeply sensible of the unjust imputation of detaining jewels that belonged to the King, which besides the disrepute, exposed her to loss and violence, as pretence of search for them. She was willing to swear that she knew of none such, and would prove that she never intermeddled with any public transaction to his present and late Majesty. She was ready to yield humble and faithful obedience to the government. She prayed therefore for protection, without which she could not expect in her old age a safe retirement in a place in his Majesty's dominions.'

In his reply Nicholas promised nothing, but said that the king was 'pleased to distinguish between the concernment of your petitioner, and those of her relatives who have been obnoxious'.[7]

Although Elizabeth and John Claypole were still plagued by creditors, she could at least relax to some extent at Narborough and enjoy the company of Bettie's children. She knew that Richard was safely out of the country, that Henry and his family seemed to be left alone in Chippenham and Bridget was living quietly in Stoke Newington without fear of reprisals against Fleetwood. There was of course the worry that their lands gained during the Commonwealth might well be confiscated and result in financial hardship, but at least they had their lives and liberty. One cheering aspect of the family was her daughter Mary. Her husband Viscount Fauconberg had of course joined Monck and expressed his loyalty to Charles II just before the Restoration. He was also the nephew of Lord Belasyse, one of the leaders of the Sealed Knot. Under these circumstances it was no surprise that in June he received the king's gracious pardon, then the next month was sufficiently trusted enough to be made Lord Lieutenant of the Bishopric of Durham and soon after Lord Lieutenant of the North Riding.

Fauconberg's Commonwealth past was forgotten, his considerable estates remained intact and he was in royal favour. This meant that Mary was not only safe, but married to a rich man who was a member of the House of Lords and enjoyed the king's patronage. Elizabeth must have found it a relief that one of her three daughters had actually benefitted from the Restoration and in time might be able to use some influence for other less fortunate members of the family. Elizabeth's only sadness about Mary was that, although she was indeed very happily married to Falconbridge, she had not yet had any children.

By the end of 1660 Elizabeth would have found that despite the Restoration she and her family were living safely and had the comfortable existence of gentry, or in Mary's case aristocracy. The so called 'Convention Parliament' that had restored the king was technically illegal as it had not been convened by a monarch. It was dissolved in December 1660 and a new parliament was summoned, which assembled on 8 May the next year. This was of a different make up from the Presbyterian dominated Convention Parliament and consisted of ardent Royalist Anglicans who wanted the full restoration of the Church of England and revenge against those who had opposed the king in the Civil War. This parliament is known to history as the 'Cavalier Parliament' and would remain in existence for the next eighteen years, trying to enforce Anglicanism and creating penalties for Non-Conformists; the form of religion practiced by members of the Cromwell family. This was to be distressing for them, but being of the gentry class, some had their own chaplains so would have been able to worship much as before, while formally attending their local Anglican church. An infinitely more distressing indication that the past had not been forgiven and forgotten was one of the last acts of the Convention Parliament; implementation of the act of attainder against Oliver, Henry Ireton and John Bradshaw.

On 30 January 1661, the anniversary of the execution of Charles I, the bodies of Oliver, Henry and Bradshaw were disinterred from Westminster Abbey, dragged on hurdles to Tyburn (now Marble Arch) where they were hanged, then later dismembered with the heads cut off and the bodies thrown into a pit. The three heads were stuck on iron tipped oak poles and set up on the roof of Westminster Hall. Oliver's was to remain there for over forty years before being blown down in a storm. The posthumous traitor's executions were horrifying for the Cromwell family, but they were accompanied by an even more distressing act, the removal of other members of the Cromwell family from Henry VII's Chapel. The body of Oliver's mother Elizabeth was exhumed as was his sister Jane's, who had been married to Desborough. Bridget not only had the horror of her husband Henry's body being hacked, scorned and desecrated, but the body of their little daughter Anne was dragged from its resting place. The bodies of Elizabeth, Jane and Anne were thrown without ceremony into a pit at St Margaret's, Westminster. Strangely the body of Bettie was left undisturbed. This may have been because it could not be located or because the belief had grown up that she had pleaded with her father for clemency towards Royalists.[8]

After the emotional shock of the dis-interments, life returned to quiet obscurity for Elizabeth, Frances and Bridget; and Mary resumed life as a peeress. However, the acts of vengeance continued. John Barkstead, John Okey and Miles Corbet, three of the regicides who had fled to the Continent, were kidnapped in Holland and returned to England for trial, then hanged, drawn and quartered. Hazelrig had died in the Tower, but in 1662 Vane and Lambert were charged with High Treason. Lambert threw himself at the mercy of the court and was sentenced to imprisonment first in Guernsey and then on Plymouth's Drake Island, where he died in the cold winter of 1683–84. Vane defended himself in court and was executed after Charles II had decided he was 'too dangerous to live'.

The King's Commissioners were sent to New England to hunt down Walley and Goffe. The two had been recognised in Boston, but managed to escape and after a long period of hiding, including living in caves, they eventually settled under assumed names in Hadley, Massachusetts where they spent the rest of their lives in constant fear of discovery. Bounty hunters began tracking down other regicides on the Continent. Ludlow had fled to Verney in Switzerland and two unsuccessful attempts were made to assassinate him. Stories of such reprisals would have made all members of the Cromwell family feel distinctly uneasy.

On the more positive side, some of those who had been close to Elizabeth managed to weather the storm of the Restoration. John Milton, Oliver's former Latin Secretary, had been released from gaol and possible execution after the intervention of Andrew Marvell, his former colleague. Marvell had managed masterly self-preservation with the new regime and became MP for Hull. Oliver's youngest sister, Robina, had died in 1660. Her second husband, the academic cleric John Wilkins, rather ungallantly declared that he had married Robina under duress and so successfully inveigled his way into favour and soon became Dean of Rippon then Bishop of Chester. The able Lockhart, husband of Robina's namesake, Oliver's niece, Robina Sewester, had been removed as ambassador to France and

Governor of Dunkirk and was allowed to quietly retire, but ten years later Charles II appointed him as a diplomat to France. Richard Beck, the husband of Oliver's other niece, Lavinia Whetstone, lost the knighthood given by Richard when he commanded the Protectorial Life Guards, but remained a Colonel after the Restoration. Most remarkable of all was Richard Ingoldsby, who had been a regicide, but who, after Richard's fall, had supported Monck and the Restoration. He insisted his cousin Oliver had forced him to sign the king's death warrant and was not only pardoned, but made a Knight of the Bath, a gentleman of the Privy Chamber and re-elected MP for Aylesbury.

The year 1662 brought a major blow to Elizabeth and the family when they heard that Bridget, Oliver's 'dear Biddy,' had died in June. Relations had of course been strained with Fleetwood and so to some extent with Bridget, but to die at the young age of 38 was tragic. Bridget was buried at St Anne's Church, Blackfriars, leaving seven small children. Fleetwood was devastated, but in time pulled himself together. Two years after Bridget's death he provided a mother for their children by marrying Lady Mary Haytopp and spent his remaining twenty-eight years living in seclusion on his estate at Stoke Newington.[9]

For Elizabeth to be predeceased by a second daughter must have been truly dreadful. She was 65 and the shocks of recent years were taking their toll. However, there would soon be some rare good news to console her. Henry had been allowed to retain much of the land he had acquired in Ireland and had bought Spinney Abbey at Wicken in Cambridgeshire from the Russells. Spinney Abbey was just five miles away from Chippenham, so Henry's wife Elizabeth would remain close to her family. Henry and Elizabeth were at last settled with a home of their own and Henry did his best to live quietly under the new regime. He put some effort into trying to demonstrate his allegiance to the monarchy, as is shown by the following extracts from summaries of two letters by him to Charles II's chief minister, the Earl of Clarendon.

In the first letter, dated February 1661, he claimed his actions in support of Cromwell were only those of a dutiful son and requested to retain his Irish lands: 'He begs that consideration of his temptations and necessities may be extenuate His Majesty's displeasure, and that he and his family may be allowed to live to expiate what he had done amis.' A second letter dated April 1662, after having been allowed to retain his lands, he stated: 'And I wish your lordship would add one favour more, which is to assure his most excellent majesty, and his royal highnes (how hard, or needless soever it bee to beleeve me) that few can wish their royall persons, family, or interest, more prosperity and establishment, then doth I.'[10]

About the time Henry and Elizabeth established themselves in Spinney Abbey it seems that his sister, the widowed Frances, came to know Elizabeth's brother, John Russell. They fell deeply in love and in spring 1663 got married at Dorothy and Richard's home of Hursley. Up to this time Frances had been living with her mother at Claypole's House. Elizabeth may well have attended the wedding, particularly after seeing Frances through her earlier grief, and also Henry and his wife Elizabeth, but we cannot be sure. Although the Cromwells were a close-knit family, weddings were small affairs in those days, and so they may not have been there. Nevertheless, the circumstances made it a truly family affair. Frances' mother must have been sad that she would be losing the company of her daughter, but relieved that she had recovered from the loss of Robert Rich and at last found happiness. Sir Francis Russell died the following year and John Russell inherited the baronetcy and estate. Frances then became 'Lady Russell' and the happy wife of a member of the upper gentry.[11]

Unfortunately, over the next year Elizabeth's health began to fail. This was not helped by the death of Bettie's 25-year-old daughter Martha, who she had helped to bring up since Bettie's own death. She was also still plagued by creditors, principally an apothecary called Robert Phelps who pursued her for £234 4s 2d for medicines supplied for both Bettie and Oliver. Although the enormous bill was at least partially fraudulent, Elizabeth paid it by selling her jewels for £300.[12] Elizabeth was not interested in ostentation, but it must have been very sad for her to part with jewellery with their memories of gifts from Oliver.

Elizabeth had now had four grandchildren die before her, not all that unusual for the times, but nevertheless very distressing. Henry came to visit Elizabeth at Narborough as her condition deteriorated. Mary also visited and wrote: 'My poor mother is so affecting a spectacle so I scarce know what to write … The Lord knows best what is best for us to suffer, and therefore I desire we may willingly submit to His will, but the condition she is in is very sad: the Lord help her and us to bear it.'[13] No doubt, Frances also visited and of course Elizabeth had Claypole and Bettie's remaining children with her. Someone who she would have loved to see, but who did not come, was her eldest son. Richard was in France or may have moved to Rome by this time, living under a number of assumed names, the principal one being 'Mr Clarke'. When he could, he wrote to Dorothy and the children, so Elizabeth would have heard from them that he was alive and well, if impecunious.

We do not know the illness from which Elizabeth suffered, but she died at the age of 67 in November 1665. She was buried at Northborough church on 19 November. The Cromwells were a close family and her departure would have been keenly felt by Henry, Mary, Frances and Bettie's children, to whom she had been something of a surrogate mother. The former Dowager Protectress had had a most amazing life married to one of the most prominent personalities of British history. Being a woman, it was not open to her at that time to directly influence that history, but she certainly had some influence on her husband's life. She had been his rock and seen him through his depression as a tenant farmer in St Ives, dramatic religious awakening and the emergence of his new life not only becoming a person of consequence in Ely, but a person who, four years later, had the confidence and local respect to return to the House of Commons and launch the career that, through a civil war, was to lead to his greatness.

Elizabeth's major contribution was to provide her husband with the love, support and encouragement that gave him the strength to achieve what he did. She made no famous speeches, took no part in government or carried out heroic acts on a battlefield, but she above all other women of her generation had the closest ringside seat to the great events of the time. There is no grave stone, plaque or marker to commemorate Elizabeth in Narborough church. This is, in a way appropriate, for a person who despite having been 'Her Serene Highness,' always remained unassuming. However, anyone who considers her life must conclude that despite her low profile and being largely forgotten in history, she must have been a lady of remarkable character.

John Claypole seems to have never recovered from Bettie's death and the fall of the Protectorate. Elizabeth had very probably given him much strength and support. After her death he continued to be pursued by creditors and neglected his estate. Although he remarried in 1670, he had an affair with a laundress then tried to disinherit his wife, resulting in long litigation, which brought about the sale of his ancestral manor of Narborough. He died an unhappy man in 1688 while living in chambers in the Middle Temple, by which time his children by Bettie had all predeceased him.

At the time of Elizabeth's death Claypole's financial circumstances were already out of hand, but it would have been a consolation to her that Henry was a prosperous landowner having retained most of his Irish estate. Also, that her two surviving daughters were more than comfortable, with Mary married to an aristocrat and Frances married in to the upper gentry. Mary and Frances remained as close as they had been since they were their father's 'two little wenches' and visited each other when time and distance permitted. Mary was of course the mistress of several mansions and estates, but Frances was the wife of a rich baronet so there was not so much difference in their life styles. A picture of Mary's life is given in an account by the Grand Duke of Tuscany who visited her and Sir John at their Chippenham manor after attending the Newmarket races with the king in 1669. The Grand Duke recalls that his host and hostess conversed with him in French and he was well entertained. He played a game of bowls, had their four children presented to him and looked through a telescope at Ely cathedral. One forms the impression that Frances lived a contented and privileged life.

Frances' happy existence was to be severely jolted later that year when her husband died at the age of only 37. The cause of death is not known, but it was a cruel blow for her to lose a second husband at so young an age. Not only had she lost the man she loved, but their eldest son William, who now became the fourth baronet, was only 17-years-old and too young to take over the effective running of the estate. Frances had been a rich woman in her own right as a result of the generous jointure she received on the death of Robert Rich. It seems that Frances was never able to fully accept giving up the luxurious life of a semi-princess in her father's court and was prone to extravagance. Grief at the loss of her husband appears to have led to her consoling herself with increased extravagance, which would lead to significant depletion of the estate by the time it came under William's control.

In 1669, the same year Frances lost her husband, Fauconberg was made ambassador Extraordinary to the Venetian Republic. On his journey there he delivered letters from Charles II to his sister the Duchess' Orleans with whom he stayed before paying his respects to King Louis. While he was away, Frances made extended visits to Mary at her house in Lincoln's Inn Fields to keep each other company. When Fauconberg returned to England the next year, he added to their mansions by buying Sutton Court in Chiswick and had a beautiful garden laid out there. A little later he purchased another town house in Soho Square. In 1673 Fauconberg succeeded his uncle Lord Bellasyse as Captain of the Band of Gentlemen Pensioners and was later made a member of the Privy Council. The close bond between Mary and Frances became even closer in 1683 when Mary's daughter Elizabeth married Fauconberg's nephew, Thomas Frankland, eldest son of the baronet, Sir William, of Thirkleby Hall, Yorkshire. Not only was this a good marriage for Elizabeth, but she and Thomas went to live in Chiswick, close to the Fauconbergs, and the young couple came to be regarded almost as their children.

Meanwhile, Henry Cromwell had been living a pleasant life as a member of the gentry with an annual income of £3,000 a year from his Irish estate on top of that from Spinney Abbey. This happy existence was brought to an untimely end in in 1674 when he died of gallstones at the young age of just 46. He left his estate to 'his dear and well beloved wife' Elizabeth. She lived thirteen more years looking after seven children and the estate by herself and was buried beside Henry in Wicken Church.

Two years after Henry's death, Richard's wife Dorothy died. It had been sixteen years since she had last seen him. Her life had been very difficult from the time Richard had found himself Lord Protector. She had been forced to cope with the anxieties of his overthrow, the debts, his flight abroad, fears of Royalist retribution and having to run an estate and family single handedly. With her father dead and husband gone, Dorothy remained at Hursley with her mother and only sister Anne. Before long her mother died, and her sister married John Dunch, of Pusey in Berkshire. Sadly, Anne was to die in November 1663 and John died three years later leaving three orphan daughters who then went to live at Hursley with Dorothy. She now had sole responsibility for them and her own four children and, at the same time, ran the Hursley estate.

We can only imagine the strains of Dorothy's life alone in the world and being mocked behind her back as the wife of 'Tumbledown Dick' or 'Queen Dick'. She had only heard from Richard very intermittently and that may not have brought much comfort. A surviving letter from Richard to one of their daughters during Elizabeth's final illness contains the words: 'Pray imbrace thy mother for me, she is deare to me. Desire her to keepe up her spirits, beg her to be cheerful.'[14] Whether Dorothy had continued to love her husband or had ended up blaming him for the situation he had left her and the family, we do not know. One thing is certain, and that is that Richard's brief time as Lord Protector had robbed her of the life of a happily married country gentlewoman.

In 1680 Richard decided it was safe enough for him to return to England using the name John Clarke. After Dorothy's death their son Oliver had taken over the Hursley estate and through poor management and extravagance slid it into debt. Richard briefly visited Hursley and saw the children he had had not seen for twenty years. Elizabeth was now 30, Oliver 23, Anne 21 and Dorothy 20. Dorothy was the baby born after Richard's departure and married a John Mortimer soon after his return, but died of child birth the next year. After his visit to Hursley Richard went to live in different places as Mr Clarke and eked out an existence on £120 settled upon him from the estate. Eventually he moved to Finchley as the lodger of a merchant called Thomas Pengelly paying 10s a week. One positive result of Richard's return to England was that he resumed contact with Mary and Frances. The Cromwell family bond remained strong and both sisters saw him discreetly from time to time.

The death of Charles II and the accession of his brother James II made little difference to Frances or Richard living in their quiet backwaters. For the Fauconbergs it was another matter. Fauconberg had been a fellow Privy Councillor with James when he was Duke of York and had even entertained him at Newburg when he and his wife came to Yorkshire during the plague back in 1665. Despite Fauconberg coming from a largely Catholic family he objected to James' pro-Catholic policies and, as a result, was removed from both the Privy Council and Lord Lieutenantship. This was no great hardship for Fauconberg and Mary as he remained a man of wealth and member of the House of Lords.

Fauconberg then joined with other peers to take a huge chance which could have gone spectacularly wrong and ended in him having his property seized and suffering a traitor's excruciating death. Fauconberg and other conspirators secretly communicated with William of Orange and invited him to take the Crown on behalf of his wife Mary, the Protestant daughter of King James. William invaded England, James fled to France in what became known as the 'Glorious Revolution' and William and Mary ruled as co-sovereigns. In April 1689 William rewarded Fauconberg by making him an earl. Mary became Countess Fauconberg–not a bad outcome for the daughter of the man who had executed William's great uncle and Mary's grandfather. Mary always tried to discreetly help members of the Cromwell family and continued to do so now her husband was in favour with the new monarchs. One example of this is that she persuaded Fauconberg to help her dead sister Bridget's son Henry to become a gentleman of the bedchamber to William III and later receive a commission in the dragoons and promotion to a major. Considering Henry's step-father was Charles Fleetwood, the Republic's Lord General, this was no mean feat.[15]

The Fauconbergs continued to thrive during William and Mary's reign, but Thomas' health failed and he died a much-respected man at the age of 73 in 1700. Mary and Thomas had had a happy life, but because there were no children the title and much of the large estate was passed to his brother's son. Mary, now dowager countess, was given Sutton Court and other London properties for life and was well provided for in terms of income, furnishings and coaches. Fauconberg also left an annuity of £50 to Frances. Mary and Frances were always close and Fauconberg's death brought them closer still as Frances went to live with Mary at Sutton Court. Frances' eldest son, Sir William, had been forced to sell the Chippenham estate twenty years before and, as a result, Mary had been a very frequent guest of her sister in the various Fauconberg residences.

In July 1712 news arrived that Richard had died at Cheshunt, in Hertfordshire, where he had lived for twelve years after his land lady, Mrs Pengelly, had moved there from Finchley. Richard's son Oliver had died seven years earlier, unmarried, with the estate mortgaged and a debt of £9,000. After Oliver's death there had been a long legal battle against Richard, instigated by the in-laws of his daughters over what little remained of the Hurley estate. Richard eventually won the case, but had to use his real name to do so and despite the upsetting legal wrangling, managed to remain on good terms with his daughters. Although Richard had good relations with his daughters, in his will he appointed Mary, his 'well beloved sister', as executrix and left everything to her. 'Everything', was not very much, but the will does show how close he was to her and probably indicates the help that she had given him over the years.

It had not been Richard's fate to remain the prosperous squire and happy family man enjoying country pursuits. An unkind Providence had turned his life upside down and brought him endless sadness. At Cheshunt he was described as 'a little and very neat old man with a most placid countenance'.[16] From this we may hope that he had come to terms with his tumultuous life and was satisfied with his moderately comfortable existence. He had died at the great age of 86. Until the record was broken by HM Queen Elizabeth II, Richard was England's longest living head of state. He did not possess the experience or temperament to rule the three nations at a time of deep financial crisis and an over powerful army. That said, he was a decent, amiable man who tried to do his duty. In more recent times he would probably have made a good constitutional monarch, with Dorothy a fitting consort. As it was he died an insignificant, rather impecunious old gentleman. Richard was buried in the vault at All Saints Parish church, Hursley, at last reunited with Dorothy after forty-two years.

Mary and Frances continued to live as reasonably contented widows through the reign of Queen Anne and into that of George I. They outlived the Stuart dynasty and the five monarchs who had replaced their father and brother as head of state. Mary and Frances stayed living in Sutton House in Chiswick and remained in high society. Frances would have been pleased that her children all prospered. Her son Sir William had the depleted, but still substantial family estate, her daughter Elizabeth had married a baronet who became Post Master General and of her two other sons, one became a general and the other, President of Bengal.

The redoubtable Mary had been known at court for her sharp wit and never hiding her pride in her father. In her later years she was described as being 'still fresh and gay although of great age'.[17] Bishop Burnet wrote of her as 'a wise and worthy woman'. She died in 1708 leaving £400 to Frances, together with a portion of her plate and other valuables including 'my carriage and one pair of my best coach horses and a set of coach harnesses'.[18] Sutton House was passed to Sir Thomas Frankland, her nephew and Frances' son-in-law. Other smaller legacies were left to some of her Cromwell nieces and nephews. Frances survived for another seven years living in a house in St Giles in the Fields, but no doubt regularly visiting her daughter Elizabeth at Sutton House. For her funeral in February 1720 Frances was not buried in St Giles, but beside her sister in Chiswick church. Oliver's 'two little wenches' inseparable to the last.

The last of the women who had been so important to Oliver had gone, sixty-two years after his own death. Mary had ended up with a long and happy life. Frances' life had been longer still, comfortable and reasonably contented, but marred by thirty-six years of widowhood. Poor Bridget's life was cut short, but she had a reasonably contented life with Fleetwood and her children, despite the anxieties of the Restoration. As for Oliver's favourite, Bettie, her untimely death had hastened his own and the eventual fall of the Commonwealth. The two principal women in Oliver's life were, of course, the two Elizabeths: Oliver's mother and wife. They were closest to him and although the records about them are few, we may be sure that they influenced him. Theirs was seldom, if ever, direct influence over Oliver's actions, but their shared religious belief, love, support and understanding must have helped provide him with the strength to achieve what he did. Few women in the seventeenth century had the opportunity to make history, but at the very least Cromwell's women saw history in the making and shared the amazing drama that was Cromwell's life.

Epilogue

The Commonwealth period, dominated as it was by Oliver Cromwell, is in many ways a *cul-de-sac* in British History. It was a revolutionary period in which England became a Republic for the first and only time and then evolved into a Protectorate. Much of the aristocratic former ruling class lost their estates and the country was ruled by the younger sons of gentry and men of humble origin who had risen to high rank in the army. The traditional world was turned upside down with the established church dismembered and the imposition of strictly enforced Puritan codes of conduct. The dramatic changes of this period, lasting just over ten years, were completely reversed by the Restoration of Charles II. The monarchy and old order returned and with it the House of Lords, bishops, Christmas, theatres, and traditional life.

Victors never give the vanquished a good press and the name of Oliver Cromwell will always have negative connotations. Some of these are quite justified, especially when judged out of context by modern standards 350 years later. Today we live in a largely secular age and find it near impossible to comprehend the religious zeal and intolerance of the seventeenth century. To us the type of spiritual fervour of Cromwell and the Puritans makes them appear unhinged, killjoys. For the Puritans, their uppermost concern was for the salvation of their immortal souls. Their salvation would be jeopardised by not strictly adhering to God's commandments or being separated from direct personal communion with God by Popish superstitious practices. It was in this context that Cromwell and the Puritans abolished Christmas, maypole dancing, theatres and many of the small joys of life. Today we regard Cromwell and the Puritans as wrong in their beliefs, which led to people being put in the stocks for swearing and the smashing of church ornaments and stained-glass windows. These Puritan anti-Papist beliefs led Cromwell to the massacres of Drogheda and Wexford Catholics. We may come to understand what motivated the extreme actions of Cromwell and the Puritans, but we can never forgive them.

It was as well for the nation that Cromwell died, the Protectorate and Commonwealth came to an end and the Restoration returned England to normality. The over powerful army was almost entirely disbanded, Dunkirk was sold to Louis XIV and it was almost as though the unfortunate episode of the Commonwealth's godly military rule had never been. However, there were still echoes of Cromwell's positive legacy. The execution of Charles I had made the point that no monarch was above the law and James II's high-handed actions to promote Catholicism let led to him losing the throne in the Glorious Revolution. The concept of the divine right of kings made way for the primacy of parliament and constitutional monarchy. Cromwell had united the three kingdoms of England, Scotland and Ireland; although this was undone at the Restoration, the United Kingdom would later be created by the Act of Union under Queen Anne. The capture of Jamaica was a small step towards the creation of a British Empire on which the sun never set. That empire was partially created by the British navy, which had won such respect under Cromwell, and his Ironsides in Flanders, who were the first to wear the red coats synonymous with the British Army. Something that Cromwell is not given credit for is religious toleration, largely because his efforts to achieve liberty of conscience were obstructed by parliament. In one area he did succeed: the Jews had been expelled from England in 1290, but Cromwell allowed them to return, practice their religion and engage in commerce. In 1664 Charles II confirmed the Jews' status as citizens and since that time a relatively few number of Jews have made a disproportionate contribution to all walks of British life.

Whether or not people are prepared to concede that there are some positive elements to Cromwell's legacy, nothing can detract from him as one of Britain's greatest generals. He introduced a new concept of close formation, tightly controlled cavalry warfare and recruited and trained his men to meet his new standard. He placed great emphasis on ensuring his men were properly equipped, and effectively cared for logistically. For this his men loved him and submitted to his iron discipline. He was brave in action and an inspiring leader whose strategic and tactical judgement would be the deciding factor in parliamentary success in the Civil Wars. To have achieved this having had no previous military experience before the age of 43 is even more remarkable. That this middle-aged East Anglian farmer should eventually become head of state is more remarkable still. Whatever one's views of Cromwell, it should be agreed that he was a great man. Even his arch-enemy, Charles II's minister the Earl of Clarendon, wrote in his 1667 *History of the Great Rebellion and Civil Wars in England* that Cromwell: 'would be looked upon by posterity as a brave bad man'.

Respect him or revile him, Oliver Cromwell is a giant of English history. He was a complex and difficult person, but a loving son, husband and father. It was this family who were closest to him and knew him best. This book has tried to describe the lives of the female members of his family, but in doing so it may provide a little insight into the man himself.

Appendix 1: Cromwell's Ancestors

Cromwell's Ancestors

Thomas Cromwell — **Kathrine Cromwell** = **Morgan Williams** **Sir Thomas Warren**
Earl of Essex d 1540   m Putney   Lord Mayor

Sir Richard Williams (Cromwell)   **Sir Ralph Warren**
d 1544   twice Lord Mayor

Sir Henry Cromwell = Joan Warren   **Sir William Steward = Catherine**   **Thomas Bourchier**   **Thomas Crane**
1537 -1603/4 'Golden Knight'   1538-1557   of Felstead, Essex   of Newton Tony, Wilts

Sir Oliver Cromwell   9 others   **Robert Cromwell = Elizabeth Steward**   **Sir James Bourchier = Frances Crane**
1563 -1555   (William, James,   1560 -1617   1565-1654   b c1560   b c1576
          Sir Henry, Col John, Philip,

Mary = Sir William Dunch (father of Edmund), Joan = Sir Francis Barrington
Frances = Richard Walley, Elizabeth = William Hampden (father of John Hampden)

Henry	Robert	Joan	Elizabeth	Catherine	Margaret	Anna	Jane	Robina	Oliver = Elizabeth
b/d 1595	b/d 1609	1594-?	1594-?	1597-?	1601-60	1603-47	1606-58	1610-60	1599-1658 1598-1665

Appendix 2: Cromwell's Siblings

Cromwell's Siblings

Sir Oliver Cromwell   9 others   **Robert Cromwell = Elizabeth Steward**   **Sir James Bourchier = Frances Crane**
1563 -1555?   1563?-1617   1565-1654   c 1560 -1635

Henry   **Robert**   **Joan**   **Elizabeth**
b/d Aug 95   b/ d.1609   1592-1601   1594 unmarried

Oliver = Elizabeth
1599-1658   1589-1665

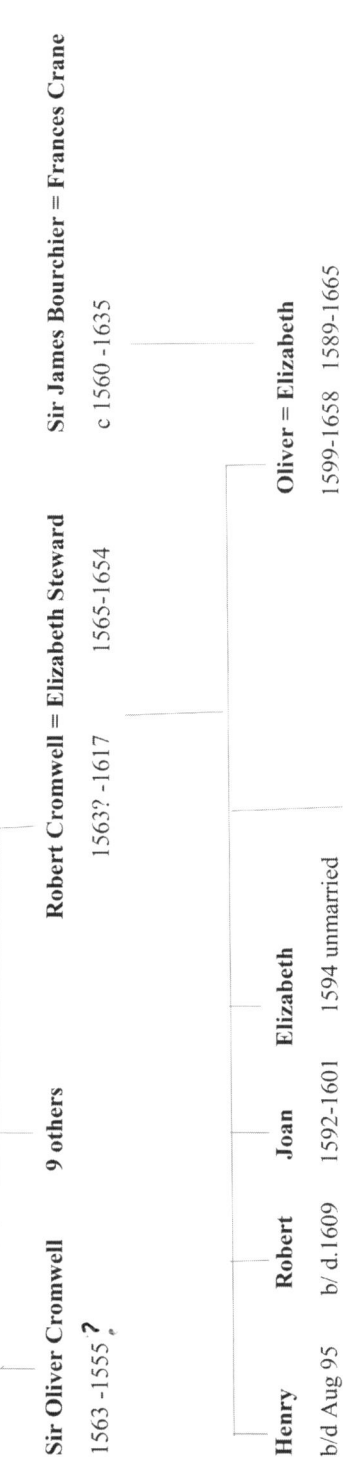

Anna= John Sewster, Catherine=[(1)]**Roger Whetstone,**   **Margaret=Valentine Walton,**   **Jane= John Desborough,**   **Robina =**[(1)]**Peter French**
1603-46   1597-?   ?-1655   1601-60   1594-1661   1606-58   1608-80   1610-60   ?- 1655

                         =[(2)]**Col John Jones**
                             1597-1660

=[(2)]**John Wilkins**
       1614-72

Lavinia = Colonel Richard Beck

Robina = Sir William Lockhart of Lee
       1621-75

Appendix 3: Cromwell's Children

Cromwell's Children

Oliver = Elizabeth Bourchier

Robert	Oliver	Bridget	Richard	Henry	Elizabeth	James	Mary	Frances
1621–1639	1623–1643	1624–1662	1626–1712	1628–1674	1629–1658	1632	1636–1713	1639–1721
		=	=	=	=		=	
		(1) Henry Ireton	Dorothy Mayor	Elizabeth Russell	John Claypole		Viscount Fauconberg	(1) Robert Rich
		1611–1651	c. 1620–1675	?–1687	1625–1688		c. 1627–1700	1611–1658
		(2) = Charles Fleetwood						(2) = Sir John Russell
		1618–1692						1632–1669
4 children		5 children	9 children	5 children	3 children			

Sir Thomas Frankland = Frances   Sir William
(nephew of Fauconberg)

Notes

Abbreviations used

Abbott — Wilbur Cortez Abbott, *The Writings and Speeches of Oliver Cromwell* (Oxford: Clarendon Press, 1988)
Burnet — *Bishop Burnet's History of his Life and Times* (London, 1715)
CSP Dom — *Calendar of State Papers Domestic* (London: Longmans, 1860)
DNB — *Oxford Dictionary of National Biography* (Oxford: Oxford University Press, 2004)
Henry Crom — Peter Gaunt, ed., *The Correspondence of Henry Cromwell* (Cambridge: Cambridge University Press, 2007)
Thurloe — *A Collection of the State Papers of John Thurloe* (London: Fletcher Gyles, 1742)

Chapter 1, The First Elizabeth, 1599–1620

1. Essex's antics in Ireland eventually led to his downfall. Instead of defeating Tyrone he made peace with him then returned to London against the Queen's orders and burst into her bedchamber, while she was un-gowned and without her wig, to beg her forgiveness. Elizabeth never fully forgave Essex, who unsuccessfully tried to raise a rebellion against Cecil, and was tried for treason and executed.
2. Antonia Fraser, *Cromwell Our Chief of Men* (London: Phoenix Press, 2000), p. 6.
3. *Cassell's History of England*, vol. 2 (London: Cassell and Company, 1901), p. 405.
4. Fraser, *Cromwell Our Chief of Men*, p. 13.
5. Huntingdon Grammar School is now the home of the Cromwell Society. Cromwell's house in the High Street was pulled down and a new one built on the site in about 1845.
6. Maurice Ashley, *Cromwell, The Conservative Dictator* (London: Jonathan Cape, 1937), p. 21.
7. The Falcon Inn no longer exists, but there is The Falcon Tavern near the same site in Princess Street, Huntingdon.
8. Fraser, *Cromwell Our Chief of Men*, p. 24.

Chapter 2, A Second Elizabeth, 1620–1629

1. The Cromwell Association, *Cromwell Four Centuries On*.
2. Barrington Hall was pulled down and replaced by a new building in 1735.
3. Ashley, *Oliver Cromwell The Conservative Dictator*, p. 21.
4. Barry Coward, *Oliver Cromwell* (London: Longman Group, 1991), p. 24.
5. Observation of the 5th of November Act 1605, it remained on statute books until repealed in 1859.
6. Maurice Ashley, *England in the Seventeenth Century (1603–1714)* (Middlesex, USA: Penguin Books, 1961), p. 61.
7. The Commons remained in the Chapel of St Stephen until 1833 when most of the Palace of Westminster was destroyed by fire.
8. *Cassell's History of England*, vol. 2, p. 535.
9. Arminianism is named after the Dutch cleric Jacobus Arminius who believed that salvation was open to all who had faith rather than the Calvinist doctrine that it was only those elected by God who would be saved.
10. Coward, *Oliver Cromwell*, p. 13.

Chapter 3, Crisis and Redemption, 1629–1638

1. Coward, *Oliver Cromwell*, p. 13; also Wilbur Cortez Abbott, *The Writings and Speeches of Oliver Cromwell*, vol. 1 (Oxford: Clarendon Press, 1988), pp. 64-5.
2. John Morrill, *Oliver Cromwell and the English Revolution* (London: Longman Group, 1990). A full account of the Fishbourne /charter incidents is on pp. 28-34.
3. Abbott, vol. 1, p. 68.
4. Slepe Hall was demolished in 1848 and nothing remains of Wood Farm, although it is thought by some to have become Green End Farm which used to stand at the junction of the Ramsey and Houghton Roads in St Ives.
5. Morrill, *Oliver Cromwell and the English Revolution*, p. 34.
6. Abbott, vol. 1, pp. 96-7.
7. Peter Gaunt, *Oliver Cromwell* (Oxford: Blackwell, 1997), p. 34.
8. Cromwell's house in Ely still exists and is open as a visitor attraction.
9. William Palmer, 'Oliver St John', *DNB*, vol. 48, p. 634.

Chapter 4, An MP's Wife, 1638–1642

1. Conrad Russell, 'John Hampden', *DNB*, vol. 24, p. 984 and Palmer, 'Oliver St John', p. 635.
2. Andrew Barclay, 'Oliver Cromwell and the Underground Opposition to Bishop Wren of Ely', in *Cromwell Four Centuries On* (The Cromwell Association, 2013), p. 16.
3. Abbott, vol. 1, p. 114.
4. John Morrill, 'Tempered Steel', in *Cromwell Four Centuries On*, p. 13.
5. Coward, *Oliver Cromwell*, p. 19.
6. Sir Philip Warwick, *Memoirs of the Reign of Charles I with a continuation to the Happy Restoration of King Charles II* (1701), p. 177.
7. Abbot, vol.1, p. 123.

Chapter 5, A Good Army Wife, 1642–1643

1. Abbott, vol. 1, p. 181.
2. Ibid., vol. 1, pp. 187-8.
3. Warwick, *Memoirs of the Reign of Charles I*, p. 177.
4. Keith Roberts, *Cromwell's War Machine, The New Model Army 1645–1660* (Barnsley: Pen & Sword, 2005), p. 98.
5. Thomas Carlisle, *The Letters and Speeches of Oliver Cromwell*, vol. 1 (London: Methuen & Co, 1902), p. 118.
6. Ibid., p. 116.
7. Coward, *Oliver Cromwell*, p. 27.
8. Robert W. Ramsey, *Henry Ireton* (London: Longmans Group, 1949), p. 15.

Chapter 6, A General's Family, 1643–1644

1. Fraser, *Cromwell our Chief of Men*, p. 109.
2. Burnet, vol., p. 175.
3. Carlisle, *Letters and Speeches*, vol. 1, p. 167.
4. Ibid., p. 167. The letter is dated 10 January 1644.
5. Fraser, *Cromwell our Chief of Men*, p. 117.
6. Abbott, vol. 1, p. 272.
7. Ibid.
8. As Oliver's letter to Warton makes no mention of his sister it is possible she may have died by this time. If so, she was spared the news of her son's death.
9. Abbott, vol. 1, p. 282.
10. Ibid., vol. 1, p. 299.

11. Fraser, *Cromwell our Chief of Men*, p. 139. For full speech see Abbott, vol. 1, pp. 302-311.
12. Coward, *Oliver Cromwell*, p. 37.

Chapter 7, Two War Brides, 1645–1647

1. Coward, *Oliver Cromwell*, p. 48.
2. Fraser, *Cromwell Our Chief of Men*, p. 17 and Ian J. Gentles, 'Henry Ireton', *DNB*, vol. 29, p. 344.
3. Abbott, vol. 1, p. 404.
4. Ashley, *Cromwell's Generals*, p. 67.
5. Fraser, *Cromwell Our Chief of Men*, p. 187.
6. Abbott, vol. 1, p. 495.
7. Ibid., p. 416.
8. Ibid., p. 585.
9. King Street is now Whitehall but the location of Oliver's house was between Great George Street and King Charles Street and now lies beneath the Treasury.

Chapter 8, Cruel Necessity, 1648–1650

1. Abbott, vol.1, p. 596.
2. Fraser, *Cromwell Our Chief of Men*, p. 268.
3. The Painted Chamber was burnt down with the rest of the Palace of Westminster, it was so called because the walls had Henry III's paintings of the Wars of the Maccabees. It was sometimes used as the House of Commons as was the case in 1605 when Guy Fawkes put his gunpowder in the cellars beneath it.
4. Abbott, vol. 1, p. 737 and Jacqueline Eales, 'Lady Anne Fairfax', *DNB*, vol. 18, p. 921.
5. Fraser, *Cromwell Our Chief of Men*, p. 292.
6. Abbott, vol. 2, p. 41.
7. Peter Gaunt, 'Elizabeth Cromwell', *DNB*, vol. 14, p. 312.
8. Carlisle, vol.1, *Letters and Speeches*, pp. 448-9.
9. Ibid, p. 452.
10. Fraser, *Cromwell Our Chief of Men*, p. 355.
11. Gaunt, *Oliver Cromwell*, p. 225.
12. Abbott, vol. 2, p. 330.
13. Carlisle, *Letters and Speeches*, vol. 2, p. 115.
14. The Cockpit is where Cabinet Office now stands in Whitehall. Whitehall Place was destroyed by fire in 1698.

15. Gaunt, 'Elizabeth Cromwell', p. 312.
16. Abbott, vol. 2, p. 375. The spelling indicates the disparity of education between the sexes.

Chapter 9, Finding a Settlement, 1651–1653

1. Ashley, *Cromwell's Generals*, p. 800.
2. Fraser, *Cromwell Our Chief of Men*, p. 379.
3. Carlisle, *Letters and Speeches*, vol. 2, pp. 189-90.
4. Ramsey, *Henry Ireton*, p. 185.
5. Gentles, 'Henry Ireton', p. 351.
6. Abbott, vol. 2, p. 412.
7. Carlisle, *Letters and Speeches*, vol. 2, p. 209.
8. Ramsey, *Henry Ireton*, pp. 199-201. John Evelyn's diary gives a good description of the funeral in his entry for 5 February 1652.
9. Abbott, vol. 2, p. 508.
10. Ibid., vol. 2, p. 521.
11. Ibid., vol. 3, p. 756.
12. Ibid., vol. 2, p. 571.
13. Hill, *English Civil War*, p. 133. Letter from Venetian ambassador, 30 May 1653.

Chapter 10, Their Serene Highnesses, 1654–1655

1. Firth, *Memoirs of Edmund Ludlow*, vol. 1, p. 379.
2. Hill, *English Civil War*, p. 138. Letter from Venetian ambassador, 4 July 1653.
3. Ibid., p. 168. Letter from the Venetian ambassador, 11 January 1654.
4. Ibid., p. 175. Letter from the Venetian ambassador, 21 February 1654.
5. Sherwood, *Court of Oliver Cromwell*, p. 25.
6. Firth, *Memoirs of Edmund Ludlow*, vol. 1, p. 380.
7. Philip Aubrey, *Mr Secretary Thurloe Cromwell's Secretary of State 1652–1660* (London: Athlone Press, 1990), p. 46.
8. Hill, *English Civil War*, p. 203. Letter from Venetian ambassador, 20 September 1654.
9. Fraser, *Cromwell Our Chief of Men*, p. 458.
10. Hill, *English Civil War*, p. 221. Letter from Venetian ambassador, 6 December 1654).
11. Firth, *Memoirs of Edmund Ludlow*, vol.1, p. 329.
12. Sherwood, *Court of Oliver Cromwell*, p. 97.
13. The fountain with many statues no longer exists but the Diana statue may be seen today in the centre of the Bushey Park fountain.

222   Cromwell and his Women

14. Sherwood, *Court of Oliver Cromwell*, p. 134.
15. Robert Latham and William Matthews, eds, *The Diary of Samuel Pepys*, (London: G. Bell and Sons, 1971), p. 296.
16. Boyle, *A Collection of State Papers*, pp. 41-43.
17. Fraser, *Cromwell Our Chief of Men*, p. 544.
18. Abbott, vol. 3, p. 802.
19. Christopher Durston, *Cromwell's Major Generals, Godly Government During the English Revolution* (Manchester: Manchester University Press, 2001), p. 3.
20. Wallingford House was on the site of the Old Admiralty Building and the Council Chamber was on what is now the car park between the Banqueting House and the Ministry of Defence.
21. Robert W. Ramsey, *Studies in Cromwell's Family Circle and Other Papers* (London: Longmans Group, 1930), p. 24.
22. *Henry Crom*, p. 85. Letter from William Stane, dated 10 December 1655.

Chapter 11, A Future Queen?, 1656–1657

1. E. S. De Beer, *Diary of J Evelyn*, vol. 2 (Oxford: Clarendon Press, 1955), p. 323. Entry for 11 February 1656.
2. Sherwood, *The Court of Oliver Cromwell*, p. 34.
3. *The Court and Kitchen of Elizabeth Commonly called Joan Cromwell wife of the late Usurper Truly Described and Represented and now Made for General Satisfaction* (Peterborough: Cambridgeshire Libraries, 1983), p. 36.
4. Sherwood, *The Court of Oliver Cromwell*, p. 60.
5. Ibid, p. 110.
6. Abbott, vol. 4, p. 314. Letter from Venetian ambassador, 10 November 1656.
7. Firth, *Memoirs of Edmund Ludlow*, p. 379.
8. Julian Whitehead, *Cavalier and Roundhead Spies* (Barnsley: Barnsley, 2009), pp. 178-80.
9. Sherwood, *The Court of Oliver Cromwell*, p. 81.
10. Abbott, vol. 4, p. 914.
11. Ibid, p. 124.
12. Fraser, *Cromwell Our Chief of Men*, p. 542.
13. Charlotte Fell Smith, *Mary Rich Countess of Warwick 1625–1678* (London: Longmans, 1901), p.137. Letter from Mary Cromwell to Henry Cromwell, 23 June 1656.

Notes 223

14. *Henry Crom*, p. 149. Letter from Fleetwood to Henry Cromwell dated June 1656.
15. Smith, *Mary Rich Countess of Warwick 1625–1678*, pp. 138-9.
16. Abbott, vol. 4, p. 420.
17. *Henry Crom*, p. 221. Letter from Richard Cromwell dated 7 March 1657.
18. Ibid, p. 260. Letter from Whalley to Henry Cromwell dated 14 April 1657.
19. Abbott, vol. 4, p. 514.

Chapter 12, Uncertain and Giddy Times, 1657–1658

1. Sherwood, *The Court of Oliver Cromwell*, p. 55.
2. *Henry Crom*, p. 145. Letter from Sir Francis Russell to Henry Cromwell dated 23 June 1656.
3. Ibid., p. 520. Undated letter.
4. Abbott, vol. 4, p. 602.
5. Ibid., p. 578.
6. David C. Hanrahan, *Charles II and the Duke of Buckingham* (Stroud: Sutton Publishing, 2006), p. 39.
7. Abbott, vol. 4, pp. 661-2.
8. Trevor Royal, *Civil War: The War of the Three Kingdoms 1638–1660* (London: Little, Brown, 2004), p. 735.
9. Ramsey, *Studies in Cromwell's Family Circle and Other Papers*, p. 172.
10. Fraser, *Cromwell Our Chief of Men*, p. 643.
11. *Henry Crom*, p. 353. Letter from Mary Fauconberg to Henry Cromwell dated 1 December 1657.
12. N. K. Keeble, ed., *Memoirs of the Life of Colonel John Hutchinson* (London: Phoenix Press, 2000), p. 256.
13. Fraser, *Cromwell Our Chief of Men*, p. 651.
14. Ibid.
15. *Henry Crom*, p. 387. Letter from Frances Rich to Henry Cromwell dated 19 June 1658.
16. The Earl of Warwick's immediate heir was the ailing Lord Rich, whose only son had been Robert. Lord Rich was briefly third earl then died and the earldom passed to his uncle.
17. *The History of the Rebellion and Civil Wars in England Beginning in the Year 1641*, VI (Oxford: Clarendon Press, 1958), p. 65.
18. Andrew Marvell, *A Poem upon the Death of His Late Highness the Lord Protector: The Poems and Letters of Andrew Marvell*, ed. H. M. Margoliouth, vol. 1 (Oxford: Clarendon Press, 1971), p. 129.

19. Sherwood, *The Court of Oliver Cromwell*, p. 126.
20. Newburg Priory was an Augustinian priory acquired by the Bellasyse family at the dissolution of the monasteries and modified by them into a fine mansion. Today it is lived in by the Wombwell family and is open to the public.
21. Robert W. Ramsey, *Richard Cromwell Protector of England* (London: Longmans, Green and Co., 1933), p. 32.
22. Marvell, *A Poem upon the Death of His Late Highness the Lord Protector*.

Chapter 13, A New Protector, 1658–1659

1. George Fox, *The Journal of George Fox* (Cambridge: Cambridge University Press, 1911), p. 327.
2. Fraser, *Cromwell Our Chief of Men*, p. 676.
3. Thurloe, vol. 7, p. 22. Letter from Thurloe to Henry Cromwell dated 7 September 1658.
4. Ramsey, *Richard Cromwell Protector of England*, p. 43, and Thurloe, vol. 7, p. 355.
5. Ramsey, *Richard Cromwell Protector of England*, p. 44.
6. Abbott, vol. 5, p. 875.
7. Ramsey, *Richard Cromwell Protector of England*, p. 69.
8. Ibid., p. 84.
9. Thurloe, vol. 7, p. 666. Letter Barwick to Hyde, 2 May 1659. For more on the fascinating espionage career of Rev John Barwick see *Cavalier and Roundhead Spies*.
10. Ramsey, *Richard Cromwell Protector of England*, p. 149.
11. *Henry Crom*, p. 516. Letter from Richard Cromwell to Henry Cromwell dated 17 May 1659.
12. Clarke, William, *The Clarke Papers V: Further Selections from the Papers of William Clarke*, ed. Frances Henderson (London: Cambridge University Press, 2005), p. 293. Letter from Richard Cromwell to Monck, 7 May 1659.
13. Narborough is now known as 'Northborough' and is today in Cambridgeshire.
14. Ramsey, *Richard Cromwell Protector of England*, p. 101.
15. Firth, *Memoirs of Edmund Ludlow*, p. 179.
16. Maurice Ashley, *Cromwell's Generals* (London: Jonathan Cape, 1954), p. 216.

Chapter 14, Survival, 1660–1720

1. Clarke, *The Clarke Papers V*, p. 167. Letter to Clarke dated 6 December 1659.
2. Thurloe, vol. 7, p. 669. Letter from Monck to Fleetwood, 12 May 1659.
3. Narborough is now called Northborough and has moved into Cambridgeshire.
4. Ramsey, *Richard Cromwell Protector of England*, p. 98.
5. Ibid, p. 119.
6. Aubrey, *Mr Secretary Thurloe*, p. 163.
7. Donald Nicholas, *Mr Secretary Nicholas 1592–1669* (London: The Bodley Head, 1955), p. 301; *CSP Dom* 1660, p. 392.
8. There is now a small stone memorial to Bettie just north of the Henry VII monument. The wording is not as impressive as that on her coffin which was: 'The body of the most illustrious Lady Elizabeth late wife of the Rt. Hon. Lord John Claypole, Master of the Horse, and second daughter of the most serene & mighty prince Oliver by the grace of God of England Scotland & Ireland etc. Protector. She died at Hampton Court on the sixth day of August in the 28th year of her age and in the year of our Lord 1658.'
9. Tony Barnard, 'Charles Fleetwood', *DNB*, vol. 20, p. 22.
10. *CSP Dom* 1660, p. 519 and Gaunt, 'Elizabeth Cromwell', p. 319.
11. *Henry Crom*, p. 414.
12. Ramsey, *Studies in Cromwell's Family Circle*, p. 26.
13. Gaunt, 'Elizabeth Cromwell', p. 312.
14. Peter Gaunt, 'Richard Cromwell', *DNB*, vol. 11, p. 364.
15. Ramsey, *Studies in Cromwell's Family Circle*, p. 55.
16. Fraser, *Cromwell Our Chief of Men*, p. 687.
17. Ramsey, *Studies in Cromwell's Family Circle*, p. 59.
18. Ibid., p. 61.

Bibliography

Anon, *The Court and Kitchen of Elizabeth Commonly called Joan Cromwell wife of the late Usurper Truly Described and Represented and now Made for General Satisfaction* (Peterborough: Cambridgeshire Libraries, 1983)

Abbott, Wilbur Cortez, *The Writings and Speeches of Oliver Cromwell* (Oxford: Clarendon Press, 1988)

Ashley, Maurice, *Cromwell: The Conservative Dictator* (London: Jonathan Cape, 1937)

——, *Cromwell's Generals* (London: Jonathan Cape, 1954)

——, *England in the Seventeenth Century (1603–1714)* (Middlesex, USA: Penguin Books, 1961)

Aubrey, Philip, *Mr Secretary Thurloe Cromwell's Secretary of State 1652–1660* (London: Athlone Press, 1990)

Barclay, Andrew, *Electing Cromwell: The Making of a Politician* (Abingdon: Routledge, 2016)

Burnet, Gilbert, *Bishop Burnet's History of his Life and Times* (London: 1715)

Calendar of State Papers Domestic (London: Longmans, 1860)

Carlisle, Thomas, *The Letters and Speeches of Oliver Cromwell* (London: Methuen & Co, 1902)

Cassell's *History of England* (London: Cassell and Company, 1901)

Clarendon, Edward Earl of, *Clarendon State Papers* (Oxford: Clarendon Press, 1970)

——, *The History of the Rebellion and Civil Wars in England Beginning in the Year 1641* (Oxford: Clarendon Press, 1958)

Clarke, William, *The Clarke Papers V: Further Selections from the Papers of William Clarke*, ed. Frances Henderson (London: Cambridge University Press, 2005)

Cooper, John, *The Cromwell Family* (London: Stanley Thomas, 1981)

Coward, Barry, *Oliver Cromwell* (London: Longman Group, 1991)

The Cromwell Association, *Cromwell Four Centuries On* (2013)

De Beer, E.E., *Diary of J Evelyn* (Oxford: Clarendon Press, 1955)

Durston, Christopher, *Cromwell's Major Generals, Godly Government During the English Revolution* (Manchester University Press, 2001)

Firth, C.H., *Memoirs of Edmund Ludlow* (Oxford: Clarendon Press, 1894)

Fox, George, *The Journal of George Fox* (Cambridge: Cambridge University Press, 1911)

Fraser, Antonia, *Cromwell Our Chief of Men* (London: Phoenix Press, 2000)
Gaunt, Peter, ed., *The Correspondence of Henry Cromwell* (Cambridge: Cambridge University Press, 2007)
——, *Oliver Cromwell* (Oxford: Blackwell, Oxford, 1997)
Hanrahan, David C., *Charles II and the Duke of Buckingham: The Merry Monarch & the Aristocratic Rogue* (Stroud: Sutton Publishing, 2006)
Hill, Christopher, *The English Civil War: A Contemporary Account* (London: Caliban Books, 1996)
Hopper, Andrew, *Black Tom: Sir Thomas Fairfax and the English Revolution* (Manchester University Press, 2007)
Hutchinson, Lucy, *Memoirs of the Life of Colonel John Hutchinson* (London: Phoenix Press, 2000)
Keeble, N. K. ed, *Memoirs of the Life of Colonel John Hutchinson* (London: Phoenix Press, 2000)
Knoppers, Laura Lunger, *Constructing Cromwell* (Cambridge: University Press, 2000)
Latham, Robert and William Matthews, *The Diary of Samuel Pepys* (London: G. Bell and Sons, 1971)
Morrill, John, *Oliver Cromwell and the English Revolution* (London: Longman, 1990)
Nicholas, Donald, *Mr Secretary Nicholas 1592–1669* (London: the Bodley Head, London, 1955)
Nobel, Mark, *Memoirs of the Protectorate House of Cromwell and the story of Dunkirk* (Birmingham: 1887)
Oxford Dictionary of National Biography (Oxford: Oxford University Press, 2004)
Peterson, R. T., *Sir Kenelm Digby: The Ornament of England 1603–1665* (London: Jonathan Cape, 1956)
Ramsey, Robert W., *Henry Ireton* (London: Longmans Group, 1949)
——, *Richard Cromwell Protector of England*, (London: Longmans, Green and Co, 1933)
——, *Studies in Cromwell's Family Circle and Other Papers* (London: Longmans Group, 1930)
Razzell, Edward and Peter, *The English Civil War: A Contemporary Account Vol 4 1648–56* (London: Caliban Books, 1996)
Roberts, Keith, *Cromwell's War Machine, The New Model Army 1645–1660* (Barnsley: Pen & Sword, 2005)
Roots, Ivan, *Commonwealth and Protectorate, The English Civil War and its Aftermath* (Westport: Greenwood Press, 1966)

Royal, Trevor, *Civil War: the War of the Three Kingdoms 1638–1660* (London: Little, Brown, 2004)

Sherwood, Roy, *The Court of Oliver Cromwell* (Totowa USA: Rowman and Littlefield, 1977)

——, *Oliver Cromwell King in all but Name 1653–1658* (Stroud: Sutton Publishing, 1997)

Smith, Charlotte Fell, *Mary Rich Countess of Warwick 1625–1678* (London: Longmans, 1901)

Thurloe, John, *A Collection of the State Papers of John Thurloe* (London: Fletcher Gyles, 1742)

Warwick, Sir Philip, *Memoirs of the Reign of Charles I with a Continuation to the Happy Restoration of King Charles II* (London: 1701)

Waylen, James, *The House of Cromwell and the Story of Dunkirk* (London: Chapman and Hall, 1897)

Wedgewood, C. V., 'The Cromwells at Whitehall', London: *History Today* 1958), vol. 8

Whitehead, Julian, *Cavalier and Roundhead Spies* (Barnsley: Pen and Sword, 2009)

Index

(Titles awarded in the Protectorate shown in brackets)

Abbot, George, Archbishop of Canterbury, 39
Alabaster, Rev William, 27
Argyll, Archibald Campbell, Earl then Marquis of, 45, 102, 106, 112, 117, 127, 143
Ashley Cooper, Sir Anthony, later Earl of Shaftesbury, 144

Barkstead, Colonel (Sir) John, 154, 157, 203
Barbon/Barebones, Praisegod, 129
Barnard, Robert, 30-2, 36, 71
Barrington, Sir Francis and Lady, 13, 16, 401
Barwick, Rev John, Royalist spy, 186
Beard, Dr Thomas, 9-11, 16, 19, 27, 29-32, 36
Becke, Colonel (Sir) Richard, 150, 158, 174
Bedford, William Russell, Earl of, 40, 42
Belasyse, John, Baron, 201
Belasyse, Thomas, Viscount, later Earl of Fauconberg (husband of Mary C),162-3, 168-9, 171-2, 176-9, 181, 184, 188-9, 193, 201-2, 207, 209
Belvoir Castle 83
Blake, Admiral Robert 145, 110, 170
Bohemia, 20, 114
Bonde, Count Christer, 146
Boteler, Colonel William, 153
Bourchier, Sir James (C's father-in-law), 13, 23, 40

Bourchier, Frances, Lady, 13
Bradshaw, John, 103, 124, 195, 199, 202
Bristol, 73, 91, 108, 111, 123, 179, 182
Broghill, Roger Boyle, Baron, 144, 158
Brooke, Robert Greville, Baron, 144, 158
Buckingham, Duke of *see* Villiers
Burleigh House, siege of, 72

Cadiz, 23
Cambridge, 10-1, 37, 40, 49, 52, 55-6, 60, 62-3, 66-7, 70, 73, 82, 90
Cantenerio Conde de, 137
Carisbrooke Castle, 98, 103
Cecil, John, 157
Cecil, Robert, Earl of Salisbury, 3, 7
Chalgrove Field, skirmish, 74
Condé, Prince de, 144-5, 189
Corbet, Miles, MP, regicide, 203
Crane, Eluzai, (C's aunt and wife of Sir Henry Cromwell), 13
Crawford, Major-General Lawrence, 83
Claypole, (Baron, Sir) John (C's son-in-law), 92, 118, 130, 138, 146, 152, 166, 171, 173, 179, 184, 188, 196, 198-9, 201-2, 206
Crequi, Duc de, 176-8
Crowland Abbey, 72
Cromwell, Anna (C's sister Mrs Sewster), 28-9, 9, 15, 25, 94
Cromwell, Bridget (C's daughter, Mrs Ireton then Mrs

Fleetwood), 18, 47, 56, 65: and Ireton, 73, 77, 86, 89, 90-8, 103, 110, 116-9, 122-4; and Fleetwood,126-7, 135-6, 146-7, 152, 166-7, 174, 181, 184, 188, 191-3, 200-4
Cromwell, Catherine (C's sister, Mrs Whetstone then Mrs Jones), 6, 9, 25, 110, 122, 150, 200
Cromwell, Dorothy Lady Protectress (née Major wife of Richard Cromwell), marriage to Richard, 96, 100, 107-9, 112-3, 120, 146, 152, 170,173, 178-9; as Lady Protectress, 181-2, 184, 186-7, 190; post Restoration, 205, 208, 210
Cromwell, Elizabeth C's mother née Steward), ancestry and first marriage, 4; marriage to Robert, 4-11; life with C in Huntingdon, 11-22, 25-6, 29, 32, 37; with C in Ely, 37-93; with C in London, 93-death, 140-1, 203
Cromwell, Elizabeth (C's sister), 5, 15, 25, 33, 38, 47, 93, 124
Cromwell, Elizabeth (C's wife née Bourchier) ancestry, 13; life in Huntingdon, 13-32; life in St Ives, 32-37; life in Ely, 37-63; Army wife, 63-93; life in London, 93-132; Protectress,133-183; Protectress Dowager, 183-205; post Restoration, 189-205; letters,113, 114, 117,119; death, 205-6
Cromwell, Elizabeth (C's daughter Bettie, Lady Claypole) early life, 28, 47; marriage to Claypole,92, 117-8, 138; health,148,152, 159, 168, 171, 176-9; death, 179-80, 203, 205-6
Cromwell, Elizabeth (C's cousin Mrs Hampden), 16, 23, 34
Cromwell, Elizabeth (C's aunt Lady Ingoldsby), 16
Cromwell, Elizabeth (C's daughter-in-law née Russell wife of Henry), 129-30, 137-8, 146, 167-8, 187, 204-5, 208
Cromwell, Frances (C's daughter Lady Rich then Lady Russell), early life, 47, 56, 73, 79, 93, 95-6, 110, 122; 'Lady Frances' 134-5, 139, 143-4, 146, 161; Lady Rich, 161-3, 168-9, 171-2, 175-8, 183, 188; Restoration, 195, 198; Lady Russell, 205-10, 211
Cromwell, Henry (son of Sir Oliver), 47, 60, 63, 100
Cromwell, Sir Henry (C's grandfather), 3-5, 7-8
Cromwell, Sir Henry (C's uncle), 13, 17, 34, 39
Cromwell, (Sir) Henry (C's son), early life 23, 33, 47, 55, 82, 90, 102; Ireland 110, 123, 126, 129; marriage, 29-30; 'Lord' Henry, 134-8; Lord Deputy, 141, 146, 148, 153, 161, 163, 167-8, 170, 172-3, 175, 181, 184, 187; fall of Richard, 187-8; post Restoration, 199-201, 204-8
Cromwell, Jane (C's sister, Mrs Desborough), 9, 15, 33, 38, 155-6, 203
Cromwell, Joan (C's aunt, Lady Barrington), 13, 16, 40-1

Cromwell, Margaret (C's sister Mrs Walton), 9-10, 16, 63, 81-2
Cromwell, Mary (C's daughter, Lady Fauconberg),early life, 39, 47, 56, 73, 93, 96, 110, 118, 122, 129; 'Princess Mary' 134-5, 137, 139, 143-4, 146, 161; marriage,162-3, 168-9,172; as viscountess, 176-8, 181, 188-9; post Restoration, 201-3, 205-9; widowhood and death, 209-11
Cromwell, Mary (C's aunt Lady Dunch), 16, 24, 44, 117
Cromwell, Sir Oliver (C's uncle), 4, 6-9, 11, 16, 20-3, 60, 63, 72, 100
Cromwell, Oliver, ancestry and family background, xi, 4-8; appearance, 14, 54; education 9-11; based in Huntingdon 10-32, 36; based in St Ives 32-37; based in Ely 37- 93; finances, 17, 32, 37, 50, 60, 64-5, 76, 82, 91-2, 124, 126, 167-9; health and depression, 27-8, 111, 117, 139, 148, 171, 179-80, 205; marriage, 13-4; military career: Civil War, 63-107; Ireland 108-111; Scotland112-122; Mother, relations with 10-12, 93-99, 140-1, MP, 22-7, 48-51, 52-128; pastimes, 10, 17, 139, 143, 171-2, 177; Protector, 130-183; spiritual conversion, 34-5, wife, relations with, 93-4,113,117-8, 119, 148, 179; death 180-183, attainder 199, 202-3
Cromwell, Oliver (C's son), 33, 40, 47-8, 55, 64, 67-9, 72, death 79
Cromwell, Richard, Lord Protector (C's son), early life, 21, 23, 47, 55, 82, 96; marriage, 106-9, 112, 118, 120; 'Lord' Richard, 130, 135, 146, 152, 163, 173, 178-9; Protector,179-86; fall,186, 188, 190, 195-9; flight and later life, 199, 205, 208-10
Cromwell, Robert (C's son), 33, 40, 47-8
Cromwell, Robert (C's father), 4-10
Cromwell, Robina (C's sister Mrs French then Mrs Wilkins), 9, 15, 25, 33, 38, 150, 152, 203
Cromwell, Thomas, Earl of Essex, 5
Cropredy Bridge, Battle of, 83

Davenant, William, 148
Desborough, Jane née Cromwell, 38, 155-6, 203
Desborough, Major-General John, 38, 66, 73, 91, 121, 129, 147, 155-6, 164, 166, 174, 183-6, 188, 190, 192-3, 203
Devonshire, Christina Cavendish, Countess of, 171
Donnington Castle, siege of, 84
Downhall, Henry, 33-4
Drogheda, siege of, 109, 111, 212
Dunbar, Battle of, 112, 114, 120-1, 181
Dunch Edmund, (Baron Burnell), 173, 24, 44
Dunch, John, 208
Dunes, Battle of, 177
Dunkirk, 43, 159, 177-8, 204, 212
Duret, Jean, 117, 153
Dutton, William, 161
Drury Lane, 93, 98

Edgehill, Battle of, 68-9
Eliot, Sir John, 27

Elizabeth I, Queen of England, xi, 3, 5-6, 18-19
Elizabeth, Queen of Bohemia, 20, 114
Ely, 32, 37-9, 42, 46, 71-3, 77, 88, 92-3, 124, 129, 207
Essex, Robert Devereux, 3rd Earl of, 3
Evelyn, John 151, 195

Fairfax, Sir Thomas, later Baron as a general,76, 80-1, 88-92, 95-8, 101-3, 105-6, 111; in retirement,169, 181; at Restoration, 193
Fairfax, Lady Anne, 92, 96; at trial of Charles I, 104; pleading for Buckingham, 169-70
Fairfax, Mary, Duchess of Buckingham, 169
Fairfax, Ferdinando Baron, 71, 73, 76, 80-1
Fauconberg, Viscount, later Earl see Belasyse
Feltham, John, 26
Felsted, Little Stanbrook Hall, 13, 40, 48
Felsted School, 40, 47, 55, 82
Finch, Sir John, Lord Keeper, 49
Fishbourne, Richard, 29-30, 32, 36
Fleetwood, Lieutenant-General Charles, as soldier, 73, 86, 94-5, 109, 112, 117, 120-2, 126-7; marriage to Bridget C, 127; in Ireland 130, 135-7,141,144, 146; in 1st Protectorate court, 146-7, 152, 158, 161, 164, 166-7, 173-4, 179; 2nd Protectorate, 181, 183-97; fall, 193, 197; post Restoration, 199-201, 204, 209

Flemming, Sir Oliver, 146
Fowey, 83
Frankland, Sir Thomas, 207, 211
French, Thomas, 49-50, 62
French, Peter Dr, 49, 65, 150
Fuller, Willian, Dean of Ely, 55

Gainsborough, siege of, 72-3, 76
Gloucester, Henry Duke of (son of Charles I), 103, 105, 125
Godmanchester, 6, 8, 34
Goffe, William, Major-General, 104, 186, 200, 203
Goring, George, Baron, 61, 80-1, 89
Grand Remonstrance, 56, 60-1, 64, 53
Grey, William Baron of Warke, 70-1, 74

Harrison, Major-General Thomas, 90, 98, 104, 128-9, 163, 183
Hammond, Colonel Robert, 93
Hampden, John, 24, 43-4, 49-56, 60-2, 66, 68, 74, 78, 98
Hampden, William, 16
Haselrig, Sir Arthur, 54, 79, 105, 112, 124, 173-4, 185, 188-9, 191-2, 196, 202
Haytop. Lady Mary (third wife of Charles Fleetwood), 209
Herbert, Henry Somerset, Lord Herbert later Marquis of Worcester and Duke of Beaufort, 118, 134
Hewett, Rev John, 172, 176-7
Hillesdon House, 79
Hingston, John, 143, 148
Hinchingbrooke House, 3, 5, 7-8, 16-7, 20-3, 29-30, 74
Hitch, Rev, 77-8

Hispaniola, 77-8
Holbeach. Martin, 40
Holdenby Hal,l 95
Holland, Henry Rich, Earl of, 49
Holles, Denzil, 53-4, 56, 62, 78, 86, 94, 102, 124
Hopton, Sir Ralph, later Baron, 73, 92
Hotham, Sir John, 59, 61, 64
Howard, Lady Catherine, 162
Howard, Colonel Charles, Viscount Howard of Morpeth, later Earl of Carlisle, 172-3, 185, 188, 160
Huchinson Lucy, xi, 173
Huntingdon, 3-6, 9-11, 14, 16-23, 29-32, 37, 39, 60, 66, 71, 90
Hursley, 107-8,152, 170, 184, 190, 196-7, 199, 205, 208, 210
Hurst Castle, 103
Hyde, Edward, later Earl of Clarendon, 55, 186, 204, 213

Ingoldsby, Colonel Sir Richard, 16, 104, 186, 188, 209
Inverkeithing, Battle of, 121
Ireton, Henry, as soldier 73, 85-6, 88, 90-2, 102-3, 107-8; marriage to Bridget, 92/3; as politician, 93-9, 102, 103-6, 130; in Ireland,107-8, 10-2, 115,118-9, 122-3; attainder, 199, 203

Jamaica, 145, 177, 213
James I, King, 6-8, 13, 18-22
James II, King, 209
Jones, Colonel John (second husband of Catherine Whetstone née Cromwell), 150, 200
Jones, Colonel Philip, 135,198,200
Joyce, Cornet George, 95

Kilbourne, William, 30-1
Kilkenny, Oath of, 61, 77, 103; castle, 111
Kinnersley, Clement, 136, 159

La Rochelle, 23, 26
Lambert, Major-General John, as a soldier, 101,112,114, 121, 183, 189, 190 192, friendship with Cromwell, 126, 137, 144, 166-7; as politician, 126, 128-30, 135, 144, 147, 158,164, 166-7; opposition to Richard, 184, 186, 188, at Restoration, 200
Lambert, Frances, 126-7, 137, 144, 167
Langdale, Sir Marmaduke, 97, 101
Langport, Battle of, 91
Laud, William, Archbishop of Canterbury, 27, 39, 43-6, 49, 53, 152
Lawrence, Henry, 32
Lawry, John 52
Lawson, Vice Admiral John (later Sir John), 192
Lenthall, William, 105, 124, 128, 186, 192-3
Leslie, David, Major General, later 1st Lord Newark, 112-3
Leslie, Alexander, General *see* Leven,
Leven, Alexander Leslie, Earl of, 45, 48, 52, 79, 80-1, 121-2
Lilburn, Colonel Robert, 98
Lincoln's Inn, 40, 96, 111
Little Stanbrook Hall, 13-4, 40
Lockhart, Sir William of Lee, 143-4, 159, 162, 170, 175, 177, 187, 203
Lostwithiel, Battle of, 83
Lowry, John, 60

Ludlow, Edmund, Major-General, 104, 124, 126, 136-7, 141, 146, 150, 156, 160, 187, 191, 203
Lucus, Sir Charles, 101
Lynne, William, 4, 28

Maidstone, Battle of, 101
Major Generals, Rule of, 148-156
Malyn, William, 152, 170
Manderville, Viscount, *see* Manchester, Edward Montague
Manchester, Edward Montague, 2nd Earl of, 56, 74-89, 172
Manchester, Henry Montague 1st Earl of, 31-2, 54, 56
Mancini, M, 177-8
Mardyck 160, 170
Marvell, Andrew, 144, 150, 154, 161, 172, 177, 179, 203
Marsdon Moor, Battle of, 80-2
Mayerne, Sir Theordore, 27
Mayor, Dorothy *see* Dorothy Cromwell,
Mayor, Richard, 100, 107-9, 112, 120, 129, 199
Meautys, Thomas, 49, 52
Milton, John, 143-4, 153, 161, 172, 203
Montagu, Henry, 1st Earl of Manchester *see* Manchester
Montagu, Edward, 2nd Earl of Manchester *see* Manchester
Montagu, Edward, later Earl of Sandwich, 170, 186-7, 190, 198
Montagu, Sir Sidney, 22
Montrose, James Graham, Earl then Marquis of, 45, 86, 89
Mortimer, John, 208

Nayler, James, 153

Narborough (now Northborough home of Claypoles), 188, 198, 201, 204, 206
Naseby, Battle of, 88, 90-1, 194
Neile, Richard Bishop of Winchester, 27
Newburn, Battle of, 52
Newbury, Battles of, 1st 76-7, 2nd 84-5
Newcastle, 52, 61, 78, 81, 94
Newcastle, William Cavendish, Earl, later Duke of, 61, 71-3, 76, 80-1
Nicholas, Sir Edward, 201
Norton, Colonel, 100
North, Sir Dudley, 60, 62, 67

Okey, Colonel John, 203
Ormonde, James Butler, 12th Earl of, 1st Marquis and later 1st Duke of, 106,108, 111, 116, 176
Osborne, Dorothy, 129

Packe, Sir Christopher, 158-9
Patient, Thomas, 118
Pembroke Castle, 100
Pengelly, Thomas, 208, 210
Pickering, Sir Gilbert, 158, 177
Pontefract Castle, siege of 102
Preston, Battle of, 101-2, 112, 143
Pride, Colonel Thomas, 102-4,
Proctor, Rev Robert, 30
Pym, John, 24, 27, 41-2, 50-7, 59-62, 65, 7, 77-8

Raleigh, Sir Walter, 3, 18, 35
Ramsey Manor, 5, 72, 100
Rathmines, Battle of, 109
Reynolds, Sir John, 170, 176
Rich, Robert (C's son-in-law), 161, 171, 175, 25, 207

Ripon, Treaty of, 52
Russell, Elizabeth (Mrs Henry Cromwell), 129
Russell, Sir Francis of Chippenham Hall, 63, 167, 173, 205
Russell, Sir John (second husband of Frances C) 205
Rupert, Prince, of the Rhine, 68-9, 73, 80-2, 84, 90-1, 106

Savoy, Duke of 145
Saye and Sele, William Fiennes, 1st Viscount, 40-1, 43, 54, 79, 94
Scot, Thomas, 173, 185, 188, 193
Sealed Knot, 189, 201
Sexby, Colonel Edward, 157
Shaftesbury, Earl of *see* Ashley Cooper
Simcott, Dr, 28
Sidney Sussex College, 10, 33, 74
Sindercombe, Miles, 157-8
Skippon, Major-General Philip, 153
Speen, 84
Sewster, John, 28
Sewster, Robina, Lady Lockhart (C's niece), 94, 143-4, 159, 203
Sexby, Colonel Edward, 157
Slingsby, Sir Henry, 176-7
Stayner, Captain Richard, 155, 166
Steward, Sir Thomas (C's uncle), 37
Steward, Sir William, 4, 10
Stoke Mandeville, 43
St Ives, 206, 32-4, 36, 38
St John, Oliver (C's cousin), 24, 40, 42-3, 52, 54, 62, 66, 76, 78-9, 86-7, 94, 103, 106, 114. 124, 144, 158, 173, 200
St John, Oliver, Baron St John of Bletso, 67-9
Stafford, Thomas Wentworth, Earl of, 51-2

Strode, William, 54, 5, 62

Thurloe, John, 137, 140, 143, 147, 153, 157-8, 162, 175, 180-1, 184, 186, 188, 197, 200
Temple, William, 129
Tookey, Job, 34
Turenne, Henry de la Tour d'Auvergne, Marshall, 177
Turnham Green, Battle of, 69

Upwood, 13, 17

Vane, Sir Henry, 78-9, 86-7, 94, 105-6, 113, 118, 124, 193, 197, 200, 203
Villiers, George, 1st Duke of Buckingham, 21, 23-6, 169
Villiers, George, 2nd Duke of Buckingham, 134, 144, 169-170, 180

Wells, Walter, 34
Wharton, Lord, 129
Waller, Sir William, 71, 73, 79, 83-5, 87, 89
Whalley, Colonel Edward (C's cousin), 73, 97, 104, 112, 147, 199, 200, 203
Whalley, Richard, 16
Walton, Valentine (C's brother-in-law), 10, 16, 60, 63, 66, 73, 81, 104, 200
Warwick, Sir Philip, 29, 54, 64
Warwick, Robert Rich, 2nd Earl of, 40-1, 43, 49, 54, 61, 74
Wentworth, Thomas, Earl of Stafford *see* Stafford
Wexford, sieges of, 108-9, 111, 212
Whetstone, Catherine, (C's sister) *see* Catherine Cromwell

Whetstone, Lavinia, (C's niece), 184, 204
Whetstone, Roger, 25, 29, 122, 200
Whitlocke, Bulstrode, 124
White, Francis, Bishop of Ely, 45
Wilkins, Dr John, 150-1, 203
Williams, Morgan, 5
Williams, Richard, 5
Winceby, Battle of, 76
Winnington Bridge, Battle of, 189
Wood Farm, 32, 218
Worcester, Battle of, 121-2, 124
Wren, Matthew, Bishop of Ely, 45-6, 50, 54-6
York, 7, 52, 60, 62-3, 80-1, 162, 178, 182, 193